WHEN LOVE GOES WRONG

For Nancy —

With thanks —

Ann Jones

3/26/92

WHEN LOVE GOES WRONG

WHAT TO DO WHEN YOU CAN'T DO ANYTHING RIGHT

Ann Jones
Susan Schechter

HarperCollinsPublishers

FIRST EDITION

Designed by Alma Orenstein

Library of Congress Cataloging-in-Publication Data
Jones, Ann, 1937–
    When love goes wrong : what to do when you can't do anything right
/ Ann Jones and Susan Schechter. — 1st ed.
        p. cm.
    Includes bibliographical references and index.
    ISBN 0-06-016306-2 (cloth)
    1. Abused women—United States. 2. Abused wives—United States.
3. Abusive men—United States. 4. Abused women—Services for—
United States. I. Schechter, Susan. II. Title.
HV1445.J67   1992
362.82'92'0973—dc20   90-56380

92 93 94 95 96 CC/RRD 10 9 8 7 6 5 4 3 2 1

Contents

Preface

We began thinking about and working with abused women many years ago—and we began with the most obvious cases of abuse. In 1976 Susan Schechter helped start new services for battered women in Chicago. At about the same time, Ann Jones was in New York writing a book that dealt, in part, with battered women who killed their partners. What struck us about the battered women we talked to was that, apart from the incidents of violence in their lives, and the terrible complications they went through as a result, they were no different from other women we knew. What's more, their partners also seemed to be ordinary people.

Over the years we came to see that the use of force, in more subtle forms, affects the lives of a great many "ordinary" women: battering is only one technique that men may use to try to keep their partners under control. Countless other controlling techniques, from yelling to withdrawing into total noncommunication, are far more commonplace, and any one of us may be subjected to them. (We may even use such controlling techniques ourselves, especially against our children.) We came to believe that much of the uneasiness and unhappiness so many women feel in their relationships—especially that frustrating feeling that you can't do anything right—is caused by a partner's control. We've written this book to help women understand what controlling behavior is, what it does to our lives, and what we can do to make our lives, and our relationships, our own.

In our research, we studied specifically how women cope with, respond to, and get away from violent men. We interviewed women mostly about their heterosexual relationships, and we draw examples only from heterosexual relationships. Nevertheless, because power dynamics are so often the same, we think lesbians, and gay men too, will identify with many of the stories in this book and will find useful information here.

When it comes to taking action and getting help, however, lesbians and heterosexual women with similar relationships face different problems. All women may be persecuted by institutions that back up male power. But the gay woman may also be harassed or not taken seriously or ignored altogether because of her sexual preference. What helps the straight woman may harm the lesbian. For that reason, when we offer suggestions in this book, we'll sometimes have special recommendations for lesbians.

Racism and class discrimination produce a similar unbalance. What works for upper-middle-class white women may be ineffective or even dangerous for minority and poor women, especially where public agencies are concerned. Consequently we'll sometimes have special suggestions for women of color, poor women, and women classified as illegal aliens, all of whom may have to look harder for help and be more resourceful.

Despite all the differences among us, women still share a common identity as women. The information and suggestions in these pages come from women, and are directed to women. It is our hope that every reader will find something here that helps.

Certainly, many people helped us. We owe thanks to all the women we've talked to over the years who have contributed to our understanding of control and violence, and particularly to Dr. Anne Ganley and Ellen Pence, who have long inspired our thinking and helped us formulate our ideas. We're especially grateful to the more than fifty women—women who represent various backgrounds, classes, races, and stages in relationships—who agreed to participate in long systematic interviews for this and other projects during the last five years. Their decision to tell their stories, in the hope that other women might benefit from them, enriched our understanding of abuse and taught us a great deal about courage.

Michelle Fine at the University of Pennsylvania helped design our interview questionnaire and tested it with the help of two of her students in social psychology, Lynn Phillips and Rhonda Jeter. Barbara Schwartz, a gifted research assistant, identified and interviewed many women for us and suggested new directions for study. As we planned the book, we received critical feedback from Sarah Buel, Mona Lou Callery, Deborah Smith-Byrne, the Duluth (Minnesota) Women's Action Group, the staff and support group of the Waltham (Massachusetts) Battered Women's Support Committee, and the staff of Boston's Transition House, especially Carole Sousa and Mary Brennick. Coral McDonell, Ellen Pence, Jill Abernathy, and Kitty Kale, all of the Domestic Abuse Intervention Project in Duluth, offered feedback as we went along. And Anne Ganley, Valli Kanuha, Ellen Pence, and Beth Richie reviewed the entire manuscript with great thoughtfulness and care.

The counseling staff at EMERGE, a men's program in Boston, allowed us to observe their group sessions and shared their ideas with us. Special thanks go to David Adams, Lundy Bancroft, and Ted German at EMERGE, and Fernando Mederos and David Douglas of Common Purpose. Sue Doucette and Ruth McCambridge provided helpful information about women's drug and alcohol problems; Teresa Swartzlander, Marilyn J. White of the Realization Center in New York, and Dan Domench of the Mid-Coast Substance Abuse Council in Maine reviewed the chapter on this subject. Laurie Woods of the National Center on Women and Family Law and Lucy Williams of the Massachusetts Law Reform Institute reviewed our account of legal issues facing abused women. Joan Duncan, Lonna Davis-Loblundo, and Susan Hoye, along with the staff of AWAKE in Boston—Lisa Gary, Emily Davern, and Josie Pandolfino—offered helpful advice and guidance. And Giulietta Swenson helped as research assistant.

Several individuals and foundations believed in this work and supported its development, no one more than our literary agent Charlotte Sheedy. We are also especially grateful to Mary Ann Snyder of the Chicago Resource Center, Sunny Fischer of the Sophia Fund, and Ann Beaver for their generous support of Susan

Schechter's research, and to our indefatigable editor Janet Goldstein and her assistant editor Peternelle Van Arsdale, who helped us put it all together.

Finally, we would like to thank Allen Steinberg and Zachary Schechter-Steinberg for their generous spirits.

PART ONE

■

What's Going On?

1

If This Is Love,
Why Do I Feel So Bad?

When love goes wrong you *feel* it—usually long before you can name or talk about exactly what the problems are. That uneasy sensation creeps up on you, like a bad case of flu. You brush it off, hoping it will go away. Or you take some precautions to "fix" things. But there it is—that awful feeling—taking up more and more of your life. Sometimes, looking back at the end of a relationship, you can see that you never were quite comfortable with it.

Haven't we all had that experience? Haven't we all said, about some relationship in our lives, "I should have figured that out a whole lot faster than I did"?

But when that uneasy feeling arises from a relationship with a controlling partner, it's very hard to make sense of it. In the midst of such a relationship, you may get all wrapped up in the immediate situation. You may become very busy, trying to keep your partner happy in order to seem reasonably happy and safe yourself.

This chapter—in fact, this whole book—will give you a chance to step back and see the bigger picture, the patterns often overlooked or ignored in the confusion of living with a controlling partner. In this chapter we'll define that key word *control,* and we'll

talk about controlling partners. Who are they? What do they do? And
most important: how can you tell if you're living with one?

BARBARA'S STORY

Barbara was a little uneasy about her boyfriend right from the start,
even though he couldn't have been nicer. Something about
Kenneth bothered her, but she couldn't say exactly what it was. The
more she thought about it, the more she felt guilty about her own
reservations, because he was usually very thoughtful and attentive.
Barbara believed that her uneasiness was a symptom of her own
fear of intimacy, and decided that if she wanted to have a boyfriend
she'd have to get over that fear. She tried to focus instead on all the
good aspects of Kenneth's personality and their relationship. She
didn't want to spoil things.

While they were going together, Barbara saw what she called
some "little problems" in Kenneth's behavior. She felt that he pressured her about sex, and sometimes he got angry or sulky if she was
not in the mood for lovemaking. He wanted to spend so much time
with her that she occasionally felt a need to get away by herself. But
she continued to believe that the biggest problem in their relationship was caused by her own "fear of intimacy"—and Kenneth
agreed. He was ready to make a commitment to Barbara, he said;
why couldn't she make a commitment to him?

Barbara convinced herself that marrying Kenneth and loving
him "better" would straighten out his problems, as well as hers. But
it didn't. After the honeymoon, her uneasy feeling didn't go away.
Barbara asked herself: Why was Kenneth so difficult? Why did he
seem to be so disappointed in her? She knew that she was far from
perfect, but Kenneth seemed to find fault not just with her lovemaking but with nearly everything she did.

NAMING THE PROBLEM

For many of us, this is a familiar story. Haven't we all spent time in
Barbara's shoes, trying to work on a relationship, trying to make a

partner happy? Perhaps your partner behaves in ways that annoy or frustrate you, but you hope that if you make him feel loved and secure, he'll behave differently, and the problems in your relationship will disappear. You may think—and he may tell you—that you and your love for him are his best hope of being happy and being able to change for the better. Or perhaps, when his behavior troubles you, you disregard it. You may find excuses for the way he acts and put the blame instead on the world we live in. You may take the blame on yourself. If he blows up at you, perhaps you tell yourself, "I should have known better than to talk to him when he was in a bad mood."

The chances are that he'll put the responsibility on you, too, just as Kenneth put the blame on Barbara. When he does something that bothers you, he says it's because of something *you* did first. And you have to admit that you're no angel. In addition, if you go to a therapist or read a self-help book, you may be reminded—quite correctly—that you can make changes only in yourself, and not in your partner.

In short, everyone points the finger at you. But in any relationship, both partners play a part in creating some of the problems, and both partners bear a share of the responsibility for fixing them. While you work hard on your part in the relationship, however, you may overlook your partner's part. Worse yet, you may not notice that some of the problems are caused entirely by your partner. Like Barbara, you may try to improve your own behavior—without really questioning *his.*

You may be overlooking cues—as Barbara did—that the real problem lies with your partner. It may be that your partner is selfish, self-centered, moody, manipulative, possessive, critical, withdrawn, demanding, pressuring, coercive, intimidating, unpredictable, exacting, domineering, bossy, bullying, unreasonable, immature, angry, tyrannical, temperamental, explosive, insistent upon always getting his own way. In short, your partner may be *controlling.*

In Chapter 3 we will discuss *why* controlling partners behave as they do. But, as you will note in the following stories, their behavior frequently undermines some aspect of the woman's freedom: her work, her ability to drive a car or to leave the house. If your partner behaves in some of these ways, it's no wonder that love is going wrong. And it's no wonder that you sometimes feel awful. But naming the problem correctly will help. You see, the controlling partner *creates* confusion, often by saying one thing and doing something else. Once you recognize that the problem is your partner's controlling behavior, you'll be able to see more clearly what your partner *does,* and you'll be less confused by what he *says.*

Let us give you some examples of the confusing and confusion-producing behavior of controllers.

▪ BETTY

Betty's husband Joe didn't object to her working, until she got a job that was better than his. Then, instead of telling her how insecure her success made him feel, he made sure she didn't keep the job. Betty describes how he did it, how confusing the situation was for her, and how hard it is to stand up to a partner who denies what he's really doing.

> I sewed in a trouser factory for about a year, and then I got a good job as an assistant supervisor at another company. I went in on a lark, and I got it. I was excited because it was a job that had a ladder to go up, and they told me that I would advance. Well, that job lasted two weeks because Joe had a fit. He wasn't going to say that he wasn't going to let me do it. He just made it as difficult as possible for me to function. He'd keep me up until 3:30 in the morning, screaming at me, when I had to be at work at 7:00. I had to quit—I was too tired. He never told me to quit. In fact he bragged to his friends about my new job. Sabotage is more what it was like. You can't put your finger on what's happening, but you know it's happening and you don't know how. You can't accuse him by saying, "You don't like me to work!" because he's never said that he doesn't like it.

▪ PATRICIA

Like Betty, Patricia got confusing double messages from her husband. She, too, gave up something she wanted to do because of the way her husband acted.

My husband didn't like it when I took the bus downtown. He would tell me it made him worry about me too much. At first I was touched by how concerned he was. But then I noticed that whenever I took the bus, he would start a fight about my family. He'd call my family every name in the book, and the fight would go on and on. I'd be furious and confused. I finally realized that the tirades were really about my taking the bus. He never gave me a direct order: "You will not take the bus." He was not that kind of person; he was a college professor. Instead, when I took the bus, I paid such a price—it was so hurtful to listen to what he was saying about my family—that I didn't do it too often. So I rarely got out by myself.

▪ INEZ

Inez was also confused by her common-law husband's double messages.

After I had my third baby and he couldn't be bothered to visit me in the hospital, I told him I was through messing with him. But he was not about to let me go. He went on and on about how much he loved me and how I was his queen and his goddess. Shit like that. Then he would do things like take the distributor cap out of my car so I couldn't drive. He would take my money out of my pocketbook. He would rip up my good clothes so I couldn't go to work. If I went out to the clubs on Saturday night with my sister or my girlfriends, it didn't matter where I went but he'd show up to give me a hard time. I'm trying to feed three kids, and this man is giving me all this grief, and all the time he's carrying on about how much he loves me and how he wants to take care of me.

▪ PHUONG

Phuong's husband established a set of unspoken rules, and he expected everyone in the family to abide by them. Most of the time Phuong could figure out what her husband wanted, but she rarely knew why he wanted it. She was often confused and frightened, but one of the rules was that the rules could not be questioned.

> He would never say, "These are my rules." But there were rules all the same. There were lots of them. And I knew what they were, and he knew what they were, and the children knew what they were. He would never say, "You cannot go in the back-yard." Instead, he would say, in a nice voice, "You'd better not go in the backyard; you know how the neighbors are." If I broke the rules, I'd know that he was not happy as soon as he walked in the door. I could tell by the way he looked. He didn't have to say anything. So he really did control me because I wanted to get along with him. I don't like to argue. I like people to be happy with me. But I could not please him.

▪ JEANETTE

Jeanette's husband also had a rule: he didn't want her to drive the car. He tried to prevent her, first by making her feel guilty, and later by frightening her and wearing her down. Like Phuong, Jeanette was confused about what her husband had in mind. To Jeanette, his opposition made no sense.

> I had two small children and we lived about nine miles from town, and my husband wouldn't let me get my driver's license. There we were, stuck out on the farm. I just pestered and pestered him for months. The whole time Carl would talk to me very sweetly and say, "Why do you need this license? I always take you where you need to go. I never say no to you." I finally got the booklets and studied all the rules and convinced him to drive me into town to the registry to take the written test. He acted like he was very hurt and insulted because I was so ungrateful to him after he'd been driving me around all this time. It was such a struggle! And then when I actually got the license, he wouldn't let me drive the car. He wouldn't give me the keys. At one point I got the keys, but I was too intimidated to use them. I knew if I drove into town, or even to the neighbors, there would be a terrible argument when I got home. It wasn't worth it.

▪ LUCY

Lucy was surprised and thrown into confusion by the fact that she couldn't meet her husband's expectations. Before she married she was a good student and a good office worker. She'd been able to do a fine job at school and at work, but at home the harder she tried, the more she failed.

> I really did a lot of work, trying to keep the lid on things, keep things happy. I would get up in the morning and adjust the thermostat to exactly what Tom required. I would turn on a particular lamp. I would prepare his breakfast. He required half a grapefruit, a particular grapefruit knife and spoon, a cloth napkin, the radio turned to a particular station. Then I was to call him. If I omitted any of these things, there was hell to pay for the next two days because, he insisted, I was trying to undermine him, make him miserable. He said that I was, in very subtle ways, making him feel unloved and uncared-for.
>
> I became compulsive. You could eat off my floors. I had to be compulsive to avoid problems. Eventually I started realizing that it didn't do any good. If I did everything all right, he still managed to find something wrong. When nothing was actually wrong, if I had everything down to perfection, then he would accuse me of being too cautious and mousy around him. He would ask: was I suggesting that he was a temperamental person?
>
> My God, I got good at anticipating every problem. I could do anything—leap tall buildings, outrun locomotives. You would be amazed at what I was able to accomplish in just a twenty-four-hour day to keep him happy. It was staggering.

▪ KAREN

Like Lucy's husband, Karen's boyfriend blamed her for his own bad temper. Then he "worked on" their relationship by telling Karen what was wrong with her. Like Lucy, Karen was thoroughly confused, and after she heard her "faults" listed time and time again, she began to believe that there must be something very wrong with her.

He and I would have an argument and he would just walk out in the middle of it and go drinking. When he came back, he'd start right where he left off—tearing me down. Then a few hours later, when I'd refuse to speak to him, he'd cry and tell me he was sorry. He wanted to talk "rationally," he'd say, about my problems—how I had made it impossible for him to stay in the apartment. He didn't want to leave, but I made him so unhappy that he had to have a few beers to relax.

He said my problem was that I was an unhappy and unfulfilled person who expected too much of a man. I wanted him to fulfill me and no person could do that. I had to learn to grow up and to really love and respect a man. What was it going to take for me to learn these things? he'd ask me. I'd say I didn't know. I couldn't figure it out. I felt awful.

▪ ANNA

Anna also found herself confused and undermined by things her boyfriend told her. He was a drug counselor, and he said he understood people very well. He said he wanted to help Anna understand herself better because he loved her so much. Anna was grateful for his attention until she noticed that whenever they had a deep, "helpful" conversation, she felt worse about herself. But how could she turn down the "help" of someone who said he loved her so much?

My boyfriend tried to convince me that my family didn't care about me, that I had been neglected as a child, that I was better off without them, that they didn't like him, and they were going to try to break us up. There was an element of truth in what he said—my family would have given me support to leave him, and he realized they were a threat in that way. Through his attack on my family and his constant repetition that I was a poor neglected child, I think he was trying to undermine my sense of respect for myself and convince me that he was my only hope, that I was in a really bad way and didn't have anyone to rely on except him.

Betty, Patricia, Inez, Phuong, Jeanette, Lucy, Karen, Anna, and most of the other women we interviewed for this book described themselves as having been "confused"—sometimes for years—as they tried one approach after another to make their partners happy and their relationships work. First they tried to be "good" girlfriends or wives, and when their efforts failed, they looked for some kind of help. Most of them talked things over with members of their family or extended family, or with close friends. Many of them also searched for outside help. Some talked to a minister, priest, or rabbi. Some confided in a social worker or a doctor. Some consulted a therapist or counselor. Some went to a community center or a women's center, looking for advice. It took some of them a long time to find the information and help they needed.

We asked them, "What information do you wish you'd had at the time? What would have helped you?" And most often we heard answers like these:

> "I wish someone had explained to me why my partner acted that way."

> "I thought I *worked* so hard on that relationship, when half the time I was really just spinning my wheels and digging the same old ruts deeper. I wish someone had explained to me what kind of 'work' is *useful* and what's not."

This book addresses these two crucial issues. It will give you some tools so that you can evaluate your partner's role in your relationship as well as your own, clear up some of the confusion you may be feeling, and figure out what to do next.

WHAT IS A CONTROLLING PARTNER?

To put it simply, the controlling person wants to have power over another. Controllers want to have their own way, and what's more, they believe that they are entitled to have their own way at the expense of others, with as little trouble to themselves as possible. Often controllers will say to their partners, "If you loved me, you would do what I want, when I want, without my having to tell you." (We'll have more to say in later chapters about how they learned to think this way.)

It's true that all of us like to have things go our way as often as possible, but controllers will go to great lengths to make sure that they come out on top. Typically, they give little or no consideration to the feelings or wishes of others, even—or perhaps especially— the people they say they love.

Controllers are not all alike. They do not all behave in the same way. Different people have different values, different experiences to call upon, and access to different resources. Controllers use whatever means they have at their disposal. A wealthy executive may use money and influence, while an attractive person may use physical allure and sex. A lawyer or college professor may forcefully "persuade," a salesperson may sweet-talk, an athlete may threaten with physical force. Each controller is out to get things his way, but different people use different tactics to achieve that goal. And what's more, different people use different tactics at different times. What works for the controller at one stage in the relationship may not work at another, or the controller may find an easier or faster way to get results. When that happens, the controller changes the way he acts. This ability to switch tactics is particularly important—because it creates confusion and makes it hard to sort out what's really going on. The willingness of many controllers to go to any lengths to get their way is also potentially dangerous. It means that the controller may switch at any time to tactics that are not just different, but more intense or more frequent or *worse*.

Such changes create more confusion. You say to yourself, "He's never done *that* before! How could he do that to me? What does it mean? What have I done to deserve this? How can I keep that from happening again?" It's hard to figure out what to do. And then again, for reasons that seem mysterious or contradictory, he may switch back. It's not simply that the controller steadily escalates control, making your situation gradually worse and worse; in fact, now and then the controller may seem to back off or relax for no particular reason, so that from time to time things may get better. The result is yet more confusion.

If a controller begins to use sexual assault or physical force and threats of additional violence, confusion is compounded by shock and fear. You worry about whether he means what he says. You wonder how far he will go. Many women in these circumstances feel frozen by a terrible sense of danger—and that danger is very real.

What matters to the controller is not what he does but what he gains by doing it. One way or another, the controller will try to coerce you into submitting to his power. He may win you by wheedling and cajoling. He may coax or seduce. He may compel by flattery and charm. He may bribe with kindness or threaten with abandonment. He may bring you around by persistence, never taking no for an answer. He may make you feel sorry for him. He may blame you for things you did or didn't do, and then manipulate you through your sense of guilt or shame. He may intimidate you, emotionally or physically, and then play upon your anxiety and fear. He may withhold what you want: his affection and attention. He may badger you with unwelcome attention and possessiveness and jealousy. He may insult and humiliate you, in private and in public. He may force you to do things you don't want to do. He may coerce you with threats and terrify you with violence. He may harass and terrorize you. He may scare you out of your wits. He may inflict painful and permanent injuries. The most extreme controllers—the ones who simply will not let a woman go—may even kill.

WHEN DOES CONTROL BECOME "ABUSE"?

There is no single word to describe the full range of controlling behavior. If the controller uses physical or sexual violence, people generally call it "abuse" and say that the woman is "battered." But many women involved with controllers who never use force (or who haven't yet) say that they feel emotionally beaten down. We believe that even deliberately throwing a partner into mental confusion and anxiety, and tearing a partner down emotionally, as controllers so often do, is abusive. Consequently, in this book, we will use the term "abuse" to refer to all controlling actions, even though some of them—like Kenneth's super-nice attentiveness—may appear at first glance to be just the opposite.

We define abuse as a *pattern* of coercive control that one person exercises over another in order to dominate and get his way. Abuse is behavior that physically harms, arouses fear, prevents a person from doing what she wants, or compels her to behave in ways she does not freely choose.[1]

We believe that the institution of marriage, which by centuries-long tradition gives husbands the right to rule "their" households, encourages men to abuse their power over women and children. In addition, male power is backed up by all the important institutions of our male-dominated society—institutions like law, religion, government . . . in short, all those things that make up what many people call "the system."

Terms such as "abused" and "battered" make many people uncomfortable, especially when these labels are pinned on us. Kay, a white woman living in a shelter for battered women, told us: " 'Abused'—that was those helpless, weak women, but not me. I've always worked. I'm tough. I take good care of my kids." Maralee, an African-American woman who became director of a battered women's shelter after she divorced her abusive husband, added: "When you think of abused women, you think *victim;* and I certainly couldn't identify with that. I always thought of myself as one strong woman."

Both Kay and Maralee felt diminished by such labels because, like most women, they had made strenuous efforts to keep control of their lives and to make their marriages work. Some women told us that such labels made them feel disloyal to a partner who was loving and decent much of the time. And no woman likes the suggestion that a relationship is hopeless and that she should do something drastic, such as leave it, before she wants to. For any of these reasons, you too may feel uncomfortable with the term "abuse." On the other hand, many women do feel alright speaking of themselves as "abused" or "formerly battered," because the terms remind them of just what their former partners did. In addition, it unites them with thousands of other women taking a stand against violence.

It might be helpful to remember that in the phrases "abused woman" and "battered woman" the words "abused" and "battered" describe *what the abuser did,* not what the woman did, and certainly not who she is. If you are intimidated by your partner and if you are experiencing the harmful effects of coercive and controlling behavior described throughout this book, then you are being abused—even if you have never been struck or injured and even though you are a strong and competent person.

We believe that the controlling partner is abusive in another sense as well. The controller abuses power, especially his power over you. Our society, with its long history of male domination, gives all men power over women. Despite our individual strengths, women are collectively at a disadvantage. When you fall in love, you may place yourself at a greater disadvantage. Simply by loving your partner and trusting him, you willingly give up some of your power to him. You give him the power to hurt your feelings, for example; and you trust that because he loves you (or says he does), he will try very hard *not* to hurt your feelings. This is not the case with the controller. That legacy of male domination not only gives him power over women but makes him think he deserves it. To exercise power over you, he'll violate your trust and use your feelings of love against you. To a partner who truly respects you as another human being, the power you entrust to his care is a gift to be safeguarded; to the controller it's probably less than he feels entitled to.

In this book, we'll refer to these controlling partners as "controllers" or "abusers." We'll use the terms "abuse" and "control" interchangeably because it's our belief that control is abusive, and that all abusive behavior—all emotional, physical, and sexual abuse—is intended to control.

Many women call controlling partners by other names as well, and often the terms they use reveal a great deal about the tactics most popular among controllers. One woman said that her boyfriend "thought he was the King of the Trailer Park." Others referred to their controlling partners as "King of the Castle," "the Great Dictator," "King Kong," "the Tiny Tyrant," "Little Hitler," "Local Hero," and "Mighty Mouse." One woman, who says her ex-husband is a cross between a couch potato and Attila the Hun, refers to him as "the TV-Room Terrorist."

Many of the same women use very different names to characterize their controlling partners earlier in the relationship—names like "Prince Charming," "Mr. Nice Guy," and "Mr. Sensitivity." But the transformation from Prince Charming to King Kong is an all-too-common scenario.

THE SHRINKING WOMAN TEST

As many of these labels indicate, the controller likes to be an important person—more important than other people. He likes to be the
center of attention. Many controllers like to flex their muscles and
throw their weight around; they like to be big shots, displaying their
power. Some choose other postures to gain attention. They may
claim to be more oppressed, more persecuted, more sensitive, more
misunderstood, more unloved than anybody else. In any case, they
demand special treatment, and they too enjoy exercising power
over other people.

Because the controller builds himself up at the expense of others, no one can remain in a relationship with him without giving up
important parts of the self, just as Betty had to give up her job and
Patricia had to give up going out by herself. First you may give up
certain activities or interests; then you find that you're giving up
your opinions, your wishes, your ambitions, your anger, your voice,
your pride, your happiness.

Nevertheless, there is a difference between supporting a partner
who also supports you and losing yourself to a partner who inflates
himself at your expense. In thinking about your own relationship,
you may want to apply this test. Ask yourself: Am I the whole person
I used to be? Am I as expansive as the person I wanted to become? Or
have I lost bits and pieces of myself without meaning to? Am I
withering away? In this relationship, who takes up the emotional and
physical space? Does he make himself bigger by making me smaller?
Do *I* make him feel bigger by making *myself* smaller? If you feel
yourself shrinking, you're probably in a relationship with a controller.

IS MY PARTNER A CONTROLLER?

The following checklists will give you an idea of the great variety of
tactics that controllers use. And they may give you a chance to
identify some tactics that you have been subjected to. As you read
the lists, check off any items that seem familiar to you. Then look
back to see how many items you checked and what they are.
Individually, many of these items seem unimportant, but your check

marks may reveal significant patterns. Keep in mind that these lists cover only *some* tactics used by controllers. The items are very specific, and many may have no bearing at all on your partner's behavior. On the other hand, you may think of coercive actions your partner uses that we haven't mentioned. If so, we suggest you write them down.

Control Through Criticism

_____ My partner makes me feel like I never do anything right. Nothing is ever good enough.

_____ My partner makes me feel like I'm not supportive and loving enough.

_____ My partner dislikes the way I cook, clean, dress, make love, carry myself in public.

_____ My partner never gives me positive support. Even compliments are backhanded: "This is the first good dinner you've cooked in months."

_____ When I confide my insecurities, my partner tells me I'm a baby and I need to grow up and join the real world.

_____ My partner calls me names: dummy, whore, cunt, bitch.

_____ My partner is always correcting things I say or do; only he can do things right.

_____ Whenever we are with family and friends, I'm on pins and needles because I expect to be humiliated about something I've done.

Control Through Moodiness, Anger, and Threats

_____ If I'm five minutes late, I'm afraid he'll be mad.

_____ My partner expects me to read his mind and is furious when I can't or won't.

_____ Living with my partner is nerve-wracking, because I never know what will set him off.

_____ When I do anything "wrong," my partner blows his top and then refuses to speak to me.

_____ My partner withdraws into silence, and I have to figure out what I've done wrong and apologize for it.

_____ My partner gets depressed and I have to work very hard to cheer him up.

_____ My partner threatens to tell social services that I'm an unfit mother if I don't do what he wants.

_____ My partner says he'll never let me leave him.

Control Through Overprotection and "Caring"

_____ My partner doesn't like it if I'm away from home because he says he worries about me too much.

_____ My partner is jealous when I talk to new people.

_____ My partner often phones or unexpectedly comes by the place I work to see if I'm "okay."

_____ My partner does the shopping so I don't have to go out.

_____ My partner says I don't ever have to work because he wants to take care of me.

_____ My partner picks out my clothes because he loves to have me look just right.

_____ My partner takes me to work and picks me up so the men I work with won't get "ideas."

_____ My partner encourages me to take drugs with him so we can share the high.

Control Through Denying Your Perceptions

_____ My partner acts very cruelly and then says I'm too sensitive and can't take a joke.

_____ My partner promises to do things, breaks his promises, then says he never promised in the first place.

_____ My partner causes big scenes in public and at family gatherings, and when I confront him about it, he accuses me of exaggerating or making the whole thing up.

_____ My partner shows excessive interest in my emotional life and tries to convince me that I need to see a psychiatrist. By contrast, he is fine.

_____ My partner says I'm always imagining things.

_____ My partner hits me and then asks how I got hurt.

_____ My partner makes me cry and then tells me I'm hysterical. He asks me why I upset myself so much.

_____ My partner says he can help me fix my character defects. He gets me to make lists of what's wrong with me.

_____ When I try to have a serious talk with him, my partner says, "There you go again. Calm down." He treats me as though I'm upset when I'm not.

Control by Ignoring Your Needs and Opinions

_____ My partner never helps me when the kids are sick, or when I'm ill. Or he promises to help me and then forgets.

_____ My partner expects me to drop my activities whenever he wants my attention, but he never pays that kind of attention to me.

_____ When I try to talk, he constantly interrupts me, twists my words, or forgets what I just said.

_____ When I want to resolve a problem, he's changed the subject before I even realize it.

_____ My partner shows up unannounced whenever he wants to, or fails to show up when he said he would, so it's hard for me to make any plans.

_____ When my partner wants to go out on his own, he does; but I can't because the kids are my responsibility.

_____ When I try to express my opinion about anything my partner doesn't respond, walks away, or makes fun of me.

Control Through Decision Making

_____ My partner has to have the last word.

_____ I think we've reached an agreement about something, and then he goes out and does just the opposite.

_____ If I bring up some decision he made but didn't consult me about, he asks me why I'm harping on something that's already been decided.

_____ My partner says some subjects are not open to discussion.

_____ My partner says that it's a man's responsibility to make the decisions for the family.

Control Through Money

_____ I can't get information about our financial situation. My partner says I have enough to do without being bothered by financial decisions.

_____ I have to account for every dime I spend and also figure out how to make ends meet.

_____ My partner spends money on whatever he wants. He gets angry and blames me when he needs money and there's none left.

_____ My partner won't give me a household allowance, so whenever I need some money I have to ask him for it.

_____ My partner says that with all he does for me I ought to be glad to support him financially.

_____ My partner gives me everything I want, but he always reminds me that I could never live so well without him.

_____ My partner doesn't work. He takes money out of my pocketbook or steals my stuff and sells it.

Control Through Shifting Responsibility

_____ If I tell my partner that he's too bossy and critical, he tells me I'm immature. We always end up picking apart _my_ personality.

_____ My partner says that he can't stay clean and sober because he lives with a bitch like me.

_____ My partner says that if I ever leave him, he'll kill himself and I'll be responsible.

_____ My partner lost his job and blamed me for it. Now he refuses to work.

_____ My partner says he wouldn't lose his temper if I kept the kids quieter.

_____ My partner says he wouldn't go after other women so much if I kept myself up better.

_____ My partner says he'd take me out more if I weren't so stupid.

_____ My partner says he's always good-natured with other people, so it must be what I do that makes him lose control of himself.

Control Through Limiting Contact with Other People

_____ When I want to go out, my partner starts a fight.

_____ My partner doesn't like me to spend time with my family, with or without him.

_____ My partner tells me I never give him enough of my time or energy, that I care more for my friends and family than I do for him.

_____ Although he never says it directly, I think my partner wants me to ask his permission before I go somewhere.

_____ My partner grills me about what happened whenever I go out.

_____ My partner accuses me of having affairs.

_____ My partner made me late for work so many times that I lost my job.

_____ When I spend time with women friends, my partner accuses me of being a lesbian.

Control Through Physical Intimidation

_____ My partner blocks the door so I can't leave during an argument.

_____ My partner scares me when he's angry by standing very close to me and clenching his fists.

_____ When we argue, I'm sometimes afraid of what he might do, so I stop arguing.

_____ My partner drives recklessly whenever he is angry at me, and it scares me to death.

_____ My partner throws things around and breaks things.

_____ My partner destroys my clothes and my favorite things.

_____ My partner refuses to leave when I ask him to.

_____ My partner won't let me sleep.

Control Through Sexual Humiliation

_____ My partner pressures me to have sex in ways that make me uncomfortable.

_____ My partner makes sexual jokes about me in front of the children and other people.

_____ My partner makes fun of my body.

_____ My partner tries to seduce my friends and family members.

_____ My partner forces me to dress in ways he thinks are "sexy" but that make me feel uncomfortable.

_____ My partner compares me to women in pornographic magazines and videos.

_____ My partner tells dirty jokes that are degrading to me and to women in general.

Control Through Physical and Sexual Violence

_____ My partner throws things at me.

_____ My partner beats my head against the wall.

_____ My partner chokes me.

_____ My partner kicks me.

_____ My partner shoves and pushes me.

_____ My partner hits me.

_____ My partner forces me to have sex with others.

_____ My partner rapes me.

_____ My partner threatens me with weapons.

_____ My partner hurts me and then won't let me go to the hospital or to a doctor.

HOW THIS BOOK CAN HELP

If you've seen reflections of your partner and your relationship in these checklists and you're feeling sad, confused, scared, or angry, it might help to remember that you're not alone. You're in the company of millions of other women. In the rest of this book we'll help you look more closely at your own situation and figure out what to do about it.

This book is designed for the woman who wants to consider changes in her life. But change may take time. Many women, like those we interviewed, travel a long path. Step by step, they gather new information and ideas, find supportive people to talk to, come to see things in a new light, build their strength—through jobs, school, friendship, and spiritual quests—and reaffirm their confidence in themselves. This book aims to help you through that process of change.

In the next few chapters we'll try to help you clarify what's going on in your relationship. In Chapters 2 and 4, we'll look at what's happening to you and consider why so many of the things you do fail to make your situation better. We'll take a hard look at what's going on with your partner, too. In Chapter 3 we'll discuss why he acts the way he does, and in Chapter 5, whether he's likely to change.

Part Two focuses again on you. It offers practical suggestions for building your own strength and making some important decisions. Part Three speaks especially to women who choose to leave their partners, and to women who are considering that choice. It also offers practical information and suggestions.

Part Four aims to help women with some more specific problems. It contains chapters for women having trouble with substance abuse, women concerned about the safety and well-being of their children, and women concerned about their own personal safety. (If you do not feel safe, you may want to turn first to Chapters 7 and 10.) Also included in Part Four is a chapter giving information and suggestions to family, friends, counselors, and other supporters of abused women. After you've read it yourself, you may want to show it to people who are helping you or people you would like to ask for help.

Now let's turn to the question: what's happening to you? As you take a deep breath and read on, don't worry that it's all going to be horribly grim and depressing. Although women have told us about thousands of terrible experiences with moody, manipulative, critical, and controlling partners, every woman we interviewed also told us wonderful stories—some funny, some sad—about the ways she found to preserve her own dignity and to rebel against the unfair, dictatorial behavior of her partner. We found the stories inspiring, and we think you will too.

2

■

What's Happening to You?

When love goes wrong, that terrible feeling that comes over you is not simple. Any person subjected to the tactics of a controlling partner is bound to go through some complicated emotional reactions. In addition, you develop some tactics of your own to cope with the way your partner behaves. And you may not like yourself for using them.

In this chapter we'll try to cut through some of the confusion the controller creates. We'll sort out some of the most common reactions experienced by women involved with controlling partners. We'll talk about strategies women use to cope with the situation and some of the emotions they commonly feel. Finally, we'll describe an additional problem that complicates the situation for many women: namely, that some strategies you use to cope with a controlling partner can get you into worse trouble.

Let's begin with Tina's story. She had every advantage. She grew up in a white well-to-do family in California, finished college and law school, became an attorney with a top law firm in a large midwestern city, married an up-and-coming businessman, and had two children—Daisy, who is now ten years old, and Tim, eight. For many years Tina volunteered free legal help to residents of an inner-city shelter for abused women. That experience made her feel lucky to have a partner who was not violent but sensitive, supportive, and helpful. Her husband Terry even sympathized with her feminist politics and called himself a feminist, too.

It took Tina eight years to realize that she was being emotionally battered by a controlling partner. She now knows that even though she was living in far less danger than women who are physically or sexually abused, she was wrong to think that Terry's behavior wasn't doing harm to her and her children.

▪ TINA

I met Terry when I was in my second year of law school. One of the things I remember most clearly was how supportive he seemed of my career goals. I thought I had found the perfect guy—he was attractive, warm, nurturing, and respectful of my commitment to help women. On a superficial level he stayed that way through the eight years of our marriage. He always applauded my career. He bragged about me all the time to his friends and family.

But once we were married, another side of him began to emerge. He'd always been extremely impatient with other people, but then he turned his impatience on me. If I were ten minutes late, he'd literally have a temper tantrum. The first few times it happened I was stunned. I don't think I'd ever seen an adult behave like that. He'd snap at me with something like, "Why did you do this to me?" And before I could answer, he'd start yelling, "Why does this always have to happen? Why can't you manage your life?" I'd explain—maybe a meeting ran over, or the traffic was bad—but it never made any difference to him. He seemed to think that the whole world was supposed to operate on his time schedule—especially *me*.

I would feel terrible after these incidents—rejected and frustrated because I didn't know how to calm him down and make things nice again. Or I'd get angry and say, "Don't be silly, just read the newspaper for ten minutes and wait for me." He might react by not speaking to me for hours, or sometimes days.

The worst silence actually lasted through an entire vacation and ruined our week in Hawaii. The fight started on our way there. I'm phobic about airplanes, and we had a horrible flight through a storm. I was sure I was going to die. He told me later that I had been a great disappointment to him. When I think back on it, it seems like he expected me to be perfect, to show no weakness, to be there to take care of him. He couldn't stand it when I needed something from him.

I was very scared of Terry's anger. I never was afraid that he would hit me, or anything like that, but I was always in a state of anxiety because I never knew how to make things better. And when we had kids, it only made matters worse because we had just that many more possibilities for disagreement—which he could never tolerate. He always had to be right, and every question became the subject for an explosion. If I was trying to discuss where we should send the kids to school and we didn't agree right away, he'd end it after five minutes with, "I don't have time for this. You always waste my time. This is where my kids are going to school and that's that."

After these blowups, he would never apologize. But I kept trying to smooth things over—for the sake of keeping things calm, for the sake of keeping my family together.

We were both unhappy and we knew we fought too much, so we went to family therapy—for years. I went because most of the time I wanted to be closer to him and to work through our problems. But sometimes I wanted to get out of the marriage because I felt so angry and trapped. I kept asking him, "Why are you so frustrated and angry at me? What's wrong?" I never got an answer. In therapy he would just list the things that I did wrong—I was too demanding, too critical. At home, after our counseling sessions, I'd try to talk about things, try to get him to express a feeling, suggest alternatives to his constant criticism of me and the kids, the blowups, but nothing changed. Everything was still my fault.

If you had asked me years ago, I would have said, "My husband's a brilliant and difficult man." I never thought of him as overly critical or intimidating. I never saw his behavior as harmful to me or the kids. Here was a guy who was supportive of my career. His surface is generous, not mean. He cooks all the time, helps clean the house. He is an incredibly involved father. It's very complicated. His persona is very mixed. I just kept saying, "Terry is a difficult man." I actually thought it must be a sign of his intelligence.

One of my friends was the first person to call Terry a bully. When I started talking about leaving him, he said he'd fight me for custody of the children. He claimed that because I had a career, I was a neglectful mother—a success at my job but a failure in my family. It made me feel terrible. I internalized a lot of guilt. When a friend heard one of his harangues—and they could go on and on—I remember her commenting, "Boy, he likes to boss people around! He's a real bully." That was the moment—the first time I heard myself saying, "Oh, *that's* the horrible feeling in the pit of my stomach when he talks to me that way. He's pushing me around." It seems amazing to me now that I was so blind. I heard about these domineering men all the time from my clients at the women's shelter, but I didn't put it together until that moment.

Now it's clear to me that there was never any give and take in the relationship. I was doing all the work. He was making all the demands. And he was absolutely unwilling to look at his own behavior or change anything about himself. In his eyes, he was just perfect, and I was the cause of all his problems. He really did a number on me. I've been divorced for three years now, but his criticism still bangs around in my head.

I still struggle against that sense of failure when it comes to the accusations he made about me as a wife and mother. Sometimes when I have to work late or leave town to see a client, I hear his taunts, "If you'd only cared about your husband as much as you do your career, you could have made this work." Or his jabs about the children: "If you'd stop putting yourself first, I'd gladly stop fighting for custody, but I can't abandon my kids like you have." (And remember, I always thought he supported my career.) I think it's going to take a long time to recover from his brainwashing and stop accusing myself. I still have to remind myself that I was the injured party. But one thing I'm sure of: this divorce was the best thing I ever did for myself and my kids.

Tina's story illustrates the fundamental problem of dealing with a controlling partner: figuring out what's really going on. As an attorney, working every day with other attorneys and clients, Tina had to be a good judge of character, and she had to be able to stand up for herself against competition and opposition. Yet in her marriage, even though she felt unhappy and knew there was something wrong, she believed for several years that her husband was an exceptionally good and supportive one. And for eight years she worked overtime on the relationship, trying to make it work by making him happy. How could she have been so mistaken?

HOW WOMEN MAY BE MISLED

Although the roles of women and men in society are continually changing, most of us have been taught some old, traditional lessons about what those roles should be. Like most other women, Tina was taught to care about relationships and to take responsibility for mending and maintaining them. Even though she worked just as hard as her husband outside her home, as many women now do, she was still influenced by the ideas she had grown up with—namely, that maintaining a happy home and a happy husband is a woman's task. But as Tina discovered, no woman can make a relationship work all by herself. Your partner plays an essential part.

There's some truth in the old cliché, "It takes two to tango." But unfortunately, a controlling partner usually calls the tune, and he is not nearly as interested in you or the relationship as he is in himself and his ability to dominate. He too has learned the traditional lessons of our male-dominated society—namely, that men are more important than women, and that women exist mainly to serve men and look after them. Consequently, the controller is unwilling to question his own behavior or his part in the relationship. He feels that he has a right to whatever he wants; and in order to get it, he'll do whatever seems to work—including some things that *seem* supportive, helpful, and kind. Thus, his actions may be extremely deceptive and confusing.

Take Terry's cooking, for example. Tina's women friends envied her because she was lucky enough to have a husband who did all the cooking. They took it as a sign that she and Terry had a "liberated" relationship, equally sharing household tasks. And Tina thought of it that way too. For a long time she felt grateful to Terry for doing this part of the "wife's job." But Terry had first prompted Tina to give up cooking by criticizing her. Then he took over—and basked in the attention and gratitude of Tina and her friends, who always praised him for being such a wonderful "liberated" man. And in any argument, Terry managed to bring up the fact of his cooking, thus making Tina feel both guilty and incompetent. "You don't take care of your own children," he'd say. "You can't even be bothered to *feed* them." And in the end, when they went to court to fight over custody of the children, Terry's cooking counted heavily against Tina's record as a mother.

If controllers were simply "bad" people who do "bad" things, our relationships with them would be a lot less complicated—and very brief. But many controllers manipulate by doing "good" things. Most, like Terry, do both. He could be wonderfully helpful on the one hand, and violently angry and intimidating on the other. He could cook dinner and shout abuse at Tina at the same time. No wonder she had trouble figuring things out.

Unlike Terry, who never apologized for his bad behavior, some controllers alternate the "good" and the "bad"—especially if they're afraid they may have gone too far. They follow a blowup with roses, a black eye with tears of "remorse." Some psychologists who study battered women—women whose partners use violence as a control tactic—call this alternation of violence and apology "the cycle of violence." They speak of a "honeymoon" phase when a batterer is kind and affectionate, until tension builds up and he becomes violent once more.

But in fact both the "bad" and the "good," the blows and the apology, the violence and the "honeymoon," are effective tactics in the overall *pattern of control* by which one person exercises power over another—the pattern we talked about in Chapter 1. Other psychologists tell us that this kind of volatile, inconsistent, on-again-off-again person is the hardest to break away from because, among other things, his unpredictability keeps us hooked on hope. If the controlling partner was *always* "bad," any woman would leave. By being "good" the controller keeps her locked into the relationship, hopeful of change. Oddly enough, a woman may hang on to that hope even when the controller is "bad" or simply ignores her almost all the time.

The controller's contradictory behavior damages a woman in another way as well: it creates ambivalence. When the controller is "good," she loves him or at least feels that it's a good idea to keep the relationship going. When he's "bad," she hates him and wants out. Like Tina, she is of two minds; she switches back and forth. That ambivalence is natural under the circumstances, but it may cause a woman to lose confidence in herself or even to blame herself. Tina explains, "I couldn't decide how I really felt, and I began to think that the whole problem was in my own mind, or rather in the fact that I couldn't make up my mind once and for all. Why couldn't I figure out how I felt about my own husband? It seemed insane. I used to make lists: 'Why I Should Try Again' and 'Why I Should Get a Divorce.' They'd come out the same. It made me nuts."

One term we often hear women apply to controlling partners is "Dr. Jekyll and Mr. Hyde." In the novel by Robert Louis Stevenson, Dr. Henry Jekyll is a respectable physician whose experiments with drugs call forth the hidden side of his personality, in the form of the evil stranger Mr. Hyde. Countless women report that their partners seem to have two such opposite personalities. A woman becomes involved with "Dr. Jekyll," just as Tina fell in love with the "supportive feminist" Terry. When "Mr. Hyde" appears, she tries to cope with him and transform him again into the good doctor. When "Dr. Jekyll" returns, she forgets about his nasty side—that *other* person. She prefers to think that her partner is a good man at heart who only occasionally does something mean or hurtful. But all too often things happen just as they did in Stevenson's novel and in Tina's marriage: the unwelcome visitor comes again and again, more and more often, until he takes over the personality of the good doctor altogether.

At the end of Stevenson's story, Dr. Jekyll's friends and servants discover that Dr. Jekyll and Mr. Hyde are not two different people, as everybody had thought, but one and the same. Tina made a similar discovery: the "supportive" Terry and the critical, bullying Terry were one and the same person, and that person was a controller.

You may want to look at your partner's behavior to see if you are being confused and misled by actions that are not what they seem. In the next chapter we'll examine your partner's behavior more closely and give you some guidelines for evaluating it. But first, let's get back to you and what you may be going through with your partner. Even if you feel confused—or perhaps we should say *especially* if you feel confused—your own reactions and feelings may be your best guide to what you're up against.

STRATEGIES WOMEN USE TO COPE

Before Tina discovered that Terry was not the person she thought and left him, she tried many different strategies to cope with his behavior. No two women face exactly the same situation or respond in the same way, of course, but many of Tina's reactions are typical. If you have a controlling partner, you may be using similar strategies yourself.

1. Disbelief and Minimizing

The controller's first verbal or physical assault throws many women into a state of shock. Like Tina, you may be stunned. You simply can't believe it happened. Your partner may be remorseful: "I'll never do it again," he promises. From your experience with him, you have good reason to believe the pledge. But even if he doesn't apologize, even if he acts as if nothing happened, you have no reason to expect that it will happen again. He has never acted this way before.

Even though you might be very upset or angry or hurt, you try to put the incident behind you and go on. That's what most women do. After all, let's be realistic. You don't walk out on the person you love at the first sign of trouble. You probably wouldn't leave your partner if he lost his job or got arrested or had an affair. And if he yells at you, or hits you, is that worse?

Most women believe it will never happen again. And at the same time, they may take steps to prevent it from happening again. They may find some outside cause to explain away what happened: he was overtired or drunk or under too much stress. Or they take their partner's criticism to heart and try to change the things that supposedly caused him to lose his temper. After Terry blew up at Tina for keeping him waiting, she tried harder to be on time in the hope of eliminating the cause of the problem.

Another way women cope with these shocking and stressful incidents is to forget them as quickly as possible. Forgetting is a common reaction that people use to defend themselves from all kinds of threatening experiences, such as accidents or natural disasters like floods and tornados. How many times have you heard the advice given to someone who suffered a traumatic event: "Don't dwell on it"? Women shocked by the behavior of a controlling partner often adopt that attitude. Tina did such a good job of forgetting Terry's first explosion that she was shocked all over again the second time he blew up, and the third. "After that," she says, "I knew it actually happened, and I knew it had happened more than once, so I started telling myself that it wasn't so bad."

Minimizing the impact of overwhelming events is another common defense mechanism people use to cut things down to manageable size. Women commonly minimize the impact of the controlling partner's behavior so that they can do what they have to do—take care of the kids, show up at work, make some money—without falling apart. Many women in abusive relationships say to themselves, as Tina did, "It wasn't so bad. It could have been worse."

Some women minimize explosive incidents because they don't happen very often. Some overlook the bad times because they feel that the good times are so good. And many have little choice but to ignore the bad times.

▪ LUISA

I was a good Catholic wife who believed in her marriage vows. I had two kids, ages one and four. I couldn't get a decent job—I never finished high school, and at that time my English wasn't so good. My family was on the other side of the country, and anyway I knew what my mother would say. She was a good Catholic too. So I could take my chances on being alone and too poor to feed my kids, or I could stay where I was. Those were my choices. So I kept telling myself, "A lot of women have it a lot worse. I can manage." And I prayed a lot.

Disbelief, denying, forgetting, and minimizing may be psychologically useful strategies in the short term. They keep many women going. But they are also signs of trouble, indications that a woman has gone through too much. Over time, they take their toll. And after a while, if a woman goes through worse experiences that she can't block out with these overworked defenses, she may turn to tranquilizers, alcohol, or drugs to do the job. Then her trouble deepens.

▪ MARY ANN

I was severely battered for two years. After every time, he'd say, "I'll never do it again," and I needed to believe that he'd never do it again. I still cared about him. But once I went to the emergency room, and when the nurse checked me over, I had bruises everywhere. I wasn't seeing them. I knew my shoulder hurt, but I didn't realize that my entire back was black-and-blue. I said, "I don't have bruises." And this nurse said, "Honey, either you've got bruises, or you're out of your mind. Now which one is it?" It took that experience to open my eyes.

Denying what was happening to me was my way of hanging on to my sanity. If I'd had to face up to it all at once, I couldn't have handled it. I think I really would have seriously freaked out. How could anybody hate me that much? And he said he loved me, so why was he doing this? It totally wiped me out, so I just denied it altogether.

2. Managing

We've never met a woman who didn't think she could "manage." As we've seen, denying, minimizing, and forgetting prepare the way by reducing potentially overwhelming problems to "manageable" size. Thus most women can believe (at least for a while) that they are able to handle their partners and improve their relationships. Even women who are very badly physically abused often believe, perhaps correctly, that they have some control over the situation. They think that if they didn't have some power—to calm a partner down, to put him in a better mood, to make him leave the kids alone—things might be much worse. This belief seems to be strongest among women like Luisa, who can't see any way out of the situation. If you can't find a way to leave the relationship, what else can you do but "manage"?

Broadly speaking, managing the situation seems to mean managing the partner. As Tina explains: "Even though his anger scared me, I always felt like I could handle him. I always thought I could coax him out of it or at least shift his attention to something else, and sometimes I could. But obviously it wasn't really true; he'd 'forgive' me when it suited him—and not before." Like Tina, most women keep trying to "manage," even in the face of mounting evidence that it's not working very well.

Managing a partner usually means keeping him calm. As we mentioned, most women try to remove the immediate "cause" of their partner's anger. Tina tried to be prompt. Gwen made sure the refrigerator always held a cold six-pack of the right brand of beer. LaVonne always said no when other men asked her to dance. Molly stopped going out with her women friends.

Unfortunately, the immediate cause of a controller's outburst is usually not what it seems to be. How many times have you heard women say, "If it's not one thing, it's another"? What this means is that no matter how much you fix, there will always be something else wrong. Keeping the controller calm becomes a full-time job. And it leaves you with an awful feeling that you either can't do enough or you can't do anything right at all. Maggie and Annette tried unsuccessfully to manage their partners by doing things "right."

▪ MAGGIE

If the least little thing went wrong, he would blow up, so I felt I had to keep everything under control. I spent most of my time making sure the kids didn't yell, supper was on time, and the house was spotless. I cleaned from 6:00 A.M. to midnight, scrubbing, waxing the floors, vacuuming every day, polishing, dusting, washing twenty-one loads of laundry a week. Then when everything was just perfect, there'd be something else—some tiny little thing, literally a tiny spot on a napkin, a tiny wrinkle in a T-shirt, a tiny bit of dust. I'd mispronounce a word. One of the kids would sneeze. I'm sure there's more leeway in the marines.

▪ ANNETTE

I spent my whole day thinking about him. What can I fix for him? How can I look? What should I do with the kids? Have I done everything I was supposed to do today? What will he want to do tonight? Maybe then he would be happy. I had to stay one step ahead of him all the time. I'd keep track of his moods, where he was going, who he was spending time with, how everything was going for him at work, how his favorite teams were doing, what the president was doing—he loved George Bush—how much he was drinking. That way I thought I was more able to predict what the weekend would be like and what to do with the kids. I thought about this stuff all the time, and I did everything I thought of. But no matter how far I went, it wasn't enough.

Women try to manage their partners to make things better, or at least prevent them from getting worse. With that goal in mind, women placate and calm and comfort and protect and please the controller. They try to help him with his problems, soothe his cares, denounce his enemies, build up his ego, support his plans, encourage his dreams. And they comply with his demands. Women stop doing things they enjoy doing and do what the partner wants them to do instead. In any difference of opinion, they give in to him. They agree with him when they know he's wrong. They accept blame for things they know are not their fault. They avoid showing their own anger for fear of prompting his. They take care of everything. They make excuses for him. They bite their tongues. They try to change their own behavior and personality to meet the criticism and demands of the controller. They adopt his definition of perfection and try to achieve it. In short, they fall under the control of the controller.

All women use some of these tactics at some time to get by in a great range of situations we face in our male-dominated society. Women in relationships with controllers use them more often. For women who live with controllers, trying to please and keep a partner calm becomes a way of life. Most of them believe that they *are* managing, but when they later look back, most of them get angry. Brenda says: "I was conned. I thought I was taking care of business, and I was. But it was all *his* business. I busted my ass for that jerk—and all just so he'd be so kind as sometimes not to scream at me in front of my kids." When a woman tries to keep a partner calm by pleasing him, he gains exactly what he wants. He exercises his power over her and gets his way on a daily basis. It is ironic that she thinks she is "managing" best when in fact she is most under his control.

3. Asserting Yourself

Even while women are being misled, they keep trying to figure out what's best for themselves and their families. They are always taking stock, reevaluating their options. Although Luisa felt bound to her Catholic marriage, she kept reconsidering her position.

▪ LUISA

I'd go back and forth in my head. I'd say, "I can't stay here. I can't stand him yelling at me and hitting me and yelling at the kids. I know it hurts them." But then I'd think about leaving and I'd get scared. This other voice in my head would say, "How can you find a place to live? How are you going to pay for it? What if you wind up in some project full of junkies? How are you going to take care of your kids then? What if you can't hack it? What if they take your kids away?" So I'd tell myself, "Okay, okay. You're right. Things aren't so bad here. They could be worse." And then he'd go off again and I'd be saying to myself, "I've got to get out of here."

Like most women, Luisa tried not just to keep her controlling partner calm but to make changes in the relationship. Many women resist their partner's demands, just as Tina did when she told Terry to stop being silly. Maggie resisted by refusing to do her husband's laundry anymore. She told him that since she obviously wasn't able to do it right, he'd better hire professionals. Gwen told her boyfriend to bring home his own beer. "You drink it, you fetch it," she told him. Some time later, she issued a bigger ultimatum: either go to AA or get out. And she herself started attending Al-Anon meetings. Tina insisted that Terry go with her to a marriage counselor. Luisa prayed—and insisted on her right to go to church whenever she wanted to.

All of these steps, however small they may seem, help a woman to maintain her own strength and pride, challenge her partner's control, and help to change the balance of power in the relationship. Some steps are more effective than others; and some may be counterproductive. In Tina's case, for example, marriage counseling did not improve the relationship; and as Tina says now, it probably delayed her decision to get a divorce. But very often, you can't tell what will happen until you try.

Women try many different ways to make change. Some turn to their own support network, or his, for advice and help. They may ask family members or friends to intervene and talk to the controlling partner. They may strike out for greater long-term independence by applying for a job or entering a school or training program. They may start saving up and hiding money, just in case. Women who are physically abused may call the police or go to court for an order of protection. They may leave temporarily, as a warning that they could leave permanently if the controller doesn't change his ways. All of these strategies to resist control and to make the controller give up some of his power, whether they succeed in that aim or not, testify to the great strength and resourcefulness of women.

4. Surviving As Best You Can

Unfortunately, standing up to a controller may put a woman in greater danger. When she sticks up for herself, the determined controller feels threatened and may redouble his efforts to maintain power over her. Even a controlling partner who has been withdrawn and distant, apparently uninterested in his wife or girlfriend, may use much more direct tactics—even violence—to keep her under control if he fears that she might slip away. It is when a woman is trying to leave that a controlling partner becomes most threatening and dangerous. Many women feel afraid to stay but become even more afraid to leave. They report feeling completely isolated, cut off, and trapped. Nevertheless, most women survive. Some do so by clinging to their religion or moral code as a source of inner strength, as Luisa did. Others echo the attitude expressed by Brenda: "I hated how he put me down and called me names all the time, but I swore that I'd never stoop to his level—and I never did." A lot of women cling to dreams and ambitions until they can put them into effect. Their lives seem to be on hold, but their hopes keep them going.

Many women who can't leave the controlling partner end up leaving in another sense. They withdraw emotionally, retreating into an internal space as a refuge from threats, verbal abuse, and physical assaults. That's what Gloria did.

▪ GLORIA

The first month he beat me I took my wedding ring off and never put it on again. I told him I lost it. In my head I separated myself from my husband right then, even though I spent another five years getting together the money to get to California and start over. When he wanted sex, I'd turn my face and I'd keep my hands right on my chest so that he couldn't be close to me. He did whatever he wanted, but he wasn't going to be close to me. From the waist up I was mine. I went somewhere else in my head.

For some women, withdrawal can be a lifesaver. Charlotte explains it this way: "There was a strong person inside me, in spite of his put-downs. The person who helped me survive was the woman I knew I was underneath." Jill says, "It's hard to explain but we are our own person within, and nobody can take that away, no matter what he does." Gwen says, "I told him, 'You can't get inside my soul. You might kill me, but you'll never break my spirit.' "

But when control and violence increase, a woman may get caught in her own withdrawal. Sheila's story illustrates what can happen as abuse escalates. Sheila is trapped by a *combination of circumstances*: her husband's increasing use of sexual and physical violence, the fear and depression she feels as a result, and the failure of others to help her. It is important to recognize that some women who get caught in this kind of trap do not get out again.

▪ SHEILA

My husband would come home from work about 2:00 in the morning, and my daughter would wake from a peaceful sleep, screaming. When I would hear his car door slam, I'd start to shake uncontrollably because it was always at night that he would rape me. And he'd put the key in the door, and she'd be screaming, and I'd be holding her and crying. This went on for months. I didn't know that I was on the verge of a nervous breakdown. All I knew was I needed help. I couldn't sleep. I wasn't feeding my daughter properly. I'd give her peanut butter and jelly and turn on the TV to get her out of my hair. I would sleep during the day, and then at night when I wanted to, I couldn't. I was so nervous that I gulped down the Valium.

Eventually I got paralyzed with fear. I'd look up help numbers in the phone book—hotlines, social-service agencies, priests, domestic violence services, all sorts of people I could call—and I would freeze. I didn't have the strength to pick up the phone. It was so embarrassing to talk about my situation. And what if my husband walked through the door in the middle of the conversation? I'd die from fright, I was sure.

I did try to tell my neighbor and my doctor, but it was obvious that they didn't want to hear about it. I felt humiliated, and I was terrified someone would criticize me, like he did. I lost so much self-confidence that it felt safer to be at home than to go out on the street. I was so glad when the phone didn't ring or the day would pass without anyone coming to my door.

About one year before I got out, I was totally numb and dead. I thought about killing myself, but I decided against it because I knew how it would hurt my daughter. I remember that during this time my mother and sister came to visit me from thousands of miles away and I said to myself, "These people love me and I'm so glad to see them, but here I sit, completely indifferent to them, and all I can think of is sleep."

But that visit was the turning point. I think it reminded me of who I used to be when I was "alive." It wasn't long after they left when I got the nerve to call a women's shelter two towns away. I was so scared James would find out. I didn't have any black-and-blue marks so I wasn't sure they would help, but they came and picked me up. They seemed to understand what I had been through. I never went back.

HOW DO WOMEN FEEL?

Most women involved with a controlling partner try out and then discard one strategy after another. As they watch each strategy fail and the partner's control increase, many also notice emotional changes in themselves. Some changes are subtle, and others are far more disturbing. They seem to be especially severe if the partner uses violence as a means of control. Some women become more short-tempered and jumpy, less patient—even abusive—with their children, more pessimistic about the future. Some notice physical symptoms as well, such as fatigue, migraine headaches, menstrual problems, skin rashes, weight changes, and sleep disorders.

A number of women involved with a controlling partner experience so many conflicting feelings that they describe their emotional lives as "a roller-coaster ride." They often feel sad, worried and anxious, angry, lonely, numb, embarrassed, humiliated, powerless, depressed, hopeless, bitter, despairing, hostile, terrified—a whole range of feelings, most of them bad. But at the core of the emotional confusion aroused by living with a controller, we most often find five key feelings, sometimes all at once. They are fear, shame, guilt, anger, and the nameless feeling of "going crazy."

1. Fear

Most women involved with a controlling partner fear his outbursts of anger and verbal abuse and try to avoid them, just as Tina did. Women whose partners use violence face the possibility of injury or even death. They have every reason to be afraid. Some women fear that anything they do will make matters worse. Some are afraid to seek help because they fear that no one will protect them and that their call for help will simply put them in greater danger.

These fears are perfectly reasonable, and many women undoubtedly save their own lives by listening to their fears and acting accordingly. Women in this situation often seem to be doing "nothing," but in fact they are usually working very hard to survive by keeping the violent partner calm. Safety must be their first consideration, as it was for Ruth. (We'll have much more to say about planning for your safety in Chapter 7.)

▪ RUTH

> He told me that he was never going to let me go. He said that he married me, and whether he loved me or not, and whether I loved him or not, I was going to stay with him, and if I tried to leave him, he was going to kill me—one day at a time, like dripping water on a rock, until I broke apart. Although I never knew exactly what he would do, I knew that he was capable of torture. He broke my arm once and dangled it in front of me, playing with it, telling me it wasn't broken.

2. Shame

Shame is the feeling that makes you want to disappear through the floor. It comes over you when your partner tells you you're stupid and ugly, or when he tears you apart in front of others. For women in these situations, the shame is twofold: they are humiliated by the incident and ashamed of their inability to make such incidents stop. Many say they are ashamed of their own sense of powerlessness. Many are deeply ashamed of their partner and consequently of themselves for being with him. A lot of women also feel ashamed of themselves for tolerating what their partner does, even when they have no other choice. This feeling is often reinforced by other people who mistakenly blame women for "asking for" and "enjoying" abuse.

Shame has complicated effects. For one thing, it discourages some women from telling other people about what's going on and seeking help. Some then become ashamed of their own silence and withdraw further, increasing their isolation. In addition, over the course of time, some women find themselves incorporating the shame, taking it upon themselves, even when they know that the fault is not theirs.

▪ CINDA

> I was embarrassed to let anyone know my problems because they seemed so stupid, so messed up. I also thought that if people knew what was going on they would say it was my fault and that I was a fool for staying. And I *was* a fool for staying. So maybe it *was* all my fault. That's how I'd think. It would go round and round in my head. And then, of course, I felt so dishonest for lying to my friends about my life that I withdrew completely. Things just got worse, and when he would physically push me around, that was the worst moment for me. I mean, I couldn't even stand on my own two feet. I felt so small.

3. Guilt

Many controllers are very skilled at making their partners feel guilty, just as Terry succeeded in making Tina feel guilty for not being a "good mother." Many women have to defend themselves from verbal attacks about their appearance, their parenting, their cooking, their housekeeping, their sexual performance, or their lack of devotion to their husbands. Constant accusations keep a woman on guard against the next verbal attack, and they wear down her resistance. And since no woman is perfect, many of us are easily convinced that we're not doing as well as we should.

Women feel guilty for many different reasons. Some feel guilty for being unable to make their partner calm and happy. Some feel guilty for doing things they believe to be wrong in order to keep him happy, things like lying, shoplifting, or engaging in unusual sex acts. Some women—especially women with strong religious backgrounds—feel very guilty that they can't seem to make their relationship work.

Some feel guilty for staying with a controlling partner, particularly a violent one; and some feel guilty for thinking of leaving a partner who is so messed up, so put down, so poor, so pathetic. Women may feel guilty on both counts at once. Similarly, mothers often feel guilty that they are exposing their children to arguments and even physical violence. On the other hand, when they think about leaving, they feel guilty about depriving their children of a father or father figure and of the economic advantages an employed father might offer the kids.

▪ GWEN

I didn't like myself for not having the strength to get out. I didn't know where I could go to get away from him. Everybody in town knew me, so it wasn't going to take much for him to find me again. So I had no idea where I could go, but I didn't like myself for not walking away. But then when I decided to leave, I knew he didn't have anybody, and I just couldn't do it to him. He's had a really hard life. He was trying to sober up—going to AA. But he never could find a job. And his mama died and he didn't have money to help bury her. That shamed him. It was sad. He was just pathetic.

Most of these guilty feelings are reinforced by other people. Traditionally, our society teaches women to stand by their men, then blames abused women for not leaving. Our society teaches that children should have a father, then often blames mothers when things go wrong.

4. Going Crazy

As we mentioned earlier, controllers often say one thing and do another, and they often act in contradictory and unpredictable ways. These things are confusing enough. But in addition, when women try to talk over with their partner the problems they see in the relationship, they may find that their own perceptions of reality are called into question. In many cases, the partner denies a woman's description and interpretation of events. He denies that problems exist. In other cases, he agrees entirely with the woman's point of view, but he changes nothing. Either way, women report, they feel like they're "going crazy."

When a woman is subjected to extreme or violent control, the feeling becomes so severe and so common that it requires special mention here. A great many women feel that they are losing control altogether and going out of their minds. Many women are troubled by insomnia or nightmares. Some have fantasies of hurting themselves or others. Some feel as though they leave their bodies—particularly if they are subjected to sexual assault—while others report the numb and "dead" condition that Sheila described. Many women have fantasies of suicide or revenge.

These feelings are understandable responses to trauma. They may be experienced by anyone who has survived a traumatic event, such as warfare or a violent crime, but they make the person who experiences them feel out of touch with reality. And that feeling may be reinforced by others. For example, many women feel great fear (often with good reason) that their partner intends to do them harm. If a woman seeking help takes a psychological exam at this point, she may be diagnosed as "paranoid"—that is, as someone who has an irrational fear of others. Her "paranoia" is a rational and healthy response to her situation in life, but the psychologist's report may confirm that she is "crazy." In such cases, women report an additional terrifying fear: that psychologists or social workers will lock them up or take away their children.

The feeling that she is losing her mind adds to a woman's fears and may deepen her feelings of depression and hopelessness. Many women speak of feeling isolated and trapped. Some report a dramatic loss of self-confidence brought on by their feeling of powerlessness and the failure of all their efforts to help themselves. That loss of the sense of self-worth is even more extreme for some women who adopt strategies that prove self-destructive, such as drinking or taking drugs.

5. Anger

Sooner or later, control almost always makes the controlled person angry. Many women, however, push down their angry feelings for fear that expressing anger may trigger even greater anger in the controlling partner. Consequently, while many women are conscious of feeling fearful, guilty, ashamed, or crazy, they may be less aware that underneath those feelings there sometimes lies a deep deposit of rage. Some women act out their anger in indirect ways. Liz, for example, sabotaged her partner and did harm to herself at the same time.

▪ LIZ

I cared a lot about my appearance, and so did my husband since he was in the clothing business and I modeled his line at shows. But slowly I started putting on weight. He was furious. I know I did this because my weight was the one thing he could not control. I had charge of it. But on the other hand, I didn't really like myself being fat.

Sometimes women act out anger much more directly. Some women fight back against violent partners, and others plan revenge. Beth and Lindsy are examples.

▪ BETH

For weeks I would do everything to please him and agree with him, and then I got to the point where I'd say, "To hell with it," and I'd call him every name in the book, and I'd lay into him with everything I had—kicking, biting, pulling hair. I knew he'd pay me back, but just at the moment it didn't matter.

▪ LINDSY

I used to fantasize about his death all the time. At first I just imagined that he'd die in a horrible accident—his plane would crash or he'd fall down an elevator shaft. Then I imagined that other people would hurt him. I hoped some street gang would beat him up or the woman he was having an affair with might stick a knife into him. Then I started thinking I might do it myself, and at that point I decided I better leave.

Many women are particularly troubled, as Lindsy was, by thoughts of getting back at their partner. But that desire for revenge is an understandable result of being abused. It is one of the few tools available to those with less power to use against those who have more. It shouldn't be surprising that many women pray or plot for revenge against their partners, and some actually assault them.

Fighting back makes some women feel better about themselves, as it did Beth. But it leaves some women feeling more shame and guilt. Women who hate their partner's abuse sometimes condemn themselves for using the same tactics. And so does their partner. "You're just as violent as I am," he may say, twisting reality to serve his purposes. But in fact, in most cases, her violent fantasies and actions are a response to his.

Nevertheless, a woman who seriously assaults or kills her partner will be severely punished and may spend the better part of her life in prison. It's best to take your fantasies of killing a partner as Lindsy did: as clear signals that it's time to leave.

WHEN YOUR SURVIVAL STRATEGIES GIVE YOU TROUBLE

As a woman feels more and more trapped by a controlling partner, she may do things that trouble her or make her ashamed of herself. Many women come to depend on alcohol or drugs to get through the day. Some lie to friends to avoid further trouble, let down people they care about, have affairs, eat compulsively, or sleep all the time. All of these tactics, like the strategies we've already mentioned, are perfectly understandable responses, given the circumstances. What matters in most cases is how well the strategies you use work, and how they make you feel about yourself.

Some strategies, however, clearly do not work. Instead, they prove to be self-destructive. They are loud and clear signals that a person is in trouble and must find some other way. One of them, which we have already mentioned, is planning to kill your partner. Another is planning to kill yourself. Don't do it. Call for help. (In Chapter 6 we'll talk about ways to build up your strength and confidence.) Two other actions that prove to be self-destructive are: depending on alcohol and drugs, and neglecting and abusing your children.

▪ LAVONNE: ON ABUSING SUBSTANCES

I used to smoke dope and drink with him every night to keep him from exploding at me. It seemed like the best way to keep him from going off, and it felt good to get a little high myself. But really I just made another problem for myself. I kept it up until one of my friends confronted me and dragged me to AA. When I got clean and sober, he left. Get this—he said I wasn't any fun anymore.

▪ NANCY: ON NEGLECTING AND ABUSING CHILDREN

I got to using prescribed Valium more than I like to remember. After months and months of abuse and tranqs it's hard to keep it together and be a loving mommy. I was angry all the time and hurt and spaced out, all at once. I'm so ashamed of this, but there were many times when I treated them just like he treated me. It wasn't just that I sat them in front of the TV for days at a time. I yelled at them. I said the most god-awful things to them. I smacked them. It was terrible.

WHAT'S HAPPENING TO YOU?

Women involved with controlling partners have to sort through their confusion, untangle the conflicting emotions they feel, and evaluate the various strategies they might use to change their lives. In this chapter, we've tried to start you thinking about how you're feeling about yourself and the strategies you may be using to cope with your partner. If sorting out your feelings and making changes seems like an overwhelming job, keep in mind that most women do what they can, one step at a time; and although sometimes the actions they take are counterproductive or self-destructive, most women come through. They do sort out their feelings, they do get clear, and they do take positive action. (Chapters 6 and 7 will help you do so too.)

We have to admit, however, that many women involved with controlling partners don't come through before they've spent a great deal of time and thought and energy on another strategy that usually doesn't get them very far—that is, trying to figure out their partner. The single most important issue for most women involved with controlling partners is a question so basic, and so misleading, that we'll devote the next chapter to discussing it.

3

Why Does My Partner Treat Me This Way?

For most women with controlling partners, the big question is: why does my partner treat me this way? How much thought have you given already to that question? In this chapter, we'll give you the answer.

You probably know your partner better than anyone else in the world does, including his own parents. Nevertheless, like many women involved with a controlling partner, you may not be able to let go of the feeling that if only you understood him *better,* you could figure out what to do to make him feel and behave differently. No matter how badly he treats you, you may cling to the belief that you could bring out his better nature, if only you were able to figure out *why* he acts the way he does.

In a great many relationships, the worse the controlling partner acts, the harder a woman tries to understand him. Some simple and obvious explanations for his behavior are: he doesn't like her, doesn't respect her, or doesn't have any feelings for her at all. If an acquaintance treated you the way your partner does, wouldn't you possibly draw those conclusions? But it hurts. It may be too hard for a woman to accept those notions. After all, he *says* he loves her. So she may go on thinking that there must be some deep and complex reason: something in his past, some problem at work, or some injustice he's suffered—some oppression, some deprivation, some injury—that *makes* him behave as he does. She can fix him, and the relationship, she thinks—if only she can figure out what makes him tick. Her intention is a good one, but it leads her in the wrong direction. It leads her smack into what we call the explanation trap—busy with her search for theories, she misses the plain facts.

The unpleasant truth is that the simple explanations of his behavior are closer to the truth. Why does he treat you this way? Because he *chooses* to. None of us can help what we feel, but all of us choose how we act upon our feelings. *Your partner could treat you differently if he wanted to.* And if he doesn't want to, then no matter how well you understand your partner, *you cannot change him.*

But why does he choose to behave this way? For one thing, he thinks he has a right to dominate. That is the role for which many men are still trained. Men grow up expecting to take charge, and expecting women to submit. And each man's expectation is backed up by the culture around him, for men (especially white upper-class men) are still very much in charge of everything, legal and illegal: the government, the military, the law, the media, business, industry, science, the professions, organized crime, the drug trade, prostitution. Despite all the advances made by the women's movement, men still run the world, and most women, both at home and on the job, still serve men and take care of them.

These are hard truths—unpleasant to think about. So, many women reject the clear, simple answer—that men act this way because they choose to and because they are allowed to—and they look instead for another explanation, more personal, more complicated, more reassuring. Keisha describes the difficulty and confusion of that search.

▪ KEISHA

I tried to reach inside myself and find out, "What am I doing wrong?" Maybe it's something he doesn't like about me. And then I'd say, "I do what's right. I treat him very well. So maybe it's something he dislikes about himself, or it's some problem at work that he takes out on me." Then I'd decide, "It's the alcohol." But that wasn't quite right either because he had these awful ways when he was sober, too.

Like Keisha, you may ask yourself, "Is it me?" Then, "Is it him?" And then you may conclude that it's just too hard to make sense of it all. It is difficult to sort through this confusion alone, but that's what many women try to do. Later, we'll talk about where they go wrong, and why. But first, let's hear some of the explanations that women often come up with for their partner's behavior.

▪ PATTI

First I blamed Ron's bad moods on his job. He had lots of financial worries at work; it was just seasonal employment, and he had a son-of-a-bitch for a boss. Then I added the stresses of family life. We lived in a trailer, a fairly good-sized one, but it was still much too small for us. The confinement was awful. There were toys all over the floor, and the kids were all over him. I kept thinking that when we moved, things would get better.

▪ KATHRYN

I came to see Eddie as lonely and sick. He was so mean to me, but he kept saying he was sorry. And he would cry. I thought, "This has got to be a sickness. He needs my help. I have to be strong for the two of us to get us through."

▪ JOSIE

At first I would say, "He lost control—he wasn't himself." But he always made it seem like I set him off. So I went into therapy to find out what I was doing wrong. My therapist suggested the idea that Ben was angry at his mother and that he was taking it out on me. And that's what I believed for a long time.

LOOKING FOR EXPLANATIONS

As we mentioned in the last chapter, many women who live with controlling partners try to manage as best they can. Looking for explanations of the controlling partner's behavior is one way of managing the situation, and maybe even the partner. It's a particularly attractive strategy because it seems to offer a chance to find what's wrong, fix it, and live happily ever after, or at least manage better in the future. Looking for explanations offers a woman hope. It helps her go on believing for a long time that things will improve—despite all the evidence to the contrary.

The more specific the explanation she can find, the more hopeful of change a woman may be, because specific problems seem more manageable than vague, ill-defined ones. If some specific circumstances now trouble her partner and cause his bad behavior, he may change when the circumstances do. She may tell herself, "Things will get better when he finds a new job. When we have more money. When we move. When the kids get older." Such explanations are particularly appealing because they promise an inevitable solution *in the future*. All she has to do is wait.

Many women find hope in the "if only" formula. They blame themselves for causing their partner's behavior. To change his behavior, they think, all they have to do is change their own. If her partner explodes because dinner isn't ready, then all a woman has to do to change his behavior in the future is to have dinner ready on time. Many women say things like, "If only I had behaved better. If only I had listened to him. If only I had watched my mouth. If only I had stayed home." Such explanations give women hope for change and the sense of being able to bring that change about, to manage. Often they make a woman feel much more in control of the situation than she actually is.

Such explanations—and the long search for other explanations when these turn out to be wrong—keep a woman's hopes up. Everyone needs hope, both to make progress and to maintain a healthy outlook on life. But for women involved with controlling partners, hope may be misleading, a waste of time, and even dangerous, if it is what keeps them with violent partners. Anyone involved with an abusive person has a right not only to hope he will change, but to *demand* that he change. And in fact, a controlling partner *may* change. But if he doesn't choose to, all the hope in the world is not going to help.

GETTING STUCK IN EXPLANATIONS

Like so many women, Beth was raised to make things "easy" and "nice" for her family. "That's a woman's role," she would say, and it made her feel good when she succeeded at it. When things went wrong—when her husband exploded—she felt responsible. She says, "I adored Ralph. I kept saying, 'He'll be okay tomorrow. That's how I wanted it to be, so that's how I made it in my head—even though he wasn't changing." Searching for explanations, she blamed his "rotten job" for his explosive behavior.

Without that theory, the world was a scary place for Beth. "I had to find a reason for the way he acted," she says. "It's too overwhelming to face the possibility that there may be *no* reason, or at least nothing you can fix."

Beth did more than merely hope that Ralph would get a better job in the future. She encouraged him to quit the job he had. She helped him figure out what kind of job would make him happier. And when things got too bad, she went out and found a job for him herself.

▪ BETH

I worked so hard because I hoped that Ralph would cheer up and one day he'd come in the front door with a big smile on his face and say, "I don't know what came over me. You're so wonderful!" Then we were going to be Mr. and Mrs. All-American couple again. I was always optimistic. If I had thought that this happy ending was never going to happen, my mind would have snapped. I would have been in the funny farm.

Ralph liked his new job. He took Beth out to dinner to celebrate after his first week at the new place—and then he went on treating her just as he had before. She says, "It was terrible, but I finally had to admit to myself, 'It wasn't the job. It's *him.*'" Nevertheless, Beth still didn't give up hope.

We're trained as women to help our partner change his life for the better, not to be "selfish" and change our own. That's another reason we spend so much time figuring out *his* problems. And let's face it: the practical problems of changing your own life—especially if you have kids—may seem too big to think about.

> I just couldn't pick up and leave with the kids. I didn't think I had the strength. So I decided that he had some kind of psychological problem, and I started trying to get him into therapy. This is going to sound terrible, but it seemed like it would be easier to keep trying to fix him than to go out on my own and fix my own life. The therapist tried to tell me I was "codependent," but I said "That's just a ten-dollar name for *scared.*"

Like Beth, Tanya felt stuck between a rock and a hard place—between her partner's behavior and the difficulty of doing things for herself.

▪ TANYA

> Whenever I'd think, "This relationship isn't going to make it," I'd get stopped cold when I tried to imagine what I could do next. I would see a big courtroom and my husband and his attorneys, pointing their fingers at me and accusing me of neglecting my kids. Or I'd hear my Aunt Bessie telling me I was giving up the best thing I'd ever get. Sometimes I'd see my minister's disapproving eyes, or I'd hear my husband's voice on the phone, threatening to slit his wrists. Or I'd imagine the inside of the welfare office with my three kids crying, "Mommy, take us home." Then I'd start to think, "How can I help him? He *did* have such a rotten childhood."

Ida was stuck for a long time too, trying to explain to herself why her partner hit her—until a conversation with a good friend snapped her out of it.

▪ IDA

One of my friends, who had listened to me talk about Dan for months, finally said to me, "Ida, what would happen if you could totally understand him? What if you had him completely figured out?" I couldn't believe what came out of my mouth next. I told her, "Nothing would change." "That's probably right," she teased me. "You'd just have the best-analyzed batterer in town."

As Ida realized, your explanation for your partner's behavior is not the problem. His behavior is the problem. Finding an explanation for his behavior won't change it. Even acting upon your explanation or insight, as Beth did when she got Ralph a new job, won't change your partner's behavior. Only he can do that.

To make this point clear, we asked several women to tell us the theories they came up with in the past to explain their partner's controlling behavior. Then we asked them to evaluate those theories, given what they know now. Let's look at some of the most common explanations they found. All of them sound good; they seem reasonable and convincing. Any one of them may contain some grains of truth. But they are merely explanations: they don't produce change.

Explanation 1:
Alcohol and Drugs Make Him This Way

We often assume that drugs and alcohol lead to abusive behavior and particularly to violent behavior. Every day in the news we hear stories of violence related to drug and alcohol abuse. And our own experience bears out the close connection. But is the relationship between substance abuse and violence this clear-cut?

▪ RAYE

I told my kids, "Look, your dad is ill. He has a disease called alcoholism." But it wasn't all alcoholism, because eventually he started abusing me when he was sober. That blew it for me. I'd sit there going, "Now what am I to do? There's no hope." I had to accept that the alcohol was a cover, and now he didn't even need it. I was going to be a punching bag with or without the booze. That was so hard to face.

Undoubtedly drugs and alcohol make abuse worse, and there is evidence that some heavy-duty drugs—mainly crack/cocaine and PCP—can produce violent behavior. But for the most part, we can't say that alcohol or drugs by themselves *cause* abuse or violence to happen. When your partner is drunk or on drugs, he probably looks and acts out of control. In his sober moments, he probably tells you that he can't help what he does when he's drunk or high because he loses control. Ask yourself, "Is it true?" Why, then, does he attack you and not his boss? Why is he nice to a friend, yet hurtful to you? How can he have so much self-control with others but none at home?

That's where a man's privilege comes in. Our culture gives him permission to assault you. "She's my woman," he may say, and drunk or sober, he believes he has the right to control you. In fact, it's likely that no one will stop him or punish him; whereas if he assaulted his boss, he'd lose his job and probably end up in jail. Since he's drunk, he gets to behave in all sorts of bizarre and antisocial ways, including beating you up. That's more or less what we expect from drunks. When he's drunk or high, he has an excuse to assault you without guilt or remorse. "I lost control," he will say. "I don't remember what happened. I wasn't myself." That's supposed to make his actions okay, or at least to put them out of the realm of his responsibility. Clearly, for all his claims of being out of control, he is making choices.

▪ LATONYA

He went into substance abuse treatment and we went into family counseling. He stopped the drugs, and for a few weeks I was in heaven. But then I realized that, without the drugs, he was still having these horrible temper tantrums, swearing at me, telling me I was ugly and selfish and that I abused him. He'd carry on that I was trying to destroy him, I was warped and twisted. I thought this might pass, but the truth was it didn't. Now I had a "clean" abuser.

Some men admit that while their drug or alcohol addiction is a very real problem, they also use it as a convenient excuse for abusive behavior. "I used my drinking as a rationalization, and the excuse worked well," a man named Roger told us. "I knew in the morning that I was going to pay my wife back that night. So I'd go out and get loaded on the way home from work. Then I could say, 'It was the booze that did it. I'm not that kind of guy, honey.' Not that it was like a big conscious plot against her. I believed it too."

Why then will a few violent men (unfortunately only a few) stop physical violence when they complete drug or alcohol treatment? In a sober state, these men disapprove of violence. When they decide to give up drugs or alcohol, they also lose their excuse to harm their partners. Consequently, they stop practicing violence, although they may turn to other forms of emotional manipulation to maintain control. It's important to remember that physical violence is only one tactic of the controlling partner. Ending violence does not mean ending control.

▪ ELEANOR

Charles stopped hitting—temporarily—after he joined AA, but my life was still hell. In fact, things got worse. He blamed me for everything. And on top of that I was supposed to be grateful to him all the time because he wasn't drinking. Then he started in with the pushing and shoving again.

David Adams, a Boston counselor who has worked for many years with abusive men, had this to say about Eleanor's husband: "Charles has two *separate* problems—one with alcohol and drugs, and a second with abuse. Eleanor believed that alcoholism caused the abuse, so logically she thought that treating the alcoholism would stop the abuse. Unfortunately, she was wrong. Charles got help in AA for his drinking, but he has yet another choice just ahead: to find counseling to stop his abuse. He can do this, too, but it's up to him."

Explanation 2:
His Childhood Made Him This Way

▪ GERI

> I used to say to myself, "Poor guy, he never was nurtured by his
> mother. His father beat him regularly and then died when he was
> eleven. This is why he's so bad to me." In the meantime he's
> telling me I'm a jerk who can't ever do anything right. One day
> I said, "Whoa, this ain't fair." He tells me that I'm a jerk, a bitch,
> a slut, but I'm still saying, "He's a poor guy." Understanding him
> is getting me nowhere.

Geri is right in thinking that childhood trauma can create adult
misery. "But," as she reminded us, "so what?" Many women and
men were abused as children, and although they may suffer from
depression and other aftereffects throughout their lives, childhood
abuse does not make them abusers. As adults they choose their
behavior. Nevertheless, for years Geri explained away Joel's behavior by seeing him—as so many women see their partners—as a
divided personality. "There are two parts of him," she told herself.
"There's a wounded child inside. That good child is often hiding
because he was so hurt, but I'll bring it out." Insisting that "the good
part is the real him" made sense to Geri. One day a friend asked Geri
a number of questions that helped: "What about *your* childhood?
Your parents treated you pretty badly at times too, didn't they? Why
aren't you beating people up?"

In fact, several studies indicate that an estimated 65 to 85 percent
of adults who were abused as children *do not grow up to abuse their
children*.[1] They choose to behave differently than their parents did.
Joel was in the same position as many other people, including Geri.
He had an awful childhood, but he could still have made different
choices.

At last Geri threatened to leave Joel—and miraculously, he
changed. She says, "I couldn't believe how nice he became. For
weeks he treated me like a queen. Suddenly he had control of his
so-called 'uncontrollable' pain, and he stopped his verbal harangues and abusiveness. I saw him do it—treat me differently—

when he needed to. I wish I had known a long time ago that he could do it if he wanted to."

Explanation 3: War Did This to Him

▪ JOANN

> Harry's stories were filled with death and brutality. It broke my heart listening to him and watching his face. His spirit was gone. Nobody should have to live through that. That's the way I felt about it for years. I still do. But then I started talking to the wives of other vets. Eventually I told one of them what Harry was doing to me. "JoAnn," she told me, "there's plenty of people with post–traumatic stress disorder who *don't* do this."

Post–traumatic stress disorder (PTSD) is the psychological label used to designate the symptoms suffered by many abused women, combat veterans, survivors of natural disasters, and other people who've gone through overwhelming stress or trauma. Some of the symptoms, which can be brief or long lasting, are: emotional and intellectual numbing, limited expression of feeling, nightmares, painful intrusion of old memories, and flashbacks. Ironically, women like JoAnn, who make allowances for their partner's violence because he's a vet with PTSD, may be developing PTSD themselves. Yet their reaction to stress and trauma does not make them attack their partners.

A number of women told us that serving in Vietnam changed their husbands. Many men were exposed there not only to particularly brutal warfare but also, perhaps for the first time, to drugs. Yet the combat veteran, like everyone else, makes choices about how he behaves. At home he does what the culture gives him permission to do. If he feels hurt, frustrated, angry, or out of sorts, he may take it out on his wife. If he suffers violent flashbacks, he can be extremely dangerous. But her suffering will not make his any more bearable. Nor will it cause him to change. As long as he can take things out on her, he has no motivation to change.

Explanation 4: Stress Is Doing Him In

▪ CINDA

When he started yelling at my kids, he wasn't like the person he was before. At first I made excuses in my mind for that: "He must have had a bad day. Work is rough right now." But then it kept going. I started to say to myself, "My kids are just kids. They're not doing anything to make him that mad." The more I thought about it, the more I knew that it was him, something inside him. The stress was an excuse. Calming things down for him did two things—it exhausted me and it spoiled him; he expected the perfect life and he always paid me back when I wasn't right there providing it for him all the time.

A lot of women we talked to worked very hard to alleviate their partner's stress. They made perfect dinners, took care of the kids, screened phone calls, paid the bills, moved their partners into new homes or new cities. Quietly, without fanfare or notice, they tried to create stress-free environments. But the controlling behavior continued. Although sometimes a relationship improved temporarily, always in the long run it went down hill. No matter how much stress the women alleviated, there was always more. Life is simply full of stress, but stress never "causes" abuse. Each of us, under stress, chooses how to deal with it. Most people do it without abusing others.

Explanation 5: He's Sick

▪ SHERI

It became painfully obvious to me, just as Richard was getting over his alcoholism, that he was going into a deep depression and was behaving very badly and abusively again. I figured, "Okay, we did the alcoholism for five years; now we will do the depression. Then we're going to do senility because he is ten years older than me." And that was too much: my whole life taken from me through his illness and abuse.

▪ JUANA

For years I thought he was mentally ill, totally out of control. But when I think of it now, I realize that he was in control. He could have killed me, but he never did. He knew where to hit me so no one else would see it. He knew when to stop. He only went so far—just far enough to show me he was in control of me.

The marriage vows say: "In sickness and in health." Clergy and kin tell us, "Good people stick it out through thick and thin." When we think about leaving, we imagine him alone, with no one to care for him. Or we imagine his suicide. In those moments it's hard to remember that we have been driven away by his abuse. Although his behavior, not ours, is harmful to others, *we* feel guilty.

It's true that a few men become violent because of organic brain disorders or psychosis; they really can't control their behavior, and neither can you. They may be dangerous to themselves and others, and they need professional medical help. But the number of men who are genuinely, uncontrollably "sick" is very small. Most people, no matter how much they may be suffering from physical or mental ills, make choices about their behavior. Although they may feel irritable and depressed, they don't take it out on those around them.

"Sickness" can also be a trap—in more ways than one—when it tempts a woman not only to forgive abuse but to take care of the abuser.

▪ LOIS

At first, even though I was scared of him, I almost developed a maternal relationship toward him: poor guy with emotional problems. I had to manage things for him because he just couldn't handle them himself. I thought about how strong I am and how pathetic he is underneath it all. Did I ever trap myself! It took years for my pity to turn to anger. Eventually I stopped feeling sorry for him. I said, "He's mentally sick, he refuses to get help, and now there's nothing I can do to change that." All along I saw myself as the strong one. Never did I realize that from his position of "weakness" he was absolutely controlling me.

Explanation 6:
Insecurity Is the Root of His Problem

▪ **COLLEEN**

> Ted couldn't stand it when I would look at another guy. So I
> stopped looking. Then he started *imagining* I was looking, and I
> knew I was in trouble.

Many women told us of partners so insecure, so uncertain of
themselves, or so jealous that reassuring them became for the
women a full-time job. And despite all their efforts to compliment,
soothe, comfort, support, and strengthen the fragile ego of the
controlling partner, these women reported failure. He remained
insecure and uncomfortable. Why?

Male privilege again. It entitles a man to be cared for by a
woman, all his needs and wishes fulfilled. Colleen's husband, Ted,
and many men like him depend almost entirely upon a woman to
make life comfortable and secure. That woman is supposed to cater
to him, put him first—before her children or herself—guess his
needs, take care of his house, manage his problems. If she fails to
do it perfectly (as any human being would) or if she resists, his
"security" is threatened and he strikes back. He behaves decently
only when he feels that he has her under control: in other words,
only when she does whatever he expects (whether or not she
knows what his expectations are). The basis of his "security" is her
subservience, dependence, and adoration. He builds himself up by
putting her down. He puffs up as she shrinks. That's what happened
to Colleen.

> It took me years to see what he really is. He's a bottomless pit
> that I kept trying to fill. Just when I thought I had it right, he
> changed the rules. He acts plenty insecure, but I don't buy it
> anymore. By putting me through hoops and making me prove
> my love all the time, Ted was reminding me that he runs the
> show. He got so much attention from his "insecure" position. All
> the while I thought I was soothing a hurt ego, and he was running
> me ragged.

Explanation 7:
Racism and/or Poverty Makes Him This Way

▪ PAM

> If the least little thing happened to him in the street, he'd come home and take it out on me. He'd always tell me later on about how sorry he was. He'd bring me some little perfume or some shit he'd lifted out of the store. According to him, the black man didn't have a chance—and him in particular. He was in prison for a while for robbing a liquor store, or some shit like that, and when he got out he couldn't get a job. The cops took him in again and beat him up for no reason. So he'd cry, and he'd tell me, "Oh, baby, you're the onliest thing in the world can make me feel good." So naturally I busted my ass trying to do the job.

Racism and poverty limited the options of Pam's boyfriend Darrell and made his life hard, but Darrell himself didn't do much to make his life easier. He expected Pam to do that for him. We heard many similar stories from women living with controlling partners who were among the least powerful men in our society: poor men of color, unemployed men, illegal aliens, migrant workers, petty criminals, physically disabled men. These men, whose place in the world made them feel small and powerless, looked to women to make them feel a little bigger and more powerful. And no matter how low they had fallen, even the least powerful men felt entitled to exercise power over a woman and demand her services. The male privilege to be cared for by a woman was just about the only privilege they had.

In addition, Darrell used racism to keep Pam loyal to him. White racism emasculates the black man and takes away his pride, Darrell said. So Pam owed it to her race, as well as to Darrell, to stick by him and help him get on his feet. If she didn't support him, he said, he'd have to deal drugs and probably end up back in prison. He swore that only Pam had the "power" to save him.

> A lot of what he said was true. I had a job, but he couldn't get one. And I saw the cops hassle him out of nowhere. I had a lot of sympathy for him. Darrell was oppressed by racism. But I was

oppressed by racism too, and then it got to where I was oppressed by Darrell. There's just no way a man's going to get into
my money—especially not while he's laying up in the bed all day
watching the TV. I had my kids to feed. . . . I told him, "If the white
man owes you a living, then you best go on and ask him for it,
'cause I ain't handling his payroll."

Explanation 8:
If Only He Could Express His Feelings, He
Wouldn't Explode

▪ SHIRLEY

I tried for years to get Lou to see a therapist. I knew he couldn't
express himself, and I could. I thought a therapist would teach
him to say what was on his mind. He wouldn't need to bottle it
up. Finally he went with me, but it wasn't at all what I expected.
Lou and I and the therapist would sit in the office and talk about
Lou's childhood. Then the counselor would encourage him to
"vent his feelings of rage toward his mother." The sessions got
kind of scary for me, and when we went home, Lou would keep
raving and threatening and throwing plates. I told the therapist
that I was frightened. He told me that I had no faith in Lou. Some
counseling that was! The therapist told me that I was undermining the process, and all the while Lou was getting more abusive
and violent.

Popular psychology—popular among the white middle class, at
least—teaches that people should express their inner feelings. Many
psychologists urge people to vent their anger, reasoning that if it
comes out, it magically disappears and leaves you feeling better. But
that advice is dangerous, even deadly, when it is handed out to
controlling and perhaps violent men. They already believe they
have a right to impose their bad moods on others. And studies show
that people who give vent to their anger become *more* angry, not
less.[2] Therapists who encourage abusive people to "vent their emotions" give them what they want: authoritative support for their
explosive tirades.

Lundy Bancroft and David Douglas, two counselors of abusive men, explain: "Women think, 'If only I could get him to express himself.' But he does express himself—often quite well. What he really needs is to stop thinking about himself and his injured feelings all day. He's far too self-centered. In counseling we try to get him to pay less attention to his feelings and more attention to the fact that there are other people in the world who have feelings and who are hurt because of his behavior. The last thing he needs to do is to blow off his anger."[3]

Ellen Pence, a founder of the Domestic Abuse Intervention Project in Duluth, Minnesota, expresses the same view in a different way: "The women we work with want their partners to have feelings. 'Put him in the abuser's group and teach him how to talk,' they tell us. It makes sense from their perspective, but it's wrong. The problem is that if we teach him how to express his feelings and he still believes that he has the right to control her, he will use his new skills at self-expression to control her even more. If his belief system is unchanged—if he still insists that she stay home with the kids, give up her job, cater to him sexually—then teaching him to express his feelings is a mistake. We have men who go home after groups and say to their wives, 'See how you're talking to me. You hurt me so much.' They twist the ideas they've heard in the counseling group and turn them against her because they're still trying to control her."

Pence continues, "Certainly some abusive men need to express themselves more appropriately. But first they need to stop harming others. We can teach communication skills only if they stop their verbal and physical abuse. It doesn't work the other way around."[4]

WHY DOES HE TREAT ME THIS WAY?
A NEW EXPLANATION

Let's review again the simple explanation we offered at the beginning of this chapter. Why does he treat you this way? Because he *chooses* too.

Despite his miserable childhood, despite his drug and alcohol use, despite his financial problems, despite the horrors he suffered in Vietnam, despite the stress he's under, despite his illness, despite his insecurity, despite his unemployment, despite the trouble he has expressing himself, despite racism, despite the recession, despite the weather, despite what the kids do, despite the way you look, and despite the way you conduct yourself, he could behave differently—if he wanted to.

But why would any person choose to behave this way? As we've been pointing out all along, the controller's behavior is not simply the result of personal psychological problems. It's largely a product of our culture. If you look at the world we live in (instead of trying to look inside your partner's head), it's easy to see that our culture sets men up to abuse women.

How does this work? As we've mentioned, our culture provides all of us with some ready-made beliefs about who women and men are, and about how they should behave. In the United States we have many different cultures—African-American, Hispanic, Asian-American, Native American—with different values and different definitions of feminine and masculine, but most people pick up some values of the dominant white middle-class culture—whether they want to or not—just by watching TV or going to the movies.

Films give us a composite image of a *man:* in control, smart, tough, cool, aggressive, handsome, sexy, rich, stylish, and very good at lying, physical combat, and keeping his feelings to himself. If he's African-American, he may also be funny, sly, dishonest, and a great talker. Whether he's white or black, women (mostly beautiful and thin) fall all over him. He's important. She's *his.*

In the real world, of course, most men aren't in control of very much. In the real world, the government, the military, the media, business, industry, science, and the professions are still mainly in the hands of well-to-do white men. But that's all the more reason for some men to feel that if they can't rule anything else, they should at least be kings in their own homes. At work or in the streets, a man may have a tough time. He expects home to be different. Home is private. Home—even *her* home—is his castle. What's inside is *his.* There he can be a *man* in control by demonstrating his power over her, again and again.

But what makes him feel that he has a right to push his partner around? And where did he get the idea that home belongs to him? These ideas have persisted for centuries; they are embedded in the family, enshrined in the church, and practiced by law. In fact, until the end of the nineteenth century, husband and wife were one person (the man) in the eyes of the law; a wife was said to be "covered" by her husband. This meant that married women could not divorce, retain custody of their children, or hold property. Although women now are legally entitled to do all of these things, a cultural, religious, and social tradition endures that proclaims men head of the household. Unless he rejects the role, your partner has every reason to think that he is in charge. In fact, for him, it may seem perfectly natural.

Our traditional marriage vows call for the bride to promise to love, honor, and *obey* her husband. Most people don't say those words anymore, and many people don't bother to get officially married at all, but everyone still remembers that word "obey." When they marry, many women still give up their own name and take their partner's. If they don't marry, many a man still sees her as *his* woman. He may find it laughable if she suggests that she has rights too, or if she informs him that it is against the law to assault her. "You're mine," he may say, and he means it.

And what is a woman expected to do? You know: she stands by her man. She cares for him and cares for her family. When anything goes wrong, a good woman fixes it—and quick. She's been taught that a real man holds a job, brings home some money, and takes charge. Her role is to back him up and to soothe him through the rough trials and tests of life.

These old-fashioned definitions of proper sex roles are bad enough in themselves. But within the institution of marriage they create the perfect setup for abuse. Within the home, many men carry possession and control to extremes. They use violence to get their way, or simply to demonstrate their power. Most people are shocked to learn that these men beat up at least two million women in the United States every year. Some estimates place the number much higher. Most of the men who do this are not crazy. Most of them do not have any particular problems that make them behave this way. Most of them behave this way because they feel entitled to. Our culture—our history, our institutions, our laws, and even our movies—gives them the right.

But if men learn from our culture to dominate and beat up women, then why don't all men act that way? That's a good question, and it has a complicated answer. First, in a broad sense, all men *do* dominate all women simply by being members of the dominant or privileged class. Just by being men, they get all sorts of privileges, from higher pay to "ownership" of the streets. (In some African-American and Hispanic communities, where many men can't get jobs and the streets are dangerous for everybody, you have to look further to find male privilege, but it's there. Ask yourself: who are the bosses?) Generally speaking, then, all men *have* power over women. Some of them act it out in their personal relationships, and some don't.

Many men learn different and contradictory lessons from our culture as well. They may learn, for example, that women are important, that women should be protected and respected, that women are people, that real men don't hit women, and so on. Many men take those lessons to heart and live by them.

But the controllers—particularly those who use violence against women—either never learn those lessons, or they *un*learn them. A boy who learns at home and in church to respect women may unlearn it in street gangs or college fraternities or military zones where gang rape is encouraged. Each man's experience of life is a little different. But once a man comes to believe that he's entitled to dominate women, he will find aspects of our culture to offer him plenty of support.

Professional counselors who work with men to change their controlling and violent behavior point out four widespread conditions in our culture that permit, even encourage, men to abuse women.[5]

1. Objectification of women. Our society turns women into objects. The way women are portrayed in much of our advertising, films, popular entertainment, and especially pornography turns women into things. This objectification creates in many men the expectation that women are there to be used for the satisfaction of men's personal sexual, emotional, and physical needs. Objectification helps explain why men who physically abuse women so rarely call their partners by their names. (She's "the wife" or "the old lady" or worse—in his eyes, she is not a person with an identity of her own.) It also helps explain why he can come home late, spend money on what he wants, and generally forget to take his partner into account. She is there to serve him.

2. A belief in male authority.[6] The controlling man has an agenda of expectations: he expects his home to be maintained, his woman to be sexually available, his desires to be met. These requirements are not negotiable. They are the fundamental conditions of life to which he feels entitled, simply because he is a man. And because he believes that he is legitimately in charge, he thinks he has a right to coerce or punish his partner when she disobeys, disagrees, asserts herself, speaks her mind, expresses a desire or feeling, or makes a "mistake"—in other words, when she acts like a separate person with a will and some ideas of her own.

3. A belief in the right to use force to get their way. Many controlling men manage to get their way through manipulation and intimidation; they decline to use physical force. But a great number of other men are willing to back up their male authority with force. The belief that force is an appropriate and effective way to get what you want is very popular in our culture. Our government often uses force as an instrument of foreign policy and few Americans object. Once individual men use force, they often find it easier and easier to turn to violence to get what they want.

4. A system that supports men. Despite the progress of the last fifteen years in combating family violence, some individuals, community agencies, and institutions still support a man's "right" to control, and they often disregard the physical violence he uses. Because threats and assault are in fact against the law, a man who physically or sexually assaults his wife or girlfriend couldn't keep doing it without this support from the very people who are supposed to enforce the law and help the victims of crime—namely, police, prosecutors, judges, the clergy, psychologists, social workers, and doctors. Some let him get away with it, look the other way, or—unsure of what to do to stop it—do nothing at all. Thus, they reinforce his "right" to use force, even if they never say, "Go ahead, hit her." The police officer who walks a man around the block or fails to show up when called, the clergyman who advises a woman to go home and pray, the doctor who gently patches her injuries but avoids asking who inflicted them, all cooperate with the abusive man in several ways. He comes to understand that no one will stop him from doing what he does. He learns that there are no consequences to his actions—even his violent actions. He can beat up "his woman" if he wants to and get away with it.

Why does he treat you this way? Because he *chooses* too. And because he can.

RECONSIDERING OUR EXPLANATIONS

As we've seen in this chapter, many women look for their own explanations for their partner's controlling behavior, and develop their own theories. Many take action in keeping with their theories. They change their explanations and their actions as one after another proves wrong, or at least ineffective in changing the way the controlling partner acts. In many cases that process takes years. Sooner or later, many women are forced to hard conclusions.

▪ LORI

I used to think that everything could be changed, that love will conquer all. When I was younger I thought that under the right circumstance each person could flower. In religious terms I believed that each of us was redeemable. Now I've learned that it's not so. If you love someone who is as hardened as my husband was, who has such a pathological way of responding, then change is very difficult, maybe impossible.

▪ GERI

I finally realized that there are choices he makes about his own history. I can't go back and dig out his prehurt person. Bad experiences produced a man who is both mean and loving. I can't get to his core and redo it for him. He has to struggle with his meanness. And I have to face that he may not want to do it.

▪ MONICA

He promised to change when he saw that I was on my way out. I'd say, "Gee, he really can do this for me." But that never worked for very long. He has to decide he wants to be different and work hard, *very hard.* I'm not sure he will, or that if he does, I can trust him again. He's put me through hell. It's hard to say that I loved someone who is so untrustworthy and mean. It's hard to say: "There's no excuse for the way he acted. It just was."

A WAY OUT OF THE EXPLANATION TRAP:
A NEW QUESTION

We get stuck in explanations the minute we begin to search our partner's history or his environment or ourselves for the cause of what he's doing. We can get out of the trap by asking a new question, not about causes but about results. Ask yourself, "What does he *gain* by doing what he does?"

If you were to make a list of what your partner achieves by treating you as he does, you might be surprised at the result. One woman we interviewed, for example, was trying to get a real estate sales license by attending night classes, supposedly with the encouragement of her husband. Yet every night that Gabriela was scheduled to go to class, Jack suddenly had to work late or needed the car or picked a fight. Gabriela was always late for class, or too upset to go at all, and finally she had to drop out.

At first she thought that her husband was under too much stress at work, and she tried to be more supportive of him. But when she dropped out of class, she noticed that the stress of his job seemed to disappear. He no longer had to work late or take the car in the evening. He seemed to be in a better mood and stopped picking fights. Gabriela was depressed about her failure and grateful to Jack for being nicer to her while she was feeling bad. But she was confused and uneasy, too. She said, "I feel like there's something going on here that I don't understand—like the way you feel when everybody else is in on a joke and nobody's told you."

At our suggestion, Gabriela asked herself: "What did Jack gain by the way he acted?" And she came up with this list:

1. He got me to stop going to school.
2. He got me to stay home and pay more attention to him.
3. Maybe, in the long run, this could keep me from ever getting the training I need to get a job and money of my own.

4. He kept me from learning new things and growing and changing, from accomplishing things on my own, from doing things separately from him, from spending time with new people, from making new friends.

5. He got things to go his way without ever saying directly what he wanted. It seems like he's set up the rules in the family, and he gets me to follow them—even though he doesn't state what they are!

6. By lying to me—by telling me he supported my going to school when he didn't—he tried to keep me from seeing what he was doing.

7. When I failed, he encouraged me to believe it was all my fault.

8. By telling me he loves me anyway, he made me feel grateful to him!

Gabriela summed up what she had figured out: "Jack's sense of security is based on keeping me down. I can't go to school. I can't be smart. I can't be separate. I can't be different from what he wants me to be. If I try to be who I am, he humiliates me and generally makes my life miserable. And then I'm supposed to be grateful to him because he loves me even though I'm such a fuck-up that only such a wonderful, kind-hearted, generous man as he is would have anything to do with me."

Why not put that new question to yourself? It can change your outlook. But let's begin by first making use of the old question one last time. We suggest you get pen and paper and take as much time as you need to write out your responses to the following questions:

1. When you ask yourself, "Why does he treat me this way?", what specific treatment do you have in mind? Does he yell, withdraw, hit you, or what?

2. Considering that specific "treatment," have you thought about why it happens? Do you have an explanation?

3. Considering your explanation, and supposing that you are absolutely right, what difference does it make? Will anything change? Will the "thing" that changes be *you* again?

4. Now, ask yourself the new question: what does he gain by treating me this way? Make a list.

What you've learned from this chapter is that your controlling partner profits by his behavior. He chooses to use it. He can change it if he chooses to. And no matter how many explanations you find for his behavior, *they* won't change him. Only he can do that. But you, with a new perspective on your situation, can make some changes for yourself. We'll talk more about that in Chapter 6.

But we may be getting ahead of ourselves. Unfortunately, looking for explanations is not the only trap that lies in the path of a woman with a controlling partner. There's a second deep pit, dug by your controlling partner, just waiting for you to fall into it. That's the trap of *self-blame*. And once you fall into it, your partner will go on making this trap a little deeper every day. In the next chapter, we'll consider the problem of self-blame as we turn to another big question that may be troubling you: why can't you do anything right? Or, to put the question another way: how does it happen that no matter how much you do for your partner and your relationship, things don't seem to get any better?

4

■

Why Can't I Make Things Better?

I n the last chapter we heard from women who got stuck in the explanation trap, searching for some reasonable way to account for a partner's unreasonable behavior. We learned that a controlling partner *chooses* the way he behaves. But doesn't everyone say that it takes two to tango? And to tangle? Most women seem to think so. When love goes wrong, most women question *themselves*. They ask, "What's my part in this relationship? Don't I bear some responsibility for the way things are?"

These questions are valid. But you'd be surprised to learn how many women phrase the question differently: many ask, "Isn't it my fault?" That's where confusion sets in. That's the trap of self-blame. Just as some women get stuck searching for explanations for a partner's behavior, others get stuck searching for explanations for the partner's behavior *in themselves,* blaming themselves for everything that goes wrong. Some women get stuck in both of these traps. Some get stuck in both at once.

In this chapter we'll consider how and why so many women blame themselves for things they really can't control. We'll describe what often happens when women start thinking this way. We believe that once you *see* the trap that lies in this way of thinking, you'll find the way out.

First let's consider what it means to be responsible. It should go without saying that every woman chooses how she behaves, just as every man does. She is responsible for the way she conducts her own life. In addition, many women also take on the responsibility of caring for children and sometimes for other adults as well, such as an elderly parent, a relative or friend who is ill, or a husband who is demanding. Our culture casts women in the role of "nurturer," both in private and public life; and because caring for others seems such an admirable thing to do, a great many women are happy to choose this role. At home, they become caring wives and mothers; at work, they take on caring professions—medicine and nursing, teaching, social work, religious work. We believe that our culture trains women to be *overly* responsible for others, while it fails to train men to be responsible enough. In any case, a lot of women find the task of caring for others, at home or on the job, admirable and rewarding work.

But there's a big difference between *being responsible for conduct* and *having a responsibility for care*. As we said, every woman is responsible for her own conduct, just as every man is. And we believe that every woman in a relationship has a responsibility to care for her partner, just as her partner has a responsibility to care for her. But the responsibility to care for another person does not make you responsible for that person's conduct. You may willingly accept the responsibility to take care of your ailing father, but if he drinks too much or gets in a fight with the neighbors or robs the convenience store or wrecks the car, that's not your fault. And when your partner sulks, blows up, gets drunk, gives you the silent treatment, or throws a beer at you, that's not your fault either.

Despite the fact that every adult is responsible *only* for his or her own conduct, many women in controlling relationships hold themselves responsible for what their partner does. Many women mistake the responsibility they feel to *care* for their partner as a responsibility for his behavior. They ask themselves over and over: "Do I make him behave this way?"

The simple and correct answer to this question is "No." But the question comes up again and again, arising in part from that overly trained sense of responsibility for others. We hear it often from women whose partners are controllers, particularly when those partners use physical abuse as a tactic of control.

As we said in the last chapter, some women believe that they could have prevented an abusive incident by behaving differently. Some women believe that they can prevent future incidents by changing whatever they did that "set him off" the last time. (Remember the "if only's"? If only I'd kept my mouth shut. If only I hadn't burned the pork chops.) Most often, women get this idea from the controlling partner himself. Controllers usually blame their bad behavior on the very person who suffers most from it. Like the child who says, "Now look what you made me do!" the controller says things like, "You should have known better than to keep bitching at me." This way of thinking blames the victim for the abusive conduct of the controlling partner. It suggests that if she had behaved perfectly or if she were a mind-reader (which none of us is) she would not have been abused. That's simply not true. But as the controller continues to load the blame on her, a woman may begin to wonder if there's some truth in what he says.

Because a controlling person must keep control, sooner or later he will find a "reason" to exercise his power over you by doing you an injury, emotionally or physically. Being "perfect" may protect you for a short while, but in the long run, it won't save you. And what if you are very far from "perfect"? If you are mean, hostile, lying, manipulative, angry, or drunk, you may want to make some changes in your own behavior, but nobody has the right to demand that you live according to his specifications. Nobody is entitled to control your life, or even to try. And nobody ever has the right to hit you.

Some women tell us that they can sometimes feel the tension building up in their partner. They know that he's going to explode soon, and they can't stand tiptoeing around, trying to keep him calm. So they "push his buttons." They do something they know he won't like in order to get the explosion over with, hoping that he'll be apologetic afterwards and easier to get along with. In that way, they exert some control over the timing of the abusive incident, but that does not mean that they cause the abuse. It would happen anyway, sooner or later.

Whether a woman chooses to push her partner's buttons or not, a controller who uses physical or sexual abuse very often accuses his victim of "provoking" violence. This charge is made so often that some people—including some people in the helping professions—believe it. They assume that battered women (or some of them at least) "provoke" or "ask for" physical or sexual abuse from their partner. This belief is hurtful to abused women because it makes some of them ashamed and afraid to seek help. It is also very silly. Does it make sense to think that a woman who can't get her partner to help with the dishes, cut down on his drinking, or look after the kids, no matter how hard she tries, can make him beat her up simply by looking at him the wrong way or raising her voice? In fact, what a woman does or doesn't do in relation to her partner is *never* the real issue. Any time a woman "provokes" her partner, he can choose not to respond abusively. What he does is up to him.

GETTING STUCK IN SELF-BLAME

When people have a healthy sense of responsibility to themselves and others, we all benefit. That's the glue that helps hold relationships and society together. But the controller's habit of blaming everything on his partner, combined with her over-trained sense of responsibility, and reinforced by the tendency of others to expect women to take on the job of keeping relationships together, can glue her into an abusive relationship. When her sense of responsibility slides into self-blame, a woman can be trapped.

And why do we call self-blame a trap? Because self-blame leads women in the wrong direction and wastes their time. Just like women caught in the explanation trap, women caught in the self-blame trap spend a lot of time and energy looking in the wrong place for causes, asking the wrong questions, and trying the wrong strategies to "fix" their troubled relationship. If you are among them, you should know that this mistaken search will not help you, your partner, your relationship, or your children.

Articles and reports about battered women often say that they "blame themselves" for the abuse they suffer. You've probably heard that view yourself. But we haven't found that to be the case—at least not at first. At the outset of emotional or physical abuse, most women are so shocked by their partner's behavior that it would never occur to them to hold themselves responsible for it. Nevertheless, sooner or later, some women ask themselves, "Am I doing something to *cause* this?"

More often than not, a woman's partner is eager to tell her how she is the cause of the trouble. He may have a whole list of complaints about her; and he is almost certain to insist that her unacceptable behavior provokes him to respond as he does. In other words, whatever she gets, she brings on herself. "If you knew how to act decently, I wouldn't mind your going out," he says as he pockets the car keys. "If you didn't bitch at me so much," he says, "I wouldn't have to drink." "If you didn't make me so mad, I wouldn't have to hit you." He may also charge her with failing in her "duties" to him: cooking, cleaning, child rearing, sexual service, and general maintenance of happy family life. According to him, she can't do anything right.

His family and friends may join in this view. "He's never treated any other woman this way," they tell her, implying that she must be causing him to behave as he does and that she is getting only what she deserves. The chorus of woman-blaming may be joined by a priest, rabbi, or minister, her (or his) therapist, social workers, the police, lawyers, judges, and even her own parents. They all chime in to ask: "What are you doing to make your husband so unhappy?"

As we learned in the last chapter, women who look for explanations come up with many different reasons for their partner's behavior. Similarly, women who blame themselves find many different specific reasons for doing so. But women don't just make these things up. In almost every case, the "faults" women find in themselves are the faults pointed out to them by their partner, and often by other people as well. Let's take a look now at some of the most common "faults" so many women are persuaded to find in themselves.

1. I Push His Buttons and I Should Know Better

Women voice many versions of the basic self-blaming idea, "I should have known better." They say things like "I should have listened to him." "I knew he was in a bad mood before I opened my big mouth." "I brought it on myself." Some women are so confused by what their partner does that they blame themselves, then their partners, and then themselves again, all in the same breath.

▪ TOBY

First I'd say, "I provoked him," and two minutes later, "It was his alcohol." It's a twisted way to live, and you start to accept twisted ways of thinking. "This man, who is drunk, has just struck me for no evident reason," I'd tell myself. Then I'd turn it inside out. "I must have done something to provoke him. Shame on me. I'll behave better from now on and it won't happen again."

Toby explained that she was raised in an alcoholic family, and she shared an attitude familiar to other children of alcoholics: "I was ready to buy that everybody would be happy if only I could find a key, if only I could behave properly." Josephine felt the same way until she recognized facts that made her stop blaming herself.

▪ JOSEPHINE

For a long time, I said, "What am I doing to him? What am I doing wrong?" The house was spotless. My floors were like a sterile operating room, I cleaned so much. I did everything a good wife was supposed to do. I refused him nothing. But I finally saw that it didn't matter what I did. I could do things perfectly right or totally wrong. And he got mad either way. I was just an object there to act out on. Whatever went wrong for him during the day, he came home and dumped it on me. I was like a kind of garbage can. Once he came home and kicked my son's dog. The dog hadn't done anything—he was just *there*. And I thought, "That's the way he treats me."

Josephine never "talked back" to her husband. But what about a woman who does? Grace told us, "I just couldn't stand the way he yelled at me. And I'd let him have it." Grace was proud to stand up for herself, but sometimes she wondered if her behavior caused her partner to become more abusive. She says, "For a while I tried to be quiet and obedient, but nothing changed. In fact, I felt worse—like a dishrag—and he kept yelling at me. So I learned that he was going to keep it up, whether I yelled back at him or not."

Do you "provoke" his abuse? Try this common-sense test: think about a person in your life (other than your partner) who irritates you and your relatives and friends. How do people respond to the "provocative" person? Most people probably ignore him. Some may choose to avoid him. Some may humor or tease him, while others just laugh at his annoying behavior. How many people decide to yell at him or call him names or hit him?

The point is that your partner makes choices about his behavior, too. No matter what you do—no matter if you lie to him, cheat on him, steal from him, hit him—he has choices. He can take a walk, cry, leave you, pray, join the marines, talk things over, laugh. It's up to him.

▪ LAUREL

I always felt that I was doing something wrong to make him do this. At the same time I thought that his behavior was wrong—that he could leave me, or something, but he didn't have to do this. There were other ways he could show me I wasn't this or that thing he wanted me to be. He didn't have to abuse me.

Laurel is right. Her partner is entitled to his opinion. But if a woman does something "wrong" in the eyes of her partner, there are many ways that he can bring it to her attention. Even if she is doing things that are illegal or dangerous or generally offensive— such as shoplifting, or using drugs, or abusing her kids—her partner can express concern and disapproval without resorting to abuse. If a woman does something wrong, or many things wrong, her partner still has no right to abuse her. Abusing another person is always wrong, no matter what that person may or may not have done. Laurel's partner, however, was abusive whether she actually did something "wrong" or not.

What Laurel failed to understand at the time is that for a controlling partner, there will always be something "wrong." A man's "reason" for exploding—or the "reason" you've come up with—

has little to do with why he really explodes. That's why correcting your "mistakes" has so little effect in the long run. Although your partner acts as if you did something "wrong," he really blows up for a different reason. He needs to demonstrate that he is in control. His abusive behavior is simply a show of power over you. That's why if you correct your "mistake" today, something else will upset him tomorrow. You can't win. And *that* really is the point he is trying to demonstrate, even though he wants you to believe otherwise.

2. I Deserved It

In one way or another, many women say, "I deserved it." Connie says, "Although I never thought it was right for him to get so jealous, I did flirt too much. I was wrong in that. He made such scenes! But in a way, I know I deserved it."

Angela, who started drinking as a way to numb herself after two years of physical abuse, describes what happened to her: "I started to think, 'Now what are people going to say about me? They'll say, "Poor Tony, he has a reason. She's a drunk. Poor guy. Look what he has to live with." ' I knew they thought I got what I deserved, and I began to think that way, too."

Connie and Angela did not deserve abuse. No woman does—it's as simple as that. Every woman has the right to live free of coercion and violence—no matter how irritating, drunk, angry, or flirtatious she may be.

You'll notice that the statement "I deserved it" is similar to the statement "I pushed his buttons" or "I provoked it." In both cases the woman who is the injured party is blaming herself. But there can be a significant difference between the two ideas.

When a woman says, "I nag too much," or "I flirt too often," she is describing behavior she thinks she can change. In addition, she believes that if she changes, he will change; if she stops nagging or flirting, he will stop abusing her. Blaming herself in this way allows a woman to maintain some sense that she is in control of her life, at least for a time. Taking this blame upon herself, she can try out new strategies. She can stop nagging or flirting. She can make better meals or quit drinking or take better care of the children. These efforts may help a woman feel better about herself, at least for a while. They enable her to keep her hopes up, take action, and maintain her commitment to her partner. But unfortunately, *these changes will not stop the partner's abuse.*

On the other hand, the statement "I deserved it" can lead a woman into a more dangerous trap. When she says to herself not only, "I provoked it," but also "I must deserve it," she suggests that there must be something fundamentally wrong with her as a person. Then what more can she do? For the woman who accepts this kind of self-blame, the situation must seem totally hopeless. If her partner is to stop being abusive, she must change her character, her whole personality—and who can easily do that? The next step after saying "There must be something wrong with me" is often terrible despair.

Why then do some women blame themselves so completely? In many cases, women believe they deserve abuse because they have undergone it time and time again. It begins to look as though being abused is their lot in life. Rosalie was abused both as a child and as an adult. Instead of finding fault with her partner's behavior or her own, she mistakenly searched for a vague, undefinable flaw within herself.

▪ ROSALIE

I tried to figure out where my share of responsibility was for my problems—because my father beat me, and then my husband treated me very badly. I said to myself, "I must be pretty rotten and don't know it. This just can't happen out of sheer coincidence—twice in my life. Maybe it's the way I express myself. Maybe it's irritating or something."

I knew that there was nothing I did to provoke the abuse. I was a good wife: I cleaned the house, I cooked for him. Yet at the same time, I was struggling with the fact that this keeps happening in my life. So I'd say, "Maybe it *is* my manner of speaking or the way I laugh. It's nothing I do deliberately, and it's nothing I have the power to change. I have no control over it." I was beaten as a kid, and the scars from my childhood were mostly psychological ones. I simply believed that I was the cause of everything wrong in my family and that I had to be perfect. So when my husband tried to convince me that I wasn't good enough for him, I bought it. I had high expectations for myself that were impossible to meet. So I always felt I deserved what I got.

Because her husband never bruised or bloodied her, Rosalie failed to see his abuse. She says, "It took me years. I didn't realize he was doing anything wrong when he bullied or pushed and shoved me." Friends convinced her otherwise, and with their support, she placed responsibility for the abuse where it belonged—squarely on her husband's shoulders.

Phyllis told us a variation of Rosalie's story: "When we were going out, I decided not to tell Mike about the incest with my father. It was too humiliating and painful. I confessed after we were married. What a mistake. He told me that I had betrayed him, that I was no good, a little whore."

Phyllis felt as if she deserved punishment for "lying" to Mike. But in fact Phyllis was the person betrayed—by her father, who sexually assaulted her when she was powerless, and by her husband, who tormented her for saying she had been powerless. She *deserved* better treatment from both.

3. I'm an Inadequate Partner

Peggy describes the way her husband opened and she closed the trap of self-blame.

▪ PEGGY

I was a full-time working mother, and he kept telling me I was bad at it, a failure at caring for my children. Then he accused me of not caring enough for him, of withdrawing my support from him when he needed it the most. That was the hook. I did feel that I didn't give enough to him, that I was angry a lot. I never associated my anger with his abuse. Instead I'd say, "Maybe it's me. I don't back him up enough. I don't trust him enough. I'm a spoiled bitch."

Julia thought about her relationship in a similar way. She says, "I decided I was an immature person who couldn't make a commitment and keep to it." She describes the experiences that made her change her mind.

▪ JULIA

At first Jeff was violent every five or six months, and I excused it or blamed myself. But then he started drinking more and being a lot more verbally abusive. He stopped giving me food money, and he assaulted me about once a month. I knew this was wrong. What helped me come to that conclusion, I'm embarrassed to say, was an affair I had with a man at work named Kevin. He was gentle and caring. Because of him, I realized that normal men don't act the way my husband did.

Julia came to see that she did not "cause" her husband to explode or to beat her up any more than she "forced" Kevin to treat her well. Both men made choices that, contrary to her belief, had little or nothing to do with Julia's behavior but everything to do with who the two men were as persons.

At the start of her marriage, Julia felt good about herself. She would have laughed at the idea that one day she would label herself an "immature person, unable to make commitments." The change, almost unnoticeable to her, happened slowly. At first, after Jeff hit her, Julia would say to herself, "He's right. I need to be more supportive. I'll learn about the details of his job." This self-blame kept Julia trying and hoping. But when her efforts to change her own behavior failed to stop the violence, Julia moved in a more dangerous direction. Instead of saying, "The abuse is not my fault. I can't change him," Julia began to believe Jeff's constant harangues about her deficiencies. Like Jeff, she attacked her own character. "I'm immature," she said. Without knowing it, Julia was experiencing the most damaging side effects of abuse: the undermining of her confidence and her perception of reality.

4. He's So Good and Then He's So Bad—It Must Be Something I'm Doing

"Abusive men play mind games. I learned this the hard way," Connie says. "One day he'd blow up about the dinner I cooked. A week later he'd ask for it again and even compliment me on it. It's a way to keep you on your toes and off balance at the same time." This inconsistent, on-again/off-again behavior is what psychologists call "intermittent reinforcement." As Connie says, it's a mind game. And as we mentioned in Chapter 3, it keeps a woman hooked on hope.

Every few months Connie's husband would calm down, especially when Connie threatened to leave him. Suddenly he would be kind and loving. Connie would think, "Now I've got the real Alan back." But it never lasted, and Alan always found a way to blame Connie for the change that came over him. "It was my vicious verbal style or my flirting with the 80-year-old parish priest or the dress I wore to confession," Connie joked.

For short periods, when Alan was kind and loving, Connie regained faith in him, only to be disappointed. The confusion trapped her in self-blame.

▪ CONNIE

Alan complained constantly about where we lived. I was a city person, but I knew urban life was making him miserable. So I bought a house in the country, with rights to a fishing dock, a boat, a horse, the whole thing. I put my heart and soul into this project. And for a while after we moved, the violence simply stopped. We were so content. But several months after the move, the abuse began again. Only this time it was worse. He threw me down the stairs. I could scream forever and nobody would hear me.

I saw that Alan *could* treat me well. He was capable of it. So I thought, "It can't be him. It must be me." The more he hit me, the more obsessed I became with improving myself. When Alan would turn angry, I couldn't figure out why. I'd never seen anger

like this. So I said again, "It's me. Something is lacking in me."
That's when I started grooming myself meticulously.

Connie's story was repeated—in various versions—by many
women we interviewed. In retrospect, most of them came to a
conclusion similar to the one Connie reached.

I kept hoping for the magic solution. I'd do it right and he'd be
good again. But it never comes. That's the reality I refused to
face, and it almost cost me my sanity, and it certainly cost me my
health. On rainy days twenty years later I still feel the pain from
his beatings every time I move.

5. I Chose This Partner—I Must Make the Best of It

This form of self-blame is different from the others we have
described. Women who hold to this belief rightfully blame their
partners for the abuse, but often they also harshly judge themselves. Yvette says, "I made a bad choice, but I thought it was my
job to live with it." Believing that she had no other choices,
Yvette minimized her partner's responsibility for his behavior,
and at the same time kicked herself. Her refrain was: "I should
have known better."

Because of religious convictions, many women conclude that
although they chose badly in selecting a partner, the choice—for
better or worse—is irrevocable. Cheryl, for example, is a devout
Catholic.

▪ CHERYL

I believe that God tests many people through suffering and that
there are rewards beyond this earth. I used to apply that to my
own life and think that I must be building up a lot of credit to get
out of purgatory by lovingly enduring an abusive relationship. My
husband was my cross to bear, and I'd practically earned saint-
hood by the time I figured out that this was not what God had
in mind for me.

Many women feel a similar strong determination to keep the family together, even though the controlling partner often makes them miserable. This determination seems to be particularly strong among some urban minority women who live in the midst of deteriorating communities where social values and human services are crumbling faster than the apartment buildings. Many minority women see their neighborhoods stripped of helpful publicly funded programs, such as Head Start and Job Corps, and ripped apart by drugs and street violence. They see more and more women raising kids on their own and sliding deeper into poverty.

▪ BEA

My husband was on my case all the time, but I tried to look on the positive side. He was a good, steady worker, and brought good money home. Between the two of us we could provide pretty well for the kids. I swore that they were going to finish school. That stuff was real important to me—giving my kids a chance. But the negative side was always there. I blamed myself for being young and dumb and getting married to *him*.

Many women say, "I made a big mistake. But I'm strong. I can take it."

▪ GENEEN

In my alcoholic family the children learned not to make waves. I learned survival strategies from being abused by my parents. I pleased people. I shut down what I really saw and felt. I replaced it with a veneer of "I can take it. I'm tough." That attitude trapped me. It kept me stuck for ten years with a guy who just shoved me around, emotionally and physically. Women think they're strong, and they are. But they're lying to themselves if they think their strength keeps them in a relationship like that. That's what I thought—"I'm making the best out of a bad thing." The truth is, he was making a mess out of me.

From her experiences Geneen learned a lesson she wants us to pass on. "You chose a partner. You didn't choose a monster, and you don't have to live with one. Nobody has to pay for one mistake for a whole lifetime."

6. It's My Fault If I Stay and Take It

Ann Marie found herself shifting the blame back and forth. "At first I'd say, 'There's something wrong with me. I let this person get by with treating me this way.' Then I'd switch and say: 'That's ridiculous, Ann Marie. He's behaving like an s.o.b., and it has nothing to do with you.' "

Lucy, too, held to several theories—some self-blaming and some not—at the same time: "If I had made a good choice in husbands, this wouldn't be happening to me. If I were not such a warped personality, he wouldn't be driven to this. If I had left him the first time, he wouldn't be doing it again now. If I were worth anything, I'd stop this." Unfortunately, Lucy's theories all pointed the finger at one person: herself. Her husband wasn't part of her account.

Maria also held herself to blame: "I was angry about his abuse. But I also had to try to figure out over and over again why he treated me so badly. That took forever; and finally, I decided that the ongoing violence was my fault because I hadn't left after the first time."

Deciding to leave is hard. There's a lot to lose: home, income, protection, and children, to name just four possibilities. Then, if he threatens to kill you if you walk out, there's your very life to consider. Most women cope with the decision for a while by *not* making it, by changing their minds, by leaving when their partner's violence escalates and returning when his behavior improves. Instead of acknowledging the costs of leaving, many women denounce themselves as weak for staying.

▪ MARIA

It doesn't help to do this to yourself. It's unproductive and wasted activity. Give it up. When you live through this stuff, you are incredibly strong, but you don't realize it at the time. Looking back, I think I took responsibility for staying as a way to avoid seeing who my husband was. If you see who he is, you have to say, "He's mean with no reason." It's too hard to believe that and say that. So you blame yourself.

7. I'm Just As Bad As He Is

Many women fight back. They tell us that they can be every bit as explosive and violent as their partners. And some tell us that when it comes to verbal abuse, they dish out more than their partners do. As a result, they often believe that they are just as "bad" and just as much to blame. Many women think of "battered women" as innocent victims who deserve support and help, but even when they are battered themselves, they don't put themselves in that category. They think that they're not "innocent."

▪ HOLLY

The very first time he hit me, I said to myself, "I'm not going to take it!" and I hit him back every time. If he yelled, I yelled. If he called me names, I called him names right back. When the hitting started, he could always win because he was so much bigger, but I'd still get back at him. Once I smashed all the lights on his car. Another time I gave his favorite clothes to the Good Will. Another time I barbecued his baseball glove. I just refused to be scared of him. He couldn't win!

I was so proud of myself for being such a strong woman. I'd tell myself that I wasn't like those poor victimized battered women who'd just lay down and let some man stomp all over them. But then I started feeling real bad about myself. My husband would tell me I had a terrible temper and a serious problem with violence, and I thought he was right.

As we mentioned in Chapter 2, women can get into trouble if their own survival strategies backfire. Some women who think of themselves as strong, proud, and able to handle their own problems get stuck at this point. Often, like Holly, they become ashamed of themselves for "stooping to his level." And eventually, they do have a new problem. Responding with verbal or physical violence may become a habit, and women who once knew better may find themselves being violent toward others—most often, the children. Then they feel guilty and ashamed for behaving in ways that go against their own standards. They think less of themselves, and consequently they are even more prepared to believe partners who tell them: "You're worse than I am." Women are then doubly caught: in the trap of self-blame, and in the terrible downward spiral of violence.

Yet most women who use verbal and physical abuse against their partners do so in self-defense. Most of them have not been verbally and physically abusive before, and a lot of them are not abusive in their other relationships. If they can recognize that their behavior is a self-defensive response (and not a very productive one) they may break out of the self-blame trap and take more effective action.

Holly was able to do just that. She says, "It finally dawned on me that I never acted like this before I started living with him. So I went home to my mama and all of a sudden my 'temper' magically disappeared. I didn't have any 'problem with violence.' My only problem was *him.*"

A WAY OUT OF THE SELF-BLAME TRAP: A NEW QUESTION

As we pointed out in Chapter 3, women get stuck in the explanation trap the minute they start examining their partner's history or his life-style to find some *cause* for the way he behaves. In exactly the same way, a woman can get caught in the self-blame trap when she begins to look within *herself* for the *cause* of what her partner does.

The way out of the explanation trap, you will remember, is to ask yourself a new question. In Chapter 3 we advised you to stop asking *"Why* does he do this?" and start asking "What does he *gain* by doing what he does?" If you followed our suggestion and made a list of some of the things your partner gains, you may now be looking at his behavior in a different light. You may have stopped— or be ready to stop—making excuses for him.

Getting out of the self-blame trap may be a little more difficult. Even though you can see that your partner gains a lot by being abusive, and even though you can see that he *chooses* to act the way he does, you may still be thinking, "But I must be at least partly to blame."

After all, you know that your partner is in the wrong, and you know that things aren't getting better. But you stay put. Doesn't that mean that *you* have a problem? Doesn't that mean that you may be "codependent" or a "masochist" or a "love addict"? Some therapists, some self-help groups, and some self-help books popular in recent years will answer *yes*.

In our view, however, the correct answer is: *absolutely not*. The problem is his abuse, not your love. These popular theories about "your" problem can only lead you in the wrong direction. The labels pin the problem on you. They suggest that there is something wrong with you or the way you act that causes your partner to abuse you. They encourage you to "work on yourself," trying to change the ways you think and act in hopes of improving your relationship with your partner.

It's true that some descriptions of "codependency" or "love addiction" may sound like descriptions of your relationship, and if you follow some suggestions for changing your behavior, you may even feel better about yourself. You may even get a different and "better" response from your partner. But the fact remains that your partner acts abusively because he chooses to. And when your partner continues to act abusively, despite all your efforts to free yourself from "addiction" or "codependent" behavior, you may be even harder on yourself. You may come to believe that because you can't stop your partner's abuse, you must secretly welcome it.

What if you are madly in love with him? As we mentioned earlier, many women believe that their partner has two personalities—a loving one and an abusive one—but each woman focuses on the loving partner. *That's* the one you fell in love with in the first place. When the controlling partner turns abusive again, you're confused and hurt and angry. You tell yourself you've been a fool. Then he turns loving again, and he's hard to resist. Besides, it's hard for a woman to give up a relationship while there still seems to be hope for it. You go on caring about the good part of your partner and hoping that your relationship will get better, as it once was.

Then you may want to label yourself a "love addict" to explain to family and friends, and to your own better judgment, why you let him back in your life. But in fact you are not an "addict." That label refers to people who are chemically dependent on substances such as alcohol and narcotics, so that when they try to quit they suffer very traumatic physical symptoms. Applying that label to human relationships is very misleading. If you feel "addicted" to your partner, you're probably feeling the confusing effects of his inconsistent, on-again/off-again behavior. As we've said before, a partner who behaves like that—a partner who uses "intermittent reinforcement"—is hardest of all to let go of. His irrational behavior may confuse you and get you stuck for a while, but that's where the problem lies—in his behavior. The fact is that you stay with your partner in spite of his abusive behavior, not because of it.

The process of giving up such a relationship may be complicated and slowed down by some of the common effects of repeated abuse. You may experience numbing and lethargy that make it hard to act. You may suffer a loss of confidence that makes you worry about whether you can survive without him or attract another lover. And you may be overcome by fear: fear of his retaliation, fear of poverty and homelessness, fear of raising kids alone, fear of living in a dangerous neighborhood without a man. All these considerations make it hard to let go.

While you're stuck in your relationship, you may find yourself clinging to the concepts of "codependency," "masochism," or "love addiction" to explain things to yourself. That's a tricky business: on one hand, these theories can make you feel better because they offer you the feeling that someone understands you, the sense that you are in control of the situation, and hope for improving your relationship. On the other hand, they keep you looking at, working on, and blaming *yourself*.

To free yourself, we suggest that you again change the question you habitually ask yourself. To help you climb out of the self-blame trap, we'll shift the focus to *you*. Stop asking "What am I doing wrong?" Ask instead: "What do I *gain* by believing that I'm doing something wrong?" Or in other words: "What do I *gain* by blaming myself?"

We suggest that you take pencil and paper again and write out your responses. Make a list. Try to be as specific as possible.

As you look back over your list, we think you'll find one important thread running through many of your responses. Blaming yourself makes you think that you are in control of yourself and your situation. It makes you think that you can change things. If you *cause* problems, then surely you can cure them.

The big catch is that you did not cause the problems. As we've said many times—and will keep repeating—the problem is that your partner chooses to behave in controlling and abusive ways. While you gain a sense of being in control by blaming yourself rather than your partner, that sense is false. You probably are fooling yourself into thinking that you have more control than you have. The downside of holding on to self-blame, then, is that it keeps you stuck, trying to change yourself, under the power of the controller. You can stay there forever.

It's perfectly natural that you should want to think that you have control of the situation. Everyone wants to feel that she has a handle on her own life. In fact, we find that some of the strongest women hold on longest to self-blame. The very things that make many women strong—the habits of hanging in there, taking care of everybody and everything, never giving in to failure—can work against them when they're holding on to the wrong partner for the wrong reasons. Taking full responsibility for your relationship—blaming yourself—can keep you busy for years, bending yourself out of shape in this way and that way, all for the sake of somebody else's happiness.

The way out is both simple and difficult. It means facing some hard facts: first, *you can't change your partner.* And second, to make your life better, you may have to make some other changes, not in yourself but *for* yourself. In the next chapter we'll turn to another question that is a key to resolving the problems you face, namely, can your partner change himself? Then in Part Two we'll begin to consider some of the decisions and changes you may want to make on your own.

In the meantime, remember that the source of the problem lies in your controlling partner. And the next time you find yourself thinking, "Maybe it's my fault," or "I must be doing something wrong," or "Maybe I deserve it," ask yourself instead: "What do I gain by blaming myself?" And one final suggestion: don't start blaming yourself for blaming yourself. Remember, you've been trained to blame yourself by some real experts: your partner, other people around you, and in fact, our whole woman-blaming culture. If you find yourself thinking, "I shouldn't have been so stupid as to fall into that trap," or, "If only I hadn't blamed myself . . ." go back and read this chapter again.

And the next time you find yourself thinking that way—just *stop*.

5

■

Can Your Partner Change?

M any a woman works very hard to change herself in order to improve a troubled relationship, even though she may know in her heart of hearts that her biggest trouble is her partner. She may try to explain away his behavior. She may take the blame upon herself. But she tries to shape up her relationship. And for a lot of women that means shaping up her partner. After all, he's the one who sulks or explodes or withdraws or yells or turns violent. Even as she works on herself, a woman knows that her partner has to change, too. Some women want a partner to change so they can live together happily ever after. Some women simply want the partner to calm down long enough for them to separate in safety and make a fresh start. In either case, the big question is: can your partner change?

The answer is: it depends—mostly on the partner's *willingness* to change. The chances that extremely violent men will change their ways are slim, but controlling men, even those who use violence, probably can change *if they want to.*

So the next question becomes: what might make him *want* to change? That's the question we'll explore in this chapter.

First of all, you must remember that *you cannot change your partner,* even though you might work on it for years. In fact, according to psychologist Anne Ganley, a leading authority on abusive men, you are the last person likely to influence your partner to change. As Ganley explains, "The man's victimization of the woman disempowers her in his eyes. He won't respond to a superhuman effort that comes from *her.*" [1] It's a vicious circle. Your partner treats you badly because he doesn't think much of you, and he doesn't think much of you because he treats you badly.

If you can't influence your partner to change, can a friend or a marriage counselor or a minister or a police officer do any better? Any of these people may make a bigger impression, but it's not likely that any one person can persuade him to change his ways. Keep in mind that the controller has had his own way most of the time, perhaps most of his life. (Even if he has suffered in the social world—from abuse, racism, poverty, and the like—he has managed to get what he wants in his personal life.) His abusive, "manly" behavior is very widely accepted, and sometimes even admired, in our culture. So why should he want to change?

Anne Ganley says that a violent man—a batterer—changes only if and when he is confronted, challenged, or punished by *many* different people, some of them at least as powerful as he is. When he hears from you *and* the marriage counselor *and* the minister *and* some friends *and* the police *and* the judge *and* his father *and* his boss all at once, then he may get the message that his controlling behavior isn't going to work any more. Counselors who work with battering men say that it usually takes a serious (and punishing) blow to get the message through. Most don't even begin to think of change until they're arrested, jailed, named in a restraining order, fired from a job, or *left* by their partner.

Since physical violence is only one tactic used by controllers, the same principles apply to controlling partners who stop short of violence. The more people who call your partner on his abusive behavior, and the more negative consequences he suffers from it, the more likely he is to get the message that his tactics aren't working.

Most women try everything they can think of to get that message across to their partner. Many go into counseling, hoping to understand their relationship better and bring about some changes. But whether they get counseling themselves or not, a large number of women eventually pin their hopes on one specific solution: getting their partner into some kind of counseling. In their desperation, they often think that any kind of counseling will do.

In this chapter, we'll discuss some of the resources that women commonly turn to, beyond family and friends, for help in getting the message across: namely, substance-abuse programs, couples or marriage counseling, and counseling programs for battering men. Substance-abuse programs are open to anyone, sometimes at little or no cost. Couples counseling is also open to anyone with a controlling partner, but for reasons that we'll explain, we strongly recommend *against* it if your partner uses physical force, threats, or intimidation, or if in any way he scares you. Except in some community or church programs, counselors charge a fee. The last option, a batterers' group, is specifically for men who use violence as a form of control. There is usually a fee, but it is often on a sliding scale.

As we discuss each of these programs, you'll see that from a woman's point of view, none of them is anywhere near perfect. More important, none of them alone can make your partner change, any more than you alone can. As you consider the various options, don't look for the right *alternative.* Think instead about how you might use each one, alone or in combination, to help you. And do remember that no single option or combination of options will necessarily change him. The best they can do is encourage him to want to change. Again, only he can change himself, and he will do it only if he *wants* to. At the end of this chapter, we'll suggest ways to evaluate these programs and the help they're giving—or failing to give—your partner.

SUBSTANCE-ABUSE TREATMENT

In Chapter 12, we'll suggest some things to do if *you* are a substance abuser, but here we want to focus on your partner. If your partner is an alcoholic or drug addict, or if he has a problem with drinking or taking drugs, that problem must be dealt with first, and the sooner the better. A person who is chemically addicted is at the mercy of his addiction. He cannot conduct life in a normal, reasonable, and reliable way. He cannot manage his own life, much less change it consistently for the better. In a sense, he is not even *there*. The addict's problem will grow worse and worse; it *always* does. It may end in his death—from overdose, accident, or general break-down of the body—unless he stops using and enters a recovery program. There is no halfway.

Treatment for substance abuse usually means spending time in a residential rehabilitation center to "kick the habit" under supervision. The recovering substance abuser then enters a long-term, twelve-step self-help program, such as Alcoholics Anonymous or Narcotics Anonymous. (Many substance abusers enter recovery through the self-help program alone.) Many enter recovery voluntarily, while others are sent to treatment by courts after being arrested for drunkenness or drunk driving. With the help of recovery programs, many drug addicts and alcoholics get "clean and sober."

But substance abuse does not cause person abuse. Your partner's controlling and perhaps violent behavior is *not* the result of substance abuse; it is a separate problem. Thus, while your partner's recovery from drug or alcohol addiction will certainly change your relationship, it will not in itself automatically end his abusive behavior. It may even make it worse.

People recovering from substance abuse in a twelve-step self-help program are encouraged to make "a searching and fearless moral inventory" of themselves, to examine their own "character defects," to ask God to remove their "shortcomings," and to "make amends" to people they have harmed. Practicing these steps, many people in recovery make an honest effort to change their lives. In this way, some are able to let go of their controlling behavior and stop being emotionally and physically abusive. But this change depends largely upon the character, the values, and the effort of the individual. Each person "works the program" in his own way. The changes he makes, or fails to make, depend upon how he works *his* recovery program—how he chooses to apply it to his own life—and not on the program itself.

Your partner's recovery program is bound to raise new issues for you. In the first place, throughout the rehabilitation program and any follow-up counseling, the substance abuser is the center of attention. You need some attention too, especially from your partner, but instead, with the encouragement of his program, he's focused even more than usual on himself. It's hard for him to quit using alcohol and/or drugs, so for quite a while he may be more unstable, more angry, more unpredictable than usual. And now that he's not using alcohol or drugs, you can't count on his passing out eventually and giving you a little peace. In addition, he may become even more controlling, demanding your appreciation and support. What's more, he may now have a counselor who supports him and "explains" his behavior. You have none.

Individual or group counseling as part of a rehabilitation program undoubtedly helps people recovering from substance abuse. But the message counselors give to women partners is often mixed and damaging. For example, when Mary's husband Todd went into a twenty-eight-day residential treatment program for alcoholism, his counselor first told Mary that she was not responsible for Todd's drinking. Like many substance-abuse counselors, he considered alcoholism a disease. He told Mary, "No matter how much Todd tries to blame you for his disease—and he will—there is nothing you do to make him drink." On the other hand, the counselor later maintained that Mary was a codependent partner in her husband's problem.

At one of the group sessions for patients and their families, Mary tried to talk about Todd's violence and its disturbing effects on her and the children. The counselor explained to Mary and the group that Todd didn't know any other way to behave. He said that because Todd's parents were alcoholics, Todd hadn't learned any other problem-solving skills as a child. But Mary had heard that excuse before—from Todd. "What do you mean by 'He didn't know any other way to behave'?" she asked. "He certainly knew right from wrong." The counselor told her to calm down. "You're being hostile," he said, "just when your husband needs your support. Your hostility can only make his recovery harder."

Mary apologized and fell silent, but she was angry that the counselor explained away Todd's violent behavior. She told us, "They keep telling me we're all ill with alcoholism. 'You're a co-alcoholic,' the counselor says to me, but I don't buy it. Todd gets drunk all the time and hits me, and I'm the one who's labeled a sicko. I'm the one who's told to be quiet because I'm doing him harm. I'm not a co-anything. I'm just getting blamed again for things the counselor himself told me were Todd's problem." A few months later, Mary separated from Todd. She says, "I'm glad for both our sakes that he got sober. It didn't improve our relationship, but it made me see that he was never really going to change toward me. I call that my 'sobering' experience."

Some women whose controlling partners join substance-abuse recovery programs find it helpful to attend meetings of Al-Anon, the self-help organization for partners and relatives of alcoholics and addicts. The companionship of other people with similar experiences relieves the shame and isolation so many emotionally and physically abused women feel. In addition, many of the principles of Al-Anon prove helpful to women involved with controlling partners—particularly those that advise you to let go of responsibility for other people, especially for your addicted partner, and take care of yourself.

To sum up, then, if your partner is a substance abuser, you should encourage him to get help for that problem. If he does, your relationship will change. It may get worse, or better, or both. A substance-abuse program will not, by itself, improve your relationship or even stop your partner's violence. But it may save your partner's life.

COUNSELING

Your partner could end up in some kind of counseling through one of several different routes, for only a few sessions or for as long as a few months. He could volunteer for individual counseling, either on his own or under pressure from you, other family members, his boss, his minister, or a friend. The two of you might decide to try couples counseling together. If he is violent, he could be sent to individual or group counseling by the court following his arrest for assaulting you or for violating an order of protection. In some communities there are specialized educational groups for physically abusive men; in others, a judge may refer an abusive partner to a local mental health center, family guidance agency, or private therapist.

No matter how your partner gets involved with counseling, the critical question to ask is: what kind of counseling? The wrong type of counseling, or the wrong counselor, can make matters worse—

and sometimes dangerously so. If your partner goes into counseling himself, whether as an individual or as a member of a group, you are outside the counseling process. You can evaluate his progress only by observing his behavior. We'll have suggestions at the end of the chapter about how to do that. But if the two of you go into couples counseling, you can evaluate the process and the counselor for yourself.

COUPLES COUNSELING

Many women persuade their partner to go into couples counseling with them because they feel sure that the partner would never go to a counselor on his own. In fact, many women begin to see a therapist by themselves, then gradually talk their partner into joining them. But if your partner is extremely reluctant—if he's unwilling even to consider the possibility that *he* might have a problem—then the prospects for change are dim.

Ideally, couples counseling may help to work out mutual differences between partners who care for one another when both partners take responsibility for their own actions and try to resolve the problem in a mutually satisfying way. But the controller has no place in this scenario. He cares much more for himself than for his partner. He refuses to own up to his own behavior, much less admit there might be something wrong with it. And he wants to continue to get his own way.

Unfortunately, some women who seek couples counseling don't recognize that what seems to be a confusing, ill-defined problem in the relationship actually *is* the partner's controlling behavior. And the counselor may not recognize it either. In that case, the counselor may suggest tasks to both partners to improve their "interaction"—when it's really the actions of the controlling partner that are causing problems.

When this happens, the controlled partner, who may genuinely want things to change, will in all likelihood follow the counselor's instructions to the letter. She will practice things like listening, offering more encouragement, offering more support, keeping questions and criticism to herself, concealing anger, complying with her partner's sexual demands—all skills that she's probably already very good at. The controller, on the other hand, will be reassured that his partner is largely to blame, just as he thought. He too will encourage her to practice these "interactive skills"—while refusing to acknowledge that his own need improvement. Thus, he continues to get his way, plus an extra measure of attention and compliance. And the controlled partner works and works and works in hopes of changes that probably will never come.

As this kind of therapy continues, she will grow more discouraged and confused, while he will grow more confident and probably more abusive. Seeing her fade, the counselor may prescribe exercises to strengthen her self-esteem—as if her shrinking self-esteem were the cause of marital problems rather than a consequence of what the controlling partner and the counselor are doing to her. In this way couples counseling can go on for years. That's exactly what happened with Tina and Terry, whose story we told in Chapter 2.

On the other hand, there are also better-informed counselors who will correctly see and name the controlling partner's abusive behavior and insist that *he* own up to it and change it. Unfortunately, when that happens, the controller may drop out of counseling, finding some convenient excuse. He might have a minor accident, for example, or suddenly be required to work late, or he might accuse his wife of having an affair with the therapist, a doubly convenient ploy because it forces her to drop out of counseling as well. One way or another, when he's threatened, he quits. And he may turn the counseling against her. One husband forbade his wife to leave the house without him after a marriage counselor told the husband to pay more attention to her.

In cases where the controller uses physical force among his tactics, couples counseling can be very dangerous. Most counselors who have experience with domestic violence strongly advise against couples counseling. They say that it may have a place *after* the abusive partner stops using force and threats, and accepts responsibility for the harm he has done. At that point, the woman may feel safe enough to speak frankly about what goes on at home, without fear of physical retaliation from her husband. Only then, if both partners agree, can couples or family counseling be considered as a way to grapple with other problems. On the other hand, many women who have been physically abused never feel safe enough to speak up, fearing that the partner who has stopped using force may simply start again. In such cases, couples counseling is a waste of time.

Too often couples counseling leads to the kind of gruesome story we heard from Suzanne the night we sat in on her support group.

▪ SUZANNE

My husband had a nervous breakdown and went into the hospital. The psychiatrist phoned me and asked me to come for marital counseling sessions. I was reluctant—Matt had been so violent before the hospitalization—but the psychiatrist made me feel that my husband needed me for his recovery. I went for eight sessions. We talked a lot about the abuse and, of course, my husband was very remorseful. Just before Matt's discharge, the psychiatrist met with me privately and assured me that his violence was a thing of the past. He persuaded me, against my better judgment, to let Matt come back home. He said it was essential for his full recovery.

Matt was home only two days before he started in on me again, and this time he broke my nose and some ribs. I had to be hospitalized for a week. But while he was pounding on my face, he said several times, "This is what you get for ratting on your husband to a stupid shrink."

That was the end for me. I had him arrested and got him evicted from the house. And I started coming to this support group so I won't let myself get talked into something stupid again. I trusted the psychiatrist's judgment because he's a trained professional. He's supposed to know more than me. But I should have listened to my gut. Someplace inside me I knew Matt was conning everybody.

We heard stories like Suzanne's from many women. In many cases, the woman initiated the couples counseling herself and saw it as the answer to her prayers. Each woman imagined that in therapy, at last, an objective third party would help sort out the mess of her relationship. These women, and the trained counselors who should have known better, failed to take into account one factor fundamental to the success of any therapy: the client must feel safe to tell the truth. This condition *cannot* be met when a therapist places a woman and her controlling partner in the same room and asks them to talk. Inevitably, week after week, the woman who is afraid of her partner agrees with whatever he says, or she bravely speaks up—and her partner retaliates, usually far from the therapist's office. Or, as in the case of Suzanne and Matt, the controlling partner lies, conning both the therapist and his wife, and then takes it out on her later.

▪ PEGGY

> Couples counseling was not even vaguely helpful to me. In it, we were supposed to be working on our interactions as a couple—as if my behavior somehow set off his. You can imagine how my husband used that one against me. For a while, at the therapist's suggestion, I even toned myself down, thinking that I could keep the situation calm. I completed silly little exercises every night in which I offered my husband support. But the abuse only got worse. We were working on our "interaction" as a couple, but we didn't *have* any interaction as a couple. What we had was a *crime*—one person committing a crime against another. That's not a relationship.

HOW TO EVALUATE A COUNSELOR

Despite these warnings, if your partner does not use physical force, violence, or threats, you may decide that you want to try couples counseling. It may be the only option in your community, or you may already have started to see a marriage counselor. How can you tell if you have a good one? The two checklists that follow may help.

Basic Requirements for Counseling

A good counselor—whatever the form of therapy used—will follow certain procedures and inquire about certain basic issues. Consider the following questions; if you have a good counselor, you should be able to answer "yes" to every one of them.

_____   Did the counselor take your history *in private,* including questions about substance abuse and about your partner's controlling behavior, threats, or violence?

_____   Does the counselor listen to your concerns, value your opinions, and support you?

_____   Does the counselor support your right to have friends, to see your family, and to make your own decisions, including decisions about sex and money? Does the counselor convey this support to your partner?

_____   Does the counselor understand that there is often a great difference between what a controller does to you and what he says to others about it? Does the counselor ever challenge or question your partner's account of his actions?

_____   Does the counselor offer you a realistic assessment of your partner's capacity for change? Does she explain that change does not happen quickly or steadily?

_____   Does the counselor warn you of potential danger, help you plan for your safety, inform you of your right to protection by the police and courts if you need it, and encourage you to use local resources for support and safety?

_____   Does the counselor hold your partner responsible for the harm he commits and not blame you for it—even if you fail to keep the house clean, have an affair, or forget to comfort your husband? Does the counselor tell your partner, clearly and frequently, that abuse is wrong and physical abuse criminal?

_____   If you reveal information privately about your partner's behavior, does the counselor respect your request to keep that information confidential and not share it with your partner? Does she understand that breaking your confidentiality could put you in danger?

_____   Does the counselor take your fears and concerns seriously? Does the counselor understand that control may take many forms—including economic, sexual, and emotional ones—and that ending violence is only one part of the counseling work with your partner to create a safe and healthy environment for you and your children?

_____ Does the counselor understand or take an interest in your particular cultural background, social conditions, and sexual preference? Is she aware of social and cultural conditioning and how it affects sex roles and relationships?

Counselors to Avoid

Now consider the following questions. If you answer yes to *any* of them, you have the wrong counselor.

_____ Does the counselor believe in keeping the family together at all costs—including your deteriorating health and well-being? Does she encourage you to stay with your partner no matter what?

_____ Does the counselor hold you responsible for your partner's abusive behavior or consider you a coequal or "codependent" partner in abuse? Does she use terms like "colluding" or "participating in your own victimization"?

_____ Does the counselor see your use of violence—in self-defense, for example—as equal to your partner's? Does she see your verbal skills as equal to your partner's physical skills? Does she define you both as abusive?

_____ Does the counselor fail to take violence and your safety seriously? Does she accept your partner's minimizing and denial of his behavior? Does she make statements like, "It only happened a few times. I see no pattern of abuse here"?

_____ Does the counselor promise your partner a "quick fix" in some form—by suggesting, for example, that abuse will end if he changes jobs, sobers up, finds God?

_____ Does the counselor encourage your partner to "vent" and express his anger and hostile feelings?

_____ Does the counselor define the abusive behavior as a symptom of other problems, such as stress, substance abuse, or childhood neglect? Does she expect the abuse to disappear after these other issues are "worked through"?

_____ Does the counselor protect your partner from experiencing the negative consequences of his abusive behavior?

———— Does the counselor disbelieve what you tell her?

———— Does the counselor become angry with you or judgmental if you leave your partner or take legal steps to protect yourself? Or, on the other hand, if you *don't* leave your partner right away, or if you go back to him?

———— Does the counselor take your partner's side?

———— Is the counselor racist or homophobic?

PROGRAMS FOR BATTERERS

The most specialized service for abusive men is provided by programs set up in many communities in the last thirteen years specifically to counsel those who use physical force. (In some larger cities and towns there are also groups for lesbians who batter their partners, but these services are not widespread.) Many of these programs are run by men and women who take a strong pro-woman, pro-feminist point of view. Of all the counseling alternatives for violent men, these programs have the best possibility of bringing about real, long-term change. But sadly, the results even of these programs are very mixed.

In the first place, only a very few physically abusive men—no more than 5 or 10 percent—ever come to batterers' programs voluntarily for help. Of those who do, a great many drop out before they complete the program. Even in the very best programs for violent men, such as EMERGE in Boston, no more than two-thirds of the men who formally enroll in the counseling program finish it, and only about one-third of those who finish remain nonviolent for some time after the program.[2] After surveying the evaluations of counseling programs nationwide, one researcher reports that if the number of successful graduates is weighed against all those who initially contacted the program but never joined, the success rate drops to about 10 percent.[3]

More important, even when abusive men change their behavior, no one knows for certain that counseling *caused* the improvement. On the contrary, many of the best counselors themselves believe that other factors—the same factors that motivate men to come to counseling in the first place—motivate them to change. These motivating factors are natural, reasonable, *negative* consequences of their actions. They encourage men to change because they hold them accountable for their bad behavior and at the same time make it clear that such behavior brings negative results. An abusive man is most highly motivated to change when (1) his wife or girlfriend leaves him or announces her intention to leave, (2) he is arrested and put in jail, (3) he is threatened with more time in jail if he acts up again, and (4) he loses his job because of violent behavior.

Perhaps because these facts about the low success rate of such programs are not widely known, women often seem to have far more faith in counseling than many counselors do. So we asked counselors from several programs, "How effective is your work, and how can a woman judge whether a counseling program is really changing her partner?" Some of these programs treat clients who come voluntarily, while others treat only those sent by the court following an arrest, but all the counselors offered surprisingly similar answers and many of the same cautions. (Bear in mind that these services work with physically violent men, and they have few clients who use *only* emotionally abusive tactics. You will have to decide how much of what these experts told us applies to your partner.)

The counselors told us that *no one changes unless he wants to.* Don Chapin of the Domestic Abuse Intervention Project in Minneapolis put it this way: "Women often ask me if domestic violence counseling programs fix men, and I tell them that they have to be real careful about that question. Men fix themselves. It's not the programs that are going to do it for them."[4]

Charles Niessen-Derry from the St. Cloud (Minnesota) Intervention Project expanded on this view: "I think change depends on what men want. If they want intimacy and closeness in their relationships, then they have to stop their violence. If they don't want these things—if they prefer to dictate what will happen in their home and insist on having their way—then they won't stop their abuse."[5]

David Adams, the executive director of EMERGE, agrees that men use counseling only when their abusive behavior no longer works to get them what they want. At EMERGE only 20 percent of the men in counseling are sent by courts; the rest come voluntarily. But most of them come to counseling only because their partners have left them. They want "their" women back. "Most of these clients have sought counseling only once it became clear that their relationship will not continue unless they attend," Adams says. "For most of these men, the problem as they see it is that their wives have left them, not that they have been violent. Some drop out as soon as they reconcile with their wives."[6] In other words, they use counseling as one more tactic of control—to fool their wives into coming back where they want them.

Some researchers believe that there are some violent men who will never change. These men are extremely abusive, inflict the most serious injuries—including sexual abuse—and use violence against other people outside the family as well. Often they have been arrested for other crimes, and in many cases they are heavy users of alcohol and drugs. Violence doesn't seem to make their lives happy or productive, yet they show no signs of giving it up. Some researchers conclude: "The hard fact may be that many of these batterers are beyond the scope of conventional treatment, especially those treatments that focus largely on anger control."[7] They seem to be just too far gone to change.

Edward Gondolf and Ellen Fisher emphasize this point in their book *Battered Women as Survivors* because they learned through their research the same troubling fact that David Adams learned through his work with batterers' groups: namely, that violent men (including many incurable ones) use their participation in a group as a tactic to persuade their partners to reconcile and come home. In their study of abused women living in shelters, Gondolf and Fisher found that only 19 percent of the women whose partners were not in counseling planned to return home. Of those women whose partners were in counseling, 53 percent planned to go back.[8] The very fact that men sign up for counseling raises women's hopes of change and encourages them to return, although many men, as Gondolf and Fisher conclude, "are highly likely to repeat their abuse and intensify it."[9]

Most professionals in your community, including those who may try to help your partner, are probably unaware of these findings. Programs for physically abusive men are relatively new, and research is scanty—so scanty, in fact, that when Dr. Jeffrey Edleson surveyed the literature, he found only eleven studies that reported on the results of abuser treatment programs, and all of them focused on the short term.[10] In other words, no one has studied violent men two or three years after they complete treatment to determine if they actually have changed.

Nor have people conducting long-term studies interviewed the

female partners of men in counseling programs about the psychological terrorism that often replaces physical force. Most experienced counselors believe that men can give up their physical violence quite easily if they choose to, but often they simply replace
violence with other tactics of control. Despite counseling, or perhaps because of it, they remain controlling men, but they take up
more sophisticated methods. And in many cases, they twist and
adapt for their purposes the new methods of self-expression or
problem-solving that they've learned in counseling. Don Chapin
says, "There is a real danger in assuming that just because the
physical violence is over, things are going to be better. Men can
learn new and improved ways to control their partners in the domestic violence program." [11]

▪ JULIA

For a short time my husband stopped the physical violence, but
the emotional abuse increased. He would come home from his
group and tell me everything I did wrong. Or, he would say
things like, "You think I'm so bad. Well, so and so took a gun to
his wife's head. You're lucky I don't do that to you. I could kill
you, you know."

He stopped beating me up because he knew he'd go to jail
if he did it again. But in some ways, he got spookier, and I was
more frightened. He would tower over me and send these intimidating barbs in my direction. I know it sounds nuts, but I'd
rather he hit me and get it over with than play these mind games
for hours. They were worse.

In his group he learned a bunch of new ways to intimidate
me. Once he said to the woman who'd been my advocate in
court, "Thanks for sending me to this program. Now I know how
to get to her *legally*." And he said to me, "I'll do what the judge
told me I have to, but it won't change me one bit."

We have been speaking of the *best* programs—all of them based
on a pro-feminist analysis of domestic violence. Many counseling
programs for abusive men, however, analyze the problem of violence differently. These programs, usually run by mental health

agencies, are based on the belief that abusive men simply lose their temper. These programs try to teach men how to control their anger and express it in nonviolent ways. But, as we've seen, loss of temper is an abusive man's *choice*. He is already in control, and more control is the last thing he needs to learn. In addition, as we've said, a man who gives up violence may still exercise control, especially if his counseling program leads him to believe that control is the *goal* rather than the problem.

The pro-woman programs for violently abusive men, on the other hand, tackle the issue of control head-on. Counselors prod the men to own up to their controlling behavior and to recognize the ways in which they abuse power. In some programs, counselors talk regularly with the partners of the men in their group, so they are prepared to challenge lies and rationalizations the men use to excuse themselves. They insist that the men stop blaming their wives and others, and start taking responsibility for their own behavior. And they point out other implications of the ways the men habitually behave: how they treat women like servants, ignore them, disregard their views, withhold support, call them names, use them for their own sexual convenience, and yet expect women to shower them with constant attention, service, and praise. Counselors insist that to have healthy relationships with women, the men have to treat women as equal and independent human beings. But few men in counseling, their counselors tell us, are willing to go that far.

Fernando Mederos of Common Purpose, a Boston counseling program, says that successful change is a process that takes place in three stages. In the first stage, which should occur within a few weeks of starting counseling, the man stops using physical force. "Without this fundamental and immediate change," Mederos says, "nothing else is possible." Then in the second stage the man gives up emotionally abusive behavior, such as intimidation, threats, insults, yelling, and name calling. "Finally," Mederos says, "he must begin to see the woman's point of view and appreciate what she has gone through and what her daily life is like." A man may give up physical abuse and emotional abuse, but until he enters this third stage, Mederos does not consider him successfully "changed."[12]

HOW TO TELL IF YOUR PARTNER IS CHANGING

Your partner may get help—through a substance-abuse program, individual or couples counseling, or a counseling group for violent men—but that doesn't mean he will change. To see if he is changing, you must examine (and periodically reexamine) the way he acts. You must ask yourself, "Is the intervention effective? Has the abuse stopped?" And to evaluate whether your partner has advanced to the third stage that Fernando Mederos describes, you must consider whether your partner is less demanding and bossy than he used to be, and more respectful, more considerate. The following checklists should help you evaluate your partner's progress.

Often it's easier to look for signs that change is *not* taking place. Our first two checklists point out such indications of negative results. The first describes signs—some obvious, some subtle—that your partner's program is failing. The second checklist points to another set of signs that his program is failing: your partner's manipulative treatment of the children.

Signs of Little or No Change

_____ Your partner drops out of counseling, or he threatens to quit and must be coaxed and pressured to continue.

_____ Your partner continues to use violence and threats.

_____ Your partner continues to abuse substances, or suggests that he will stop harming you sometime in the future when he stops drinking and/or taking drugs.

_____ Your partner attends counseling irregularly, complains constantly about how much it costs, or expects you to pay for it.

_____ In spite of continued counseling, your partner fails to see the damage he has done to you.

_____ Your partner admits he has a problem, but he physically abuses you again and blames you for it.

_____ Your partner uses what he learns in counseling against you.

_____ Your partner continues to accuse you of having affairs, or he follows you, harasses you, and monitors what you do.

_____ If you separate from him, your partner pressures you to come back with statements like, "You're the only wife who is acting this way." Or he makes you feel guilty by saying, "How can you do this to your husband?" He might use charm or guilt ("Can't you see how hard I'm trying for you?"), and if these methods fail, switch to anger and threats: "I'll never give you a penny if you leave me."

_____ Your partner makes you feel that you should be grateful to him by saying things like, "I haven't hit you in six months."

_____ Your partner says repeatedly, "Now it's your turn to change."

_____ Your partner refuses to tolerate your expression of anger about his abuse. He says things like, "You have no right to rub it in." Or he suggests that your anger will set off his violence again.

_____ Your partner makes you feel that he will change only if you are around to motivate him. Counseling is a bargaining chip for him, and he says things like, "I can't do it without you."

_____ Your partner sabotages your efforts to attend a women's support group and to make other positive changes in your life.

More Signs of Little or No Change: Control Through the Children

_____ He acts extremely depressed, even suicidal, in front of the children and blames you for the depression.

_____ He criticizes the way you discipline the children, suggesting that you can't control them.

_____ He tells the kids that he didn't mean to hurt you and that you hold grudges.

_____ He questions the children about you and your activities; he tries to turn them into spies.

_____ He tries to control your movements through the children, by insisting, for example, that you always take the children wherever you go.

_____ He threatens to punish you by fighting for custody even though he doesn't want to raise the kids.

_____ If you have separated from your partner, he blames you and makes statements to the children like, "Mommy won't let me visit."

_____ He tells the children that mommy is responsible for kicking him out and disrupting their lives.

_____ He shows up for visitation unexpectedly and is angry with you if you refuse him permission to see the children. Or, he stays longer and longer when he visits, even though it makes you uncomfortable.

_____ He punishes you and the kids by "forgetting" to show up for visitation or by canceling it repeatedly.

_____ He gives the kids expensive gifts and hints that they could have more if mom let him back in the house.

_____ He tells the kids that you left him for another man.

_____ He suggests that you are ruining the children's lives by depriving them of a father. "Think about what you are doing to them," he says. He fails to acknowledge that his abuse created the problem and that you had a right to protect yourself and the kids.

Signs of Positive Change

Now we turn to a list of signs that may indicate change for the better. (We say *may* because it's always possible for a person to behave differently in order to get what he wants without undergoing fundamental, long-term change in attitudes and beliefs. In other words, people can and do fake change.) Answer the following questions yes or no. Yes answers *may* indicate change.

_____ Has your partner stopped using physical force, threats, and other intimidating tactics?

_____ Do you feel safe to disagree and argue with him, to get angry, to complain about his behavior, to say no to sex—all without apologizing or qualifying what you say?

_____ Can you lead an independent life, have friends and outside interests, without his trying to belittle you, stop you, check up on you, or make you feel guilty?

_____ Does your partner take responsibility for his violence and his life, and has he stopped blaming you for his problems?

_____ Does your partner praise and support you?

_____ Does your partner show gratitude for the things you do for him?

_____ Has your partner stopped putting you down and humiliating you?

_____ Are you able to be with him without feeling tense or afraid of his temper?

_____ Can you negotiate so that your partner does not always have to get his way? Do you sometimes get your way?

_____ Are you happier with your partner than you used to be?

_____ Has your partner stopped pressuring you to forgive and forget? Has he stopped expecting your gratitude? Has he given up statements like "See how lucky you are that I don't do that to you anymore?" or "Lots of people are a lot more violent than I was"?

_____ Does your partner listen to you? Does he remember what you say?

_____ Does your partner take an interest in the things that interest you, without trying to take over or tell you what to do?

_____ Has your partner stopped denying, hiding, and minimizing his abuse?

_____ Has your partner maintained positive changes over a period of at least six months?

KEEPING TRACK

To help you evaluate your partner's progress more specifically, we borrow and adapt a form designed by the Domestic Abuse Intervention Project in Duluth, Minnesota. When you live with control and abuse, *it's very important to keep an accurate written record* because your memory can so easily play tricks on you, especially when your partner engages in on-again/off-again behavior. By filling out this form at regular intervals (for example, once a month, or every three months), you can see if your partner's abusive behavior is increasing, decreasing, or staying the same. The form lists many different kinds of controlling tactics, including many kinds of physical force. Simply cross out those that don't apply to your partner, and add any other controlling behaviors your partner uses that we've neglected to include. We think you'll be surprised to find what a big help this form will be in evaluating any services your partner receives and any promises he makes.

Recording My Partner's Change

MORE THAN BEFORE	LESS THAN BEFORE	ABOUT THE SAME	
____	____	____	My partner drinks.
____	____	____	My partner uses drugs.
____	____	____	My partner neglects me and the kids.
____	____	____	My partner withholds affection and praise.
____	____	____	My partner sulks and gives me the silent treatment.
____	____	____	My partner doesn't listen and twists my words.
____	____	____	My partner lies to me.
____	____	____	My partner refuses to respect my privacy, wishes, or opinions.
____	____	____	My partner insults my family or friends, or refuses to let me see them.
____	____	____	My partner bosses me around.
____	____	____	My partner withholds money.
____	____	____	My partner criticizes, blames, and ridicules me.
____	____	____	My partner pressures me in order to get his way.
____	____	____	My partner follows me around and harasses me.
____	____	____	My partner won't take no for an answer in regard to sex.
____	____	____	My partner throws things to scare me.
____	____	____	My partner destroys things I care about.
____	____	____	My partner drives recklessly.
____	____	____	My partner yells at me.
____	____	____	My partner blocks doorways when I want to leave the room.
____	____	____	My partner twists my arms or fingers.
____	____	____	My partner restrains me.
____	____	____	My partner pulls my hair.
____	____	____	My partner grabs or pushes me.

—— —— —— My partner threatens to hurt or does hurt the kids.
—— —— —— My partner threatens to hurt me.
—— —— —— My partner chokes me.
—— —— —— My partner hits me.
—— —— —— My partner punches me.
—— —— —— My partner kicks me.
—— —— —— My partner sexually assaults me.
—— —— —— My partner forces me to commit crimes.
—— —— —— My partner uses or threatens me with knives, guns, or other weapons.
—— —— —— My partner threatens to kill me, himself, or others.

WHAT ARE MY OPTIONS?

If you think counseling is a possibility for your partner, do some investigating to find out about programs and services in your community. You might begin by calling Alcoholics Anonymous, a shelter hotline, a community mental health clinic, a community center, or your church. Be wary of any program that promises a quick end to your problems. Remember that while a good counseling program may help a man who *wants* to change, counseling is not what *motivates* controlling men to change.

If your partner enters a program, don't just sit back and wait for the happy ending. You owe it to yourself to keep evaluating what's going on. For one thing, counseling can go on for a very long time without producing significant changes in behavior. While you wait for future change in your partner, you may postpone decisions and actions that could improve your life. Keep in mind, too, that your partner's counseling is *his*. It's designed to make him feel better—not you. If he does change, you may find the changes welcome. But then again, you may not.

Only one thing is certain: your partner will make only the changes he *wants* to make. Whatever happens to your partner in counseling, it's up to you to keep track, and to do what's best for you. You can make whatever changes you choose, according to *your* standards, in *your* life. Let's move on, then, to consider in the next chapter how you can create safety and support and strength for yourself.

Making Choices, Making Changes

6

Strengthening Yourself

Intimate relationships have an immense impact on self-esteem. They can make us feel loving and intelligent, or they can leave us with a growing sense of despair and incompetence. As we've seen in the preceding chapters, when you're stuck in an unhappy relationship with a controlling partner, you may try to improve the relationship by "improving" yourself. As you worry about what you are contributing to the relationship, you may not keep track of what the relationship is doing to you. But all the while your pride and dignity and aspirations—your self-esteem—will be collapsing under the pressure of a controlling partner.

Let's talk a little about that self-esteem, where it comes from, and how our relationships bear upon it. Clearly, it is affected by our interactions with the social and cultural institutions of our society, or the people who represent them, and how they treat us—the caseworker at the welfare office, for example, the principal at our children's school, the police, the family court judge. It's affected by the images we see on TV and in movies and magazines and ads of ourselves as women, and particularly by images of ourselves as white women, black women, Hispanic women, Asian women, Native American women, rich women, poor women, lesbian women, and so on.

As women, we all belong to a group that is undervalued and underprivileged in comparison to men. We do far more of the world's work, and we're paid far less for doing it (if we're paid at all). We don't even have equal rights under the United States Constitution, and when we try to get equal rights, state legislators all across the country vote against us. Women of color are even less valued than white women, poor women are valued less than women of "higher" social classes, and lesbians are valued less than heterosexual women. And when attention is paid to women, we are often "valued" for the wrong reasons—as sexual objects, for example. What this means is that our self-esteem comes in for a beating every day that we live in our sexist, racist, class-biased society.

We can take action to change these conditions, through the women's movement, the civil rights movement, and other groups working for equality and social justice. But at the same time, as women, we have to create and develop our self-esteem largely through personal interactions with people whose opinions we value: parents, friends, coworkers, children, and intimate partners. That may help to explain why women place a higher value on personal relationships than men do and work harder to maintain them. And it may help to explain why our most personal relationship of all can have such a big impact on our sense of ourselves.

When that relationship is with a controlling partner whose on-again/off-again behavior supports you one minute and attacks you the next, your self-esteem can be thrown onto very shaky ground. In addition, a controller's thoroughgoing criticism can undermine the sense of self-worth you draw from other relationships in your life. Your interactions on the job, for example, may make you feel competent and well-respected. You may feel proud of being a good doctor or office worker or teacher. And even if the only job you can get seems demeaning or boring, you may still feel proud that you are bringing in money, being responsible, and setting a good example for your kids. But your partner may discount your work or disapprove of it, and in his interactions with you leave you feeling inadequate and depressed. The more a controlling partner succeeds in isolating you—in cutting you off from work and social life and family—the more you become dependent upon him to maintain your faltering self-esteem. And of course, the more you turn to a controlling partner for support, the more thoroughly your self-esteem is undermined.

When that happens, you may be inclined to look for the cause of your low self-esteem outside your relationship. You might blame your parents or your unhappy childhood or racism. You might blame a physical disability or a poor education. Any of these things may play a part, but the fact is that you feel better or worse about yourself depending upon your current experiences. No matter what you've experienced in life, the level of your self-esteem today depends in large part on what's going on in your daily life *now*.

Even many "experts" get things backwards, and some suggest that your low self-esteem is what leads you to be unhappy in your relationship. Some have even suggested that a woman who has low self-esteem *causes* men to physically abuse her. If you want a good relationship, they advise, get high self-esteem first. We now know that the low self-esteem of so many emotionally and physically abused women is the *result,* not the cause, of the abuse they've gone through. The advice should be stated the other way around: if you want higher self-esteem, get a better relationship.

Now, however, as you let go of the responsibility you assumed for your relationship, as you pull yourself out of the traps of explaining your partner's behavior and blaming yourself, you are freeing yourself to shift focus and try some new strategies to strengthen yourself. You can reach beyond your relationship and build an external support network to revive your faltering sense of self-worth, change the conditions of your life, and, if you should decide to uproot yourself and your children, provide you with the help you need to do it.

Making real change is not easy. As Maria told us, "I felt like a ping-pong ball, I changed my mind so many times. Everybody said I was nuts, and I thought so, too." We talked to so many women who, like Maria, had made enormous life changes, that we began to ask each of them, "Where did you get your strength? What helped you?"

A lot of women told us that they drew strength from familiar sources of support. Maria, for example, turned to her best friend and "talked her head off." Sarah turned to her spiritual beliefs. She told us, "I thought and thought about it for months, and I finally decided mine was a God who cherished body and soul and did not want me to live this way." Other women found strength and support in unexpected quarters. But all the women we talked to had one thing in common: each one made the journey for herself, but she reached out for help along the way. They gave this advice:

1. Find the right person to talk to.
2. Build a good support system.
3. Become your own advocate and fight for your rights and the rights of women like you.

Let's look at each of these suggestions in greater detail.

SUGGESTION 1: FIND THE RIGHT PERSON TO TALK TO

When we met Janet, a devout Catholic and mother of six, she had recently ended her twenty-year marriage to an emotionally abusive alcoholic. During her marriage, Janet frequently reached out for help and reported her husband's abuse to the only source of comfort she could think of: her parish priest. Whenever she discussed Bob's threatening tirades or her desire to leave him, the elderly priest would roll his eyes and say, "Janet, marriage is a holy sacrament. We must pray for Bob and give the poor, sick man a chance. There's a devil inside Bob, and it's your duty as his wife to stand by him." After these meetings, Janet always felt frustrated, but she always renewed her efforts to make her marriage work.

In the months preceding her separation, Janet grew more frightened of Bob. Although she couldn't explain why, she felt a sense of impending doom. It disturbed her so much that she sought out a young priest who had recently come to her parish. When she told him about Bob's alcoholism and emotional abuse, the priest responded very differently from his older colleague. He told her that she was God's temple, sacred and valued. God's temple was not meant to be harmed. "Janet, we love you very much," the priest continued, "and we all know Bob, and we don't like what he's doing to you. One of these days," he concluded, "a door is going to open and you will see a light and, I hope, find a way out of these difficulties."

A few days after she spoke to the young priest, Janet went home one evening to find Bob standing in the doorway waiting for her. He yelled at her, "Get in this house! You've got some things to account for." In terror, Janet turned, and for the first time in her life, fled. Thinking back on that evening, Janet remembers only two things: the look in Bob's eyes when he threatened her, and the priest's words—"a door is going to open and you will see a light"— words that gave her permission to leave.

Like a number of women, Janet took a risk and told her story to a second person—in this case another priest—after the first person she confided in failed to help her. She believes this choice was a lifesaving one.

On the other hand, many women make other choices; and some (though distinctly in the minority) choose not to tell anyone about what they are going through. As women explained their situations to us, their reasons for not telling made good sense. So before we go on to consider how you might find the right person to talk to, let's look at this alternative: the option of silence.

Women Who Decide Not to Tell

Jill's husband abused her sexually, but she kept it a secret, right up to the time she finally fled. She had an explanation for her silence.

▪ JILL

> Although I felt terribly isolated and alone, I couldn't talk about it because I knew somebody in my family would say, "Why are you with him?" And what do you answer? Because I have my kids? Because I have my house? Because I don't know who would want a woman with three children? Because I'm terrified that if I do leave, he'll kill me? You know if you say something like that to people, they will say, "Oh, he's not going to kill you. You're exaggerating." They don't understand. I'd rather lie.

Gloria came to the same conclusion. She told us, "My family sat in their houses and they never saw him do this to me. They would never believe it. They only saw him quiet, respectful. They would say that I'm nuts."

Other women were convinced that telling would only make

things worse, so they decided not to. Fear is the most important factor that keeps women in controlling relationships, especially violent ones, and it is also the most important reason women don't tell.

▪ **SYLVIA**

> Fear guides everything you do. Fear that the authorities would take away the kids. Fear that if I told he would kill himself and for the rest of my life I would have to live with the thought that I drove him to it or I could have prevented it. Fear that one night he would retaliate against the people I told and murder them.

Many women, particularly poor women and women of color, feared that if they told about their partner's violence and someone reported it to the authorities, the child protective services might take their kids away. (In fact, poor women and especially women of color do lose their children more often than white middle-class women.) Some women felt that if they told, they would then have to leave their partner, and they weren't ready to make that decision. The thought of telling about abuse and staying with the person who abused them made them ashamed, and they remained silent—at least for a time.

As you think about your situation, it might help to review the following checklist of barriers to telling. Perhaps some of these barriers are standing in your way, or you may have other reservations to add to the list. We think that each woman must take her reservations seriously and make her own decision. But we also believe that in most cases the reasons *for* telling—especially if you find the right person to tell—are more persuasive than the barriers. We suggest that after you've read the next two sections, "Women Who Decide to Tell" and "Finding the Right Person to Tell," you return to this list of barriers and consider whether they still apply.

Barriers to Telling

_____ I'm not sure anyone will believe me. Maybe they will laugh at me.

_____ I feel too ashamed to tell.

_____ I'm scared that my partner will hurt or kill me if I tell.

_____ My partner threatened to take the kids if I talked about the abuse.

_____ My partner will find out that I talked. I'm not sure I can trust anyone to keep my story confidential.

_____ I may set something in motion that only makes matters worse.

_____ My partner told me I would be deported for telling.

_____ My partner will cut me off financially if I tell.

_____ The authorities will take my kids if I tell them what has happened in my home.

_____ I'm afraid people will think I'm sick; they'll think I like it.

_____ Despite everything, I feel sorry for my partner.

_____ In my ethnic group, we solve our own problems. We don't talk about them, especially not to white people.

Women Who Decide to Tell

Lisa believes that it's important to tell someone what you're going through.

▪ LISA

> I knew that I was a decent human being. No matter how hard he tried to take that away from me, he couldn't. But toward the end he was succeeding. I began to say, "What am I here for? I feel worthless." I started to think about suicide. That's when I called the women's crisis line and met my counselor, Carmen. Did she ever help me figure things out! I realized I wasn't crazy.

Stephanie, too, found that talking helped. One night at dinner she poured out part of her story to Sally, a friend from her old neighborhood. Stephanie confessed that she was worried about her marriage and terrified that if it ended, she would be penniless. To Stephanie's surprise, Sally confessed that she, too, had been trapped in an emotionally abusive marriage because of financial concerns.

Later that night Sally gave Stephanie the phone numbers of one woman friend who was a financial planner and another who was a lawyer specializing in divorce cases. This meeting changed Stephanie's life. She says, "Until that night, I never had a language to put on my problems. Afterwards I not only knew I was abused, but I saw some solutions to the mess I was in."

For years Renee chose not to "bother" her elderly parents and older sister with her troubles. When she did, she was pleasantly surprised by their response.

▪ RENEE

My mother came up for a few weeks to stay with me and try to help me figure out what to do. My father sent me a little money. My sister had me to stay at her house to have a safe place to think things over. They completely rallied around me. They took chances for me. It felt real good to hear my sister say "You don't have to take this," and to walk into a court hearing—in front of my husband—with my family surrounding me.

We asked women to tell us why it helped to talk about abuse, and certain themes came up again and again in their answers. They told us that psychological manipulation, or emotional abuse, robbed them of clarity, twisted their perceptions of reality, and clouded their judgment. Talking to a trusted outsider reminded them of what was real. They learned to listen to *themselves* again, to hear the sound of their own voices, rather than the voice of the controlling partner that had silenced them and filled their heads for so long. Many women also reported suffering from exhaustion and fear, which left them little energy to think. Friends, counselors, and advocates brought them relief from the depression and confusion that abuse creates. As Clare told us, "My husband would tell me that I was a dummy, and my best friend would remind me that I was an all-A student to whom everyone at school turned for help. She saved my soul."

Finding the Right Person to Tell

Although many women find it very helpful to tell someone what's going on, it's helpful only if you find the right person. Some women tell the wrong person, as Janet did when she told the elderly priest. It's important to look, as she later did, for a person who seems likely to be supportive and respectful of your confidence. Carol told us, "Telling the wrong person can set a woman back for years and make her never want to disclose again." It can also make matters worse, as Heather says: "My mother-in-law and I called the family doctor, who came to our house to talk to my husband. But my husband was so enraged by his visit that he punched his mother in the face. Before the doctor left the house, he wrote *me* a prescription for tranquilizers. At that moment I wanted to die, and I vowed I would never tell another soul about the abuse."

Some women talk to family members and friends who minimize the seriousness of their partner's behavior, take the abusive partner's side, point out that "there are two sides to every story," or make guilt-inducing comments like, "Give the guy a break, he doesn't really mean it." Because of these experiences, many women have strong opinions about the kinds of people to talk to. Here are some suggestions:

1. Tell your story to a person who will believe you.
2. Choose a good listener, someone who will let you talk.
3. Find a person who will keep what you say confidential.
4. If you consult a professional, ask if she has worked before with women who live with emotionally or physically abusive partners. Ask what training and experience she has.
5. Search for a person who cares about you, one you trust, one you've shared confidences with before.
6. Share your experiences only if you feel safe with the person.
7. Tell your story to someone who is knowledgeable about resources in your community and who specializes in this work. Or tell a supportive friend and ask her to find out about resources for you.
8. If you call a hotline, ask if you can talk to a woman who has lived through an abusive relationship.
9. Find someone who knows and shares your particular back-

ground and life-style—in other words, someone who will have a realistic view of what your options are.

Heather, the woman who got only tranquilizers when she confided in the doctor, did muster up the courage to tell her story again, but not for several years. Then she sought help from a mental health center and there met a counselor who was a former drug addict and former abused woman. They talked for hours, and Heather began the process of making some important changes in her life. Reflecting on those years of silence, Heather says, "I wish now that I had tried to tell a second, third, or fourth person about the abuse. I told the wrong person, and I should have tried again. I almost died, and all the while there were people out there who wanted to help me."

What to Do If You've Told the Wrong Person

In some cases the "wrong" person makes blatantly hostile or blaming comments to you, such as, "What did you do to set him off?" Others may express sympathy and concern but still be wrong. For example, whenever Laura confided in her sister that she was thinking of leaving her husband, her sister always ended the conversation with the words, "Are you sure you want to do this to your kids? Why don't you think about them for a change?"

It's a clue that you have told the wrong person if that person acts indifferent to you, urges you to forgive and forget, insists that things can't be that bad, suggests that everybody goes through this, makes excuses for your partner such as "He's had a rough time lately," wants to hear your partner's "side" of the story, blames you for doing things wrong, makes you feel guilty, or angrily turns on you. If, after making a sincere effort to describe your situation to another person, you feel that you never want to see that person again, you've definitely picked the wrong one. At these moments—when shame and despair may overwhelm you—it's important to remind yourself that you did not make a mistake by telling. You did the right thing, but you told the wrong person.

What if the person you told—a child protective worker, for example—has the power to bully or force you into choices you don't want to make? Although it may feel uncomfortable and you be more afraid than ever, this is precisely the moment you might consider telling your story again, but this time to an advocate or attorney who knows how the system operates and will help you fight for your rights within it. In these circumstances you will need all the help you can get.

Establishing Standards for the Person You Tell

If you have ever told the wrong person or are afraid of that possibility, you might want to make a list of what you want to happen when you tell. Of course, there's no guarantee that you'll get the reactions you want, but this preparation may help you judge the response more quickly and move on to other, more supportive people if you need to. Each of us may have different hopes and expectations when we tell another person about our relationship.

What I Need When I Talk About the Abuse

We start the list with examples of some things that are important to many women. We suggest that you list the things that are important to you.

I want my friend to listen. I don't want any advice— at least not until I ask for it.

I want what I say to be kept confidential.

I need reassurance that I am okay.

The Right Person, the Right Results

When you find the right person, you'll know—though perhaps not right away. Remember that what the young priest told Janet didn't become clear to her immediately. Right after you tell about your experience you may feel more vulnerable, more afraid, or more ashamed. That's perfectly natural any time you take a big risk and can't be sure how the other person will respond. But you should begin to feel some hope as well. We've compiled a list of some of the most common positive results women get from telling. We suggest that you compare this list to the checklist on page 126, "Barriers to Telling." We think you'll find that the positive results to be gained from telling outweigh the reasons for keeping silent. But that's not true in every case. You have to weigh your own situation as carefully and realistically as you can and come to your own decision.

Results of Telling the Right Person

_____   I found hope when I thought there was no way out.

_____   I felt much less isolated and crazy when I started to talk.

_____   I believed that someone cared about me.

_____   I learned about resources like shelters and restraining orders.

_____   I heard someone declare that my partner's behavior was wrong.

_____   I found people who wanted to help me.

_____   I felt relieved of the burden of being a liar and keeping secrets from people who cared about me and were being hurt by my distance.

_____   I got a different view of myself. My partner cut me down constantly, but outsiders built me up.

_____   I could let go of the shame and guilt I was experiencing.

_____   I realized I deserved a whole lot more in my life.

_____   I realized that I was carrying a bigger burden than anybody should have to.

_____   I found the strength inside me that I had forgotten was there.

_____ I became more like myself again, a more open and loving person, instead of this terrible shriveled-up silent shadow I'd turned into living with him. And people who'd known me before welcomed me back, like I'd been on a long trip.

_____ I started to see alternatives I couldn't see before. I could actually think of things to do.

SUGGESTION 2: BUILD YOUR SUPPORT SYSTEM

A controlling partner will often try to isolate you—to cut you off from family, friends, and outside interests, or at least to control your interaction with them. The more isolated a woman becomes, the more abuse robs her of her strength. Tammy told us, "I knew he was wrong when he told me how crazy I was, but as time went on, a part of me began to think, 'Maybe he's right. Maybe I do want him to act this way.' My world had gotten so narrow, with everything focused on him, and to survive in it I stopped trusting my own perceptions. I stopped believing in what I knew to be true."

In spite of her partner's objections, Tammy reached out to many different people, and she found support. Friends, coworkers, people in self-help groups like Al-Anon, advocates, and professional counselors alike—all in their own way—helped Tammy develop more positive ideas about herself, and greater clarity about her relationship.

Work or School

In one way or another, many controlling men discourage their partners from working or going to school. Most of them feel threatened by anything that might bring a woman greater independence and freedom from their control. They get nervous when a woman earns her own money or puts herself in a better position to do so by taking classes—whether she's picking up English as a second language, working on a GED, learning a trade, or entering graduate school. But some controllers, who at first frustrate or forbid a woman's interest in doing anything outside the home, finally give in—usually after a prolonged struggle. Bonnie had to battle her way out of isolation.

▪ BONNIE

I told Brad that I wanted to get my real estate license. And I sweet-talked him. "I'll probably never use it," I said to him, "but I want to go to school in the evenings. I need something to do." He only let me because my son was going to college at the same time, and we agreed that my son would drop me off at class and pick me up. I knew this was the only way Brad would permit it. He would never let me go by myself.

When I finished my courses and was studying for my license, I had to convince Brad that I should work. I picked a real estate firm in town owned by a family he looked up to and I started talking to him about how much it might help his business if I were there. I told him I'd work just a few hours a week. It would be just a little part-time job. By the time I got my license, I'd talked him into it. I'd convinced him that my working for that particular firm would make *him* look good.

Soon after Bonnie started her job, she increased her hours, and her salary. This is when "the fights got much worse," and Bonnie had to struggle with Brad about everything. Although he tried to get her to quit her job, he was too late—by years. From the time she received her first A in a real estate course, Bonnie had changed.

I had books with me every minute of the day, I wanted this license so bad. I studied so hard that I got high scores on everything. Of course, my teachers started praising me, encouraging me to go on. And there was Brad at home, making fun of it, mocking me. Something snapped when he started tearing my schooling down. I wouldn't take it anymore.

School was a way to get Brad out of my mind and my soul. He could *not* get into my brain. That's the only place he couldn't get into. It was mine. I was happy when I was at school. And when my teachers treated me respectfully and politely, I realized there was a different way to live. Before I went to school I thought I was stupid—and Brad, of course, told me I was stupid—but I learned we were both wrong.

Like Bonnie, Ella found support through her job. Although she found her work on a parts-assembly line exhausting, especially after the birth of her daughter, she refused to give it up. "Having a job," she says, "meant that I could leave home in the morning and act like I wasn't taking all the abuse I got there. It was my survival—a way to tell myself that I was okay, that I was competent, that I could function, that I could accomplish what I had set out to do that day."

Ella believed that at home she was "aging and dying." In fact, for as long as she lived with her husband, she was hospitalized annually with stomach pains, although the doctors could never find anything wrong with her. At work, however, Ella was a different person. She told us, "I had friends there. I had people who really liked me—and it was one of them who finally said, 'Ella, come to a meeting with me. You deserve more than you're getting.'"

Recovery Groups

Ella was nervous as she thought about attending her first Al-Anon meeting, a support group for the partners and adult relatives of alcoholics. What would happen? she wondered. Would people force her to talk? By the end of the first meeting she was still wary, but she felt a little better—reassured by the warmth and friendliness of the people in the group, and by the fact that no one had tried to force her to speak.

It would be weeks before Ella said a word in a meeting. In the meantime she listened, soaking up ideas and trying to make sense of them. In Al-Anon she realized that her husband was an alcoholic, and by listening to other members, she understood that she had been trying fruitlessly to manage his life and make it run smoothly. She understood that she did not cause James to drink, nor was it up to her to fix his life.

Ella found the meetings so helpful that she decided to attend a second one during her lunch hour, closer to her job. Attending this meeting would be easier, she thought, because she wouldn't have to explain her whereabouts to James. But she was disappointed and confused by the group. "It's a pity-pot," she told a friend in her first group. "The members moan and groan about everything, and one man keeps saying that we are all enablers of the disease of alcoholism, and every bit as sick as the alcoholics." The more Ella thought about it the more she knew this group was not for her. She told her friend, "It's beating up on myself to say I'm sick, too. I don't need it." Ella also resented the idea that she "enabled" James's drinking. "Of course I give him drinks," she said. "Then he passes out and doesn't hit me. I'll keep doing it if I have to."

Intuitively Ella knew that she was right, that she was not an "enabler" of James's illness. She knew that her decision to give James alcohol was not a very good one because it brought her only temporary safety and made her long-term problem worse. But she also knew that she was not "sick" for doing it. When Ella learned that the AA program was originally developed by men and mainly directed at men, she understood that a man's point of view is built into many of its teachings and carried over into Al-Anon. Some recovery groups still maintain that male orientation, but as a woman, Ella was bound to see some things differently.

She returned to her first Al-Anon group and immediately felt better. Her Al-Anon friends agreed that she had done the right thing, and their support had come to be very important to her. Over coffee after the meetings, they told one another, "You're valuable. You count." Ella also loved the energy of the members who had been in Al-Anon the longest. "These are brave women, trying all kinds of things for the first time," she told a friend, "and I want to be like them."

As Ella continued to attend meetings, she began to call Al-Anon her "life-support system." And it was to this system she turned when it was time to do something about James's abuse.

Support Groups

One night after an Al-Anon meeting, Ella poured out her fears about James's ongoing—and increasing—physical violence. Would it ever stop, she wondered, and what should she do? Why couldn't she think straight? She told her friend, "In Al-Anon I keep hearing that alcoholism is a disease. But what about the violence? Is it a disease, too?" "Whatever it is," her friend replied, "it's certainly another big problem. Why not join a support group at the women's shelter? That might make things clearer for you."

Ella didn't want to call the shelter because she thought of it as a place run by white women for white women. No one she knew had ever used the shelter. And she'd heard that women's shelters talk women into hating men and force them to leave their husbands, neither of which she was prepared to do. Nevertheless, she bravely phoned the shelter and spoke to the group's counselor, who calmed some, though not all, of her fears. The counselor told her that many different kinds of women attend support groups— women of different races and social classes, women who live with their partners and women who have left them. The goal of the twelve-week group, the counselor explained, was to offer support and new information to any woman who needed it. "Never do we tell women what to do with their lives," she said.

The counselor also applauded Ella's decision to call her. "Violence is different from alcoholism," she explained. "It's definitely not a disease. It's a choice." She went on to say that some Al-Anon teachings might be positively dangerous for Ella and women like her who live with violent men. "In Al-Anon and similar recovery programs," she said, "you're encouraged to 'detach' yourself emotionally from the alcoholic and live your own life, but we know that it's just when you try to detach, emotionally or physically, from a violent man that he's likely to become far more violent." The counselor recommended that Ella join the group. "Here," she said, "you'll have a chance to decide what's best for you."

Although Ella was jittery beforehand, she was reassured during the first group meeting by the members' friendliness and promises of confidentiality. Besides, she could see that some other women were just as nervous as she was. After the meeting Ella felt a surge of relief. The stories that other women shared were so like her own. "It helped," she said, "to get it out and to realize I'm not the only one."

As the weeks went by, Ella still had reservations about the group. "I don't like how they bad-mouth men," she told her friend. "It makes me feel guilty even though I do it myself when I'm furious at James." But she continued to attend meetings faithfully. "I'll never miss one," she explained, "because I learn so much."

Ella made good use of the shelter, too. One weekend, when James blew up and threw a lamp across the room, narrowly missing her head, she called the shelter and stayed there for a few nights. "It's so important to know I have a safe place to escape to if I need it," she told her friend. "I thought the women in the group would make me feel terrible for going back to him, and a few of them did, but I got through it okay. I know they care about me."

Ella recommends support groups to other women for one additional reason. "We have great discussions," she says. Different groups have different procedures. Ella's chose weekly topics, such as "Do I need a man to survive?" "In a discussion like this," Ella says, "one of the women might say, 'I've finally learned I want a man, but I don't need one to make me a complete person. I can take care of myself just fine, and I realize I've been doing it for years.' Then another woman might respond, 'I feel like I can't live without him'—and we're off on an intense debate." Ella feels that these discussions have helped her clarify many issues. "I'd still be in a muddle if it weren't for these groups. I've started to think straight, and I've found strength I never knew I had."

Talking to an Advocate

During her first day as a resident at the shelter, Ella was introduced to Sandra, a women's advocate. Sandra explained that an advocate is a woman whose job it is to speak up for other women and work for their rights. Many different community organizations and agencies have advocates on staff, either as paid employees or as volunteers, to help clients. Unlike traditional social workers, who are supposed to be "professional" and "objective," advocates try to put themselves in the place of the women they help and speak for them.

Because they see how unequal the power is between a woman and her partner, and how unfair the criminal justice system often is, advocates take a stand on the abused woman's side. Most women's advocates, however, are on the side of women's rights in general, and there are times when the needs of an individual woman conflict with what the advocate believes to be in the best interests of all women. For example, an advocate might believe that all physically abused women should take their husbands to court, but some women think it's too dangerous for them to do so. In such cases, the advocate may help the client see her situation in a new light: in terms of what's best for all women. But it's up to the client to decide what she wants to do, without pressure from the advocate.

Although some advocates are professionally educated and others are not, each is specially trained for the work she does. In fact, as Sandra went on to explain, many lawyers turn to advocates—and advise their clients to do the same—whenever they need expert information about domestic violence. "As an advocate," Sandra said, "I've seen every situation imaginable, and I've helped women with the worst of them."

After listening to Ella's story, Sandra explained that each guest at the shelter—whether she stays one day or thirty—and every woman who calls and asks for help is assigned an advocate who provides information about court, housing alternatives, welfare, and other resources in the community. Recognizing how difficult and frightening it is for some women to navigate through the criminal justice system or the housing bureaucracy, Sandra said that she would accompany Ella to appointments, if Ella wanted her help. Ella was grateful for the information, but she explained to Sandra that she was going home, and that, for now, she needed time to think. Sandra poured her a cup of coffee, and they talked. To her surprise, Ella learned that Sandra had once been a guest in the shelter, searching for answers to the same questions that now haunted Ella.

Ella liked Sandra right away and felt lucky to have her support. Later she learned that, as in any other occupation, some advocates are better than others. Some push their own agenda, instead of trying to understand yours. Some are simply overworked. One of the women in Ella's support group told of a discouraging experience she'd had with a victims' advocate in the district attorney's office who paid no attention to her case and never returned her phone calls. This story prompted a discussion of advocacy, and the members of the support group decided to draw up a list of the qualities they'd like to see in good advocates. We include that list here because it echoes suggestions that were made to us by good advocates around the country, all of whom urged women to reject unhelpful "helpers" and to keep searching until they found good ones.

Another important thing to keep in mind is that any person who knows the ropes can advocate for you, whether she officially works as an advocate or not. Think about people who've helped you in some way already: perhaps an immigration counselor, a resettlement sponsor, an English teacher, a church worker, or perhaps a neighborhood youth leader or a teacher who works with your children. Anyone who has helped you or a member of your family before may be able and willing to do so again—or to help you find someone who can. You may find a very good advocate in an unexpected place.

Qualities of a Good Advocate

_____ She believes your story and supports you.

_____ She is well-informed about resources and explains them clearly, thereby expanding your ideas about your options.

_____ She asks good questions and helps you as you try to make a realistic assessment of your alternatives.

_____ She informs you of your rights.

_____ She treats you like an adult. She expects you to make your own decisions and to carry out your plans.

_____ She offers help, if you want it.

_____ She cares about you and lets you know it.

_____ When she promises to do something, she does it.

_____ She is not afraid of the system and helps you get what you need from police, courts, housing, welfare, and mental health workers.

_____ She takes your fear of your partner seriously but does not let it overwhelm the two of you. She helps you assess danger and plan for your safety.

_____ She helps you sort through and clarify your ideas.

_____ She teaches you what she knows so that you can become an advocate for yourself.

Talking to a Counselor

Some programs for abused women provide what they call supportive counseling. Some programs call it "empowerment" counseling because its purpose is to help women regain their full power. Sometimes this counseling is done on an individual basis, sometimes in groups. For the individual client, it is rather like working with an advocate in that it aims to inform her and make her into her own advocate. Other programs purposely have no professionally trained counselors. Instead, they stick strictly to the idea of one woman helping another, and they refer any women who ask for professional counseling to local mental health centers or private therapists. If counseling is a service you want, you might call your local shelter hotline for suggestions. If it is doing its job well, the shelter (or another local agency specializing in services for abused women) will have a list of therapists who have been helpful to other women.

Starting with such a reference is critical. "It's better to have no counselor at all than to have a bad one," women say over and over again; and listening to women's stories convinced us of the truth of that statement. "For two years I worked with a therapist who wanted to explore my childhood," Milagros told us. "I came in every week more anxious than the last. I couldn't sleep, I had terrifying nightmares, I was scared to death of my boyfriend—and the thera pist kept asking me about my parents." Milagros finally dropped out of counseling, more confused than when she began.

On the other hand, many women told us that they had been helped by professional therapists. Francine told us that she first went to a professional counselor against her will. Her boss insisted she go for help after she missed twenty days of work because of fights at home.

"Why do I have to be here," she asked the therapist, "when he's the violent one?" The therapist acknowledged that the situation was unfair and that Francine was not the cause of her own abuse. She asked Francine, "Isn't there anything you want for yourself?" Fran- cine persisted, "He's the problem. Treat him." He, unfortunately, would not go for help. In Francine's eyes, walking through the doors of a mental health center confirmed what she most feared— that she was crazy. That was what her husband and her family always said. "Not true," said the therapist. "In fact, my guess is that you've been managing a pretty insane situation with a great deal of strength."

"This was the first sign," Francine told us, "that this woman might have something to offer me. I felt better, less tangled in knots, when I left her office." During the following weeks, Francine found the counseling "powerful and affirming." The therapist gave her articles to read about abuse, urged her to join a women's support group, and regularly inquired about her safety and well-being. "My therapist would tell me, 'Your husband is dangerous, Francine. I worry about you.' He'd brainwashed me so badly that I didn't even know how scared I was, but she saw it and named it." When we asked Francine what was most helpful about the therapy, she responded quickly, "My therapist really liked me and wanted more for me—more than my parents or my husband did. With her encouragement, I started behaving like a different person."

If you are considering counseling, we suggest that you ask yourself the question Francine's therapist asked her: "Isn't there anything you want for yourself?" Think carefully also about what you *don't* want from a therapist. You might want to write down what you want and don't want, and carry these lists to your first session; use them as guidelines as you interview the therapist and decide whether you want to work with her. Try to interview several therapists before making up your mind.

To find a counselor, you can:

1. Call a local program or your state toll-free hotline for abused women (see the list of phone numbers in the Resources section at the end of the book) and ask for a referral.
2. Ask a friend who has had a good experience in counseling.
3. Call a women's center at your local college, a rape crisis hotline, the YWCA, or a community service that specializes in helping women.
4. Ask women in Al-Anon or other recovery groups.

It's perfectly all right not to stay with the first person you see, or the one whom everyone else recommends. It's also alright to change your therapist at any time, even if your therapist doesn't think so. It's *your* therapy. Shop around. (It also might help to review "Basic Requirements for Counseling" on page 105, "Counselors to Avoid" on page 106, "Finding the Right Person to Tell" on page 129, and "Qualities of a Good Advocate" on page 140. Whether you talk with a friend, an advocate, or a therapist, what you're looking for is essentially the same in every case: support.)

Signs That You Are Working with the Wrong Counselor

_____   Even after giving the counseling process some time, I still don't trust the therapist or feel safe when we are together.

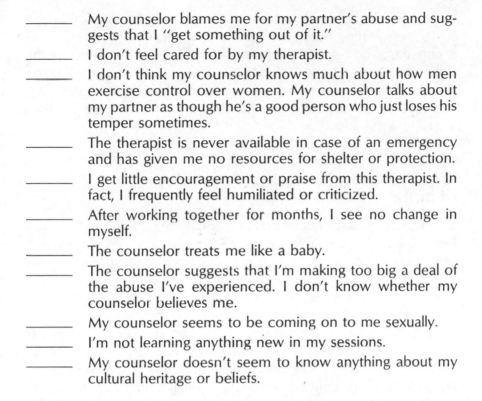

_____ My counselor blames me for my partner's abuse and suggests that I "get something out of it."

_____ I don't feel cared for by my therapist.

_____ I don't think my counselor knows much about how men exercise control over women. My counselor talks about my partner as though he's a good person who just loses his temper sometimes.

_____ The therapist is never available in case of an emergency and has given me no resources for shelter or protection.

_____ I get little encouragement or praise from this therapist. In fact, I frequently feel humiliated or criticized.

_____ After working together for months, I see no change in myself.

_____ The counselor treats me like a baby.

_____ The counselor suggests that I'm making too big a deal of the abuse I've experienced. I don't know whether my counselor believes me.

_____ My counselor seems to be coming on to me sexually.

_____ I'm not learning anything new in my sessions.

_____ My counselor doesn't seem to know anything about my cultural heritage or beliefs.

If you have any of these negative feelings about your counselor or the counseling process, you may want to voice them to your counselor. Or you may want to leave and look for another counselor. When you find the right one, you should experience many positive results, just as women do who find the right person to tell. In particular, talking with the right counselor should make you feel less isolated. It should give you a sense of being understood, supported, and cared for. And most important, it should help you regain your strength and hope.

SUGGESTION 3: BECOME YOUR OWN ADVOCATE

Women often end their interviews with us by offering a piece of advice to others. Edith put it this way: "Tell women that nobody will do it for them. They'll have to do it by themselves." Laura said: "I was lucky to have friends who said, 'Come to our house, if you need to,' but other than that, I was on my own. It was very lonely and frightening, and I seldom got any affirmation that I was doing the right thing. In fact, I often felt punished, but I persisted." Even those women lucky enough to find a good advocate or counselor learned that they had to take their lives into their own hands—step by scary step.

Step 1. Learn to Trust Your Perceptions of Reality

"The first time I saw a therapist," Charlotte told us, "I slunk into her office and asked her to help me figure out why I was insane. After an hour of talking, she laughed at me and said, 'It's quite likely you are not nuts—maybe a little eccentric, but definitely not nuts.' " The problem, her therapist told her, was that Charlotte was relentlessly examining herself and overlooking the behavior of her husband John. After years of listening to John tell her that she was selfish and uncaring—the cause of all the trouble in the family, he said—Charlotte had lost her perspective. Her task now was to regain it. Charlotte could do it, the therapist assured her, but she had to trust herself again.

Step 2. Find What You Need

Many years ago a therapist in a mental health center in Duluth, Minnesota, realized that several of her clients shared the same problem: each lived with an abusive partner. She invited them to form a group to talk about their experiences, and thus the therapist unwittingly set in motion a powerful force for change.

As the women exchanged stories, several things became clear. First, they realized that there was no safe place in town for women like them who might need to leave an abusive partner. Second, they wondered why they were in counseling when their husbands were the abusive ones. They quickly concluded that mental health was not their problem. Therapy was not what they needed; instead, these five women formed a mutual support group and a few months later founded the Duluth shelter for battered women. Without professional degrees and with no experience in administering organizations, they set out to meet their own needs; and through their success, they helped many other women in their city.

Give some thought to what you really need. What heads the list? Is it counseling? Or would your mental health be helped most by having a support group or a child care center in your apartment complex or neighborhood? Do you know any other women in the same boat? Remember that the problems in your life are not in your head. Consider whether you and your friends might be helped most by taking action together.

Step 3. Take Action

When we visited Duluth, the women there urged others to find ways to meet their own needs. "Ask your local YWCA, women's center, mental health agency, or church to help you start a support group," they advised. "It's a beginning, and you may be the only one—at first—with the interest to see it created." All of the women spoke enthusiastically of the strength they gained as individuals from working together to help other women. Sharon told us: "I know that when you're lying around down there at the bottom of your life, it seems impossible that you could do anything like what we did. None of us ever could have imagined it when we first crawled into the mental health center one by one. But we found out that a political action like this is worth years of psychological counseling. Nothing does more for your mental health than working hard with a bunch of 'crazy' women who share the same problems you do. And nothing raises your self-esteem like success. The cure for that horrible feeling of powerlessness is *power.*"

Step 4. Fight for Your Rights

"I had never been inside a courtroom until the day I went for a restraining order and asked for temporary custody of my kids," Lee told us. "I was shaking in my boots, but I was determined my husband was not going to take those kids from me. And did he try!" Lee spent the next two years caught in a terrible mess. She had to obey a court order to take her kids for counseling to therapists she didn't like, return to court every time her husband harassed her, and watch the kids slump into depression when they visited their father.

Although she had always thought of herself as "mousy," Lee soon learned that she had a different side to her character. "I became the most organized person in the world," she told us. "I had lists with the names of every person in town who might help me, and next to the name was a phone number and a summary of what they said they could do. To get some people to carry out their promises, I had to call them over and over again. I made copies of every document I sent to anybody. I played the role of charming and gracious pest," she concluded, "but it paid off. Finally professionals in the community saw how disturbed my husband was, and they decided to limit his contact with my daughters."

As you decide what you want to do, and what's best for you and your children, you will probably feel discouraged. Every woman we talked to reported times of feeling deeply downhearted and hopeless. We asked them, "What got you through those moments?" In response, many talked about sympathetic family, friends, and helping professionals. Some spoke of religious or spiritual faith. But we were struck by how many women told us that they'd had a heart to heart talk *with themselves.* Some gave themselves "lectures" or "a good talking-to." Others repeated words of encouragement at the beginning or end of every day, or at every scary moment. They told themselves things like, "I deserve more than this," "I have the right to be who I am," or "God does not want me to live this way."

Taking any of the steps to strengthen yourself that we've discussed in this chapter should also help to reacquaint you with the best side of yourself. It will remind you of the hopes and dreams you had for yourself before you got bowled over by a controlling partner. It will put you back in touch with the sources of your own dignity and pride and strength. It will encourage you to say "I deserve a better life," and to reach for it.

7

■

Deciding About Your Relationship

Women involved with controlling partners are always thinking about the relationship. They're always sizing up what to do next. Again and again they draw up what economists call a cost-benefit analysis, measuring what they gain from the relationship against what it costs them to stay in it. They think about what it might cost them to leave. And sooner or later they begin to think about what they might gain by getting out.

The costs and benefits of the relationship change over time. Often the costs gradually increase until they far outweigh the benefits. But many relationships with a controller go up and down, for no particular reason except the mood he's in. Whatever the course of your relationship, if your partner is a controller, you will probably reevaluate the relationship time and time again, making different decisions at different times.

The first time you think of leaving you may feel overwhelmed by the tasks that face you, things like getting a job, finding a place to live, transferring the kids to a new school—the high costs of leaving. Later you may be ready to try anything. The first time you leave and he comes after you with tears and flowers, you may feel you have good reason to go back to him, believing he's changed. The fourth or fifth time you may not feel the same way. But as long as you are involved with a controlling partner, the cost-benefit analysis will go on, and you'll keep facing that double-sided question: should I stay?/should I leave?

In this chapter we'll talk about that crucial decision, and how women make it. We'll discuss some of the most common reasons why women stay or return to controlling partners, and why they leave. We'll give you some guidelines for evaluating your own relationship, making a decision, and making preparations to carry it out. This chapter is about making choices—big ones. If you don't feel ready for this, you may want to spend more time with the previous chapter: "Strengthening Yourself." But if you do feel ready, keep reading.

Between the early, hopeful days of the relationship with a controlling partner and the later, more depressing ones, most women experience extremely confusing moments. Trying to think things through means unraveling layers of complicated emotional and economic needs.

▪ YOLANDA

I would tell myself that I should get out of the relationship because I didn't feel as if he was giving me any support. I was handling everything. But then I would say that I should stay because maybe it was possible that I wasn't trying hard enough to rectify the situation. Also I would tell myself, "The kids need a father." And financially I didn't think I could handle it without him. Who wants to be a failed divorcee? If a man divorces, he's a good catch, but when a woman does, everyone wonders why. And, worse, no one wants her kids.

Allyce went through what she describes as "torment" trying to decide what to do. She says, "On the one hand, I wanted him to get help, and on the other, I wanted him dead—by my hand or somebody else's. On the one side, I needed a man in my life, somebody to help me out financially; and on the other, I wanted him out."

Such decisions are not simple. Invariably, women have multiple reasons for the choices they make. And they make those choices only after considering many things. For most women, the economic and emotional factors so crucial to their decision snarl into a tight little knot. Considerations of money and love and fear have to be untied, each strand patiently sorted out.

In their book *Violence Against Wives: A Case Against the Patriarchy,* sociologists R. Emerson Dobash and Russell Dobash point out that these considerations change over time. Early in a relationship, women often leave if they feel that they or their children are in danger, but they usually don't intend to stay away. They simply want to protect themselves and give notice to their partner that they won't stand for being treated badly. Often women seem to communicate that message well. The partner does what the woman hopes for: he apologizes, acknowledges his fault, promises to change, and pleads for her to come home.[1] In the later stages of the relationship, women still continue to leave to protect themselves, and they still return to their partners, but for different reasons. They no longer hope or expect that their partners will change; they go back to them because of religious beliefs, economic hardship, and especially fear—fear of what their partner will do if they try to leave for good.

No matter what decision a woman makes— to stay, to go, to return, or to leave for good—the financial costs may be very high. In 1989 the median annual income for two-parent households in the United States was $38,547; for those headed by a woman the figure was only $16,442.[2] Almost 43 percent of all female-headed households with children live in poverty, while only 18 percent of male-headed households do.[3] Those facts put women in a bind. As Marian put it, "I didn't want to live under his thumb, but I didn't want to be poor, either. So I hedged my bets by telling myself, 'Maybe I'm leaving too early, and one day he really will change.' If I'd had a million dollars, would I have waited so long to leave? I doubt it."

On the other hand, even these financial considerations are not simple. Many women—especially women who are already poor—complain that their partner is a financial burden, not a contributor. The controlling partner may take a woman's money and may force her into illegal activities such as drug sales, shoplifting, or prostitution to get more. Each woman's circumstances are a little different. Each woman has to evaluate her situation for herself.

YOUR OWN COST-BENEFIT ANALYSIS

As you consider your choices, you might want to use the charts below. In them, we ask you to answer some basic questions about your relationship—namely, what's good and what's bad about it, and what are the benefits and costs to you and your children of maintaining it? As you fill out the charts, think about your relationship *now,* not as it may have been in the past. And consider the question: does the good still outweigh the bad? As you complete this exercise, remember that it is normal to change your mind. You might find yourself redoing these lists several times in the future.

Evaluating My Relationship

WHAT'S GOOD ABOUT IT? | WHAT'S BAD ABOUT IT?

Maintaining My Relationship

BENEFITS | COSTS

WHAT'S KEEPING YOU HERE?

As we said, every woman has many reasons for the choices she makes. If you're staying with, or thinking of returning to, a controlling partner, it's useful to figure out what's really keeping you in the relationship. That will help you figure out what to do next. If you're staying because you think your partner is changing, for example, then you should work out a systematic way to evaluate the changes. On the other hand, if you're staying out of fear of your partner's violence, you should be talking to an advocate or counselor in your community to plan for your safety. We'll go on shortly to discuss the most common reasons women give for choosing to stay in relationships with controlling partners, but first we suggest that you make note of your own reasons by checking them off on the following lists. Please remember that there aren't any right or wrong reasons here. Don't worry about evaluating your reasons. Just record them.

Reason 1: I'm Still Hopeful

_____   I love my partner.

_____   The good far outweighs the bad.

_____   My partner is in counseling and changing in positive ways.

_____   I believe the control (or violence) is not really my partner's true nature.

_____   I have a special bond with my partner that I'll never find with anyone else.

_____   I believe I can help my partner.

_____   I refuse to fail.

_____   I want my relationship the way it used to be.

_____   The abuse is not so bad.

Reason 2: I'm Afraid of My Partner

_____   I'm afraid he'll get custody of the kids, or kidnap them.

_____   I'm afraid he'll hurt the kids or other people.

_____   I'm afraid he'll track me down no matter where I go.

_____   I'm scared to act—anything I do might make it worse.

_____   He'll attack or kill me if I try to leave.

_____   He'll commit suicide if I leave, and I couldn't live with that.

Reason 3: I'm Afraid That I Can't Make It Financially

_____ I'm terrified of being poor and I will be, at least for a while, if I leave.

_____ I can't find housing I can afford.

_____ I'll never get a decent job.

_____ I'm scared I won't be able to support my kids, and maybe I'll lose them.

_____ I'm terrified I'll end up homeless or a bag lady.

Reason 4: I'm Afraid of Being Alone

_____ I'm afraid of being alone—at least I'm used to this life with my partner.

_____ I don't want to have to raise my kids alone.

_____ I'll never find anyone better out there. He's the best I can do.

_____ I've lost my confidence and feel mentally beaten down. I don't think I can make it on my own. I need him.

_____ I can't see living by myself. It's too dangerous.

Reason 5: I'm Staying Here for My Children

_____ He loves the kids so much and is so good to them that I can't take them away from him.

_____ I don't want to ruin my kids' future and deprive them of nice things or a good education.

_____ I want my children to have a father. They need a role model.

_____ My kids need a disciplinarian.

_____ My father left us when I was a child, and I vowed this would never happen to my children.

_____ I know it's not good for my kids to see him treat me this way, but the alternatives—like leaving—seem worse for them.

_____ If I leave him, he'll get the children away from me somehow.

Reason 6: I'm Bound by My Sense of Responsibility

_____   I owe it to him: he stuck with me through hard times.

_____   A good wife stands by her man.

_____   I vowed we would never be a divorce statistic. I refuse to give up.

_____   I can't bear the responsibility for the relationship failing.

_____   He needs me. He'll fall apart or kill himself if I leave.

_____   I'm not so easy to live with either. The responsibility for this is mine, too.

_____   I will never break my marriage vows; they were given to God.

_____   I can't leave him—he's not well.

_____   I support him—he needs me.

Reason 7: I'm Still in the Process of Making a Choice or Plan

_____   I need more time to save money or finish school.

_____   I am watching and evaluating: is he changing?

_____   I still have not found the help I need to leave.

_____   I'm trying to stop the abuse but keep the relationship.

REASONS TO STAY

Most women carefully and slowly make their decisions—who among us gives up a relationship without one last try? But when women look back on relationships they've left, many conclude that they stayed too long or returned once too often. At the time, of course, they thought they were doing the best thing; but now they see their decisions and their actions differently. (Incidentally, we've never met a woman who said she left a relationship with a controller too soon.)

We asked women what held them in their relationships too long, and they gave us many different answers. Besides financial considerations, five items came up again and again: Many women stayed to await the outcome of their partner's counseling program, in the hope that he would finally change. Others felt duty bound by their religion or by the traditions of their cultural community to stay with their husband, no matter what. A number of women stayed for the sake of their children. Many stayed because they feared a partner would make good his threats of suicide. And a lot of women stayed because they were afraid of serious injury or death. All in all, a great many women tell us that they're confused, angered, drained of energy, or trapped by these issues. We'll discuss each of the issues in turn.

1. Waiting for the Outcome of Counseling

As we've seen, almost every woman in a relationship with a controller hopes her partner will change. As long as this hope remains alive, she may stay with her partner, or if she leaves, she may consider going back. In many cases, a woman who has just about given up on her partner renews her hope if he goes into a counseling program. Unfortunately, as we mentioned in Chapter 5, many men enter counseling not to change, but for just that reason—to persuade a woman to take them back.

If your partner goes into counseling, how can you tell if he's sincere? How can you trust him? This judgment is often difficult to make. Janice told us, "I thought my husband was transformed until I let him live with me again. Then I found out that I'd acted too quickly. His first week home he assaulted me for the embarrassment I'd caused him." Many women have made the same mistake.

More important, even if a man completes counseling "success-fully," a woman may find the outcome less than successful for her. One researcher studied a small number of women whose partners had successfully completed a counseling program for batterers and had stopped using physical violence. (Many of the men, despite having given up physical violence, continued to abuse their wives verbally.) The researcher found that of ten women who remained with their partners, three expressed satisfaction, four regretted their decision, and three were neutral about it. The three women who were "neutral" continued to share their homes with their partners, but they lived very separate lives. The four women who regretted their decision described continuing problems caused by their partner's jealousy and drinking. All of the women found it difficult to trust their partner again, and some found it impossible. None of them ever forgot the experience of being physically abused, even if it only happened once.[4]

If your partner is in counseling, and you stay with him or think about going back to him in hopes that he will change, we suggest that you think again about what *you* want. The fact that he's in counseling is no reason to put your life on hold. In fact, making changes of your own is one way to measure his ability to accept change and give up control of you. Keep in mind that even if your partner changes for the better, he still may not change enough. Like so many women, you may find that you've gone back too soon or once too often unless you concentrate on what *you* want.

2. Abiding by Religious Beliefs or Cultural Concerns

For many women religion plays a big part in their decision to stay too long with a controlling partner. Gloria, a physically abused wife and a devout Christian, says, "The Bible commands, 'Wives submit to your husbands.' I was taught to believe that marriage is a sacred thing. Once you take a vow, you have no choice. You can't say about a vow, 'Oops, God, I changed my mind.' You have to make the best of it."

Many feminists have pointed out that all the world's most powerful religions were developed by men and are still headed by men, so we shouldn't be surprised if they seem to support men's interests at women's expense. But some religious leaders are also feminists, and they bring new interpretations to some old, sexist religious doctrines. In her book *Keeping the Faith,* for example, Reverend Marie Fortune, director of the Center for Prevention of Sexual and Domestic Violence in Seattle, Washington, offers very helpful answers to some questions that often trouble Christian women. Here are three questions frequently asked and her answers.

Question 1: "The Bible says that the wife must submit to her husband. Does this mean that I must submit to his abuse?"

Answer: "Actually, the scriptural passage that refers to the husband—wife relationship begins by saying: Be subject to one another out of reverence for Christ (Eph. 5:21) . . . Here the words 'be subject to' also mean 'accommodate to' or 'give way to.' This means that we should all, including husbands and wives, seek to be flexible with each other. . . ."

Question 2: The Bible says, "The husband is the head of the wife as Christ is the head of the church." What does this mean?

Answer: ". . . the husband's headship suggested here does not mean a role of unquestioned authority to which you are to be blindly obedient. What is described here is a model based on Christ's relationship to the church: Jesus was the servant of all who followed him and he gave himself up for them. Never did he order people around, threaten, hit, or frighten them. . . .

"[The husband] is to be to [the wife] as Christ was to the church. This means he is to serve her needs and be willing to sacrifice himself for her. . . . He is to love his wife as himself, to nourish and cherish her. Another passage is even more specific: Husbands, love your wives, and do not be harsh with them (Col. 3:19)."

Question 3: "In Matthew, Jesus . . . says, 'What therefore God has joined together, let no man put asunder' (Matt. 19:6). How can I leave?"

Answer: "Any man who brings violence and abuse into his family life is putting asunder the marriage covenant that God has blessed. The violence is what breaks up the marriage, and the one responsible for that violence is the one responsible for the breakup. The actual divorce is in fact only the public acknowledgment of the private truth that a marriage has been long since destroyed by abuse. So if you consider whether or not to get a divorce . . . you are not taking steps to break up a marriage. Emotionally, that has already happened. You are taking steps . . . to remove yourself and your children from a destructive situation, and to get on with your life."[5]

The Reverend Ms. Fortune points out that the abusive partner—not the abused woman—is responsible for breaking up a marriage. In fact, she suggests that the most helpful thing a Christian woman can do for her partner is to leave him, at least temporarily, to give him a chance to take responsibility for his sin and change his ways.[6]

"Unfortunately many women feel abandoned by God and rejected by their church when they leave an abusive partner," the Reverend Ms. Fortune says, "but it should not be this way. If a woman feels that her church is against her, she may need to change churches. But she should know that she can keep her faith, that God is still with her, and that she will not go to Hell for leaving an abuser. In fact, by leaving and protecting herself, the woman is making the right decision."[7]

Christianity is only one faith that presents problems for religious women. The teachings of other religions as well may bind women in abusive relationships. Virtually all modern religions are patriarchal; that is, they honor a male god on high, and male persons on earth. Consequently, any devout woman, no matter what her particular faith, may find herself torn between the teachings of her religion on the one hand, and her own safety and freedom on the other.

In addition, many women are pressured by the traditions, beliefs, and values of their religious or cultural group to remain too long in abusive marriages. Many Jewish women, for example, have been taught that divorce simply doesn't happen in the Jewish community. Muslim women are taught to devote themselves to husband and family, and Black Muslim women are taught in addition that Islam is the best hope for the future of their race. For such women, to "fail" in marriage seems like a betrayal of their religious beliefs as well as of the traditions and hopes of their community, all at once. It requires great courage for a woman in such circumstances to end a marriage.

Furthermore, some women of color remain too long in abusive relationships because, for many reasons, they don't want to be disloyal to their men, and either they are afraid to seek help from the white "system" or they think it won't help them anyway. If most police officers and social workers in a community are white, some women of color won't report abuse, even when it is serious, violent, and life-threatening. Betty, who is African-American, told us, "I couldn't turn him over to the cops. They might've beat him to death, and then I'd have to live with that. I never could have held up my head again. If we'd had some brothers on the police, it would've been different."

Each woman must make her own decisions about staying, returning, or leaving. But if you are a woman of strong religious beliefs or strong loyalty to your own cultural group, we suggest that you think first of your duty to safeguard yourself and your children.

3. For the Sake of the Children

Most of us grow up with an idealized image of the family. We are led to believe that children are harmed when their homes are "broken." We're told that every little boy needs his father as a male role model, and every little girl must have her daddy too. Consequently, many women feel that their children will be damaged beyond repair if the parents' relationship breaks up, no matter how bad that relationship is. Many women whose own parents divorced vow never to put their children in similar circumstances.

To a certain extent, they're right, for a woman who leaves a marriage with her children is very likely to suffer financially in almost every case. A woman who is already poor may become even poorer, at least for some time. She will undergo the stress of single parenthood, and her children will suffer real losses. If the woman stays with her husband, her children are more likely to have a roof over their heads, food on the table, a nicer home, possibly a better education, better clothes, a vacation once in a while, a daddy to protect them, discipline them, and take them to the ball game. If she leaves, who knows what will become of her and her kids? In such a dilemma, many women say to themselves, "I'm strong. I can take it. I've got to think of what's best for my kids." But what *is* best for your kids?

Even if you think your husband is a good father and provider, if you are living in a controlling relationship, the chances are that your children know it and are affected by it. If your husband uses force, he certainly is not a good father, for studies reveal that children suffer a variety of damaging effects simply by witnessing physical or sexual abuse. In addition, many controlling partners exercise control over the children, too, and a partner who uses physical force on you may use it on the children as well. If your husband or partner is not the father of your children, they may be at even greater risk. Studies show that children are more likely to be abused by a stepfather or mother's boyfriend than by their natural father.[8]

Even when a woman comes to believe that her children are suffering emotionally or physically, however, she may have to think twice about leaving. If her husband has greater resources than she has—resources like money and access to lawyers—she may be afraid that he will fight for and gain custody of her children. That danger becomes even greater if the woman has entered a lesbian relationship or formed a close friendship with another woman that might be mistaken for a lesbian relationship. Similarly, many women who know that the controlling partner is in fact physically or sexually abusing the children are afraid either to leave or to report the abuse for fear the authorities will take their children away. In some cases the controlling partner who is abusing the children threatens to report the abuse and blame it on the woman if she leaves. In this way a controlling partner may hold the woman and her children hostage. If you find yourself in a situation like this, you should start looking for a trustworthy advocate to tell and ask for help. (We'll talk more about problems like these and what you can do about them in Chapter 11, "Protecting Your Kids.")

Only you can judge what is best for your children, but that means facing up to hard facts. That's not easy. Maralee says, "I was in so much pain that I couldn't see that my kids were in pain too. I didn't want to see it. I felt so guilty. I thought that it was my fault that they were in that situation. If I recognized their pain, it would be like saying I was a bad mother."

You've probably thought of all the advantages to your children of remaining with your partner. But if you've added up the benefits the kids receive, you must also ask yourself, "What does it cost them?"

4. The Threat of Suicide

Maralee stayed with her husband because she feared he would carry out his threats to harm himself. She says, "I would tell myself that I have to leave, and then I would say, 'Maralee, you got to be here to make sure he doesn't hurt himself, that he doesn't burn down the house or jump off the roof.' I worried about him all the time, even after I left him."

Maralee finally fled the night her husband broke every window in her car, as she and her daughters sat inside it. She says, "I realized that while I was staying there to stop him from hurting himself, he was getting ready to kill me and the kids. I felt like somebody was going to get hurt real bad, and I'd rather it was him than us."

A great many controlling partners threaten to kill themselves if you leave, or if you do not behave as they want you to. Threatening suicide is an extremely common tactic of control, and it is often no more than that—a manipulative technique designed to keep you worrying about your partner and doing whatever he wants. On the other hand, some suicide threats are sincere. Men say they will kill themselves and they do, particularly just when their wives or girlfriends are leaving, or soon after. Fairly often, suicidal men kill their partners just before they kill themselves, and sometimes they run amok, killing the children, other family members, or bystanders as well. Unfortunately, it is not easy to distinguish a real threat from a manipulative one.

If your partner threatens suicide and you are uncertain whether he means it, take the threat seriously. You may be mistaken, but it is better to be too cautious than not cautious enough. You should consider him a real danger to himself *and others*. Author Ginny NiCarthy suggests in *Getting Free: A Handbook for Women in Abusive Relationships* that you help your partner find the phone number of a suicide hotline, hospital, or counselor. (Whether he uses the number or not is up to him.) You can also ask his family or friends to help him get to a hospital or mental health center for psychological evaluation or help. If he threatens suicide when you talk about leaving or if he makes a suicide attempt before or after you leave, he needs professional help. You cannot prevent his suicide by staying. As NiCarthy observes, "It is beyond any reasonable expectation to risk your sanity or life for him."[9] He has to take care of himself. Your task is to make safety plans to protect yourself and your children, a process we will talk about shortly. Again, your first duty is to yourself.

5. The Threat of Homicide

While many controlling men threaten to kill themselves, a great many more threaten to kill their partners, their children, or others.

Just as controllers often use hollow threats of suicide to manipulate women, they may also use hollow threats of homicide, with no intention of carrying them out. On the other hand, threats to kill may be perfectly sincere. And as we have mentioned before, a controller is most likely to try to kill his partner when he thinks she is leaving or slipping out of his control. In the United States, at least 2,000 men every year make good on the threat to kill a partner, and countless others inflict serious injuries in the attempt. The danger to women and children is real and must *always* be taken very seriously.

Many women take murder threats so seriously that they feel trapped by fear. When a controller intensifies that fear with emotional abuse and physical violence, a woman may find it almost impossible to think straight. As Kerry puts it, "It's a little difficult to make good decisions when you're running down the street in your pajamas in the middle of the night." Yet that is the level of desperation of thousands of women. In some communities police and judges still do little, if anything, to protect women from violent men. "There was nobody in my town willing to stop my husband," Candace told us, "so for a while I decided that it was safer to stay put, where I could keep an eye on him." Many other women make the same decision.

If you are involved with an abusive and dangerous person, you must eventually get away from him. But getting free will probably not be easy—particularly because he's likely to become more dangerous when you try to leave. We urge you first to call a hotline or make an appointment to see an advocate. When you are living in such danger, it is extremely important that you talk over your situation *confidentially* with a knowledgeable person who can help you plan for your future. It is doubly important to do so if your circumstances, like Kerry's, make it hard to think clearly and to make decisions. An advocate for abused women can't work miracles, but because she deals with similar situations all the time, there's a good chance she can suggest options you may have overlooked and resources you didn't know about. In addition, talking confidentially with a knowledgeable person gives you time and space to think for yourself about your options, a luxury you probably don't have when your partner is around.

Safety for you and your children must be your first consideration. And this is where fear can be your best friend. If you are scared, you are scared for a good reason. Listening to your own fears and acting on the warning signals you pick up may save your life. "The night I left," Connie told us, "I saw the look in his eye and I knew I had to run."

It may be that for some reason you are not ready to leave your partner, even though he is threatening suicide or homicide. If that is the case, you should think again about your safety and your partner's behavior. Watch for any of the following danger signals. Many of these danger signals indicate that your partner needs professional help. Do not make the mistake of thinking that *you* can give him that help. You should plan for your safety and, if possible, leave.

You May Be in Danger If . . .

_____ You have a feeling or intuition—clear or vague—that your partner is going to hurt you.

_____ Your partner threatens to kill you, himself, the children, other people, or pets.

_____ Your partner has a history of suicide and/or homicide attempts.

_____ Your partner's abuse and threats escalate or change for the worse; his behavior grows more violent, sexually brutal, humiliating, reckless, scary, or bizarre.

_____ Your partner has weapons, or he has used or threatened to use weapons against you or others.

_____ Your partner follows you, checks up on you, accuses you of having affairs, and wants to control your every move. He says things like, "If I can't have you, no one will."

_____ Your partner is abusing drugs like alcohol, cocaine, sleeping pills, marijuana. As the drug use continues, your partner seems more suspicious, jealous, paranoid, controlling, and abusive.

_____ Your partner voices suspicions or fears that you are leaving him, and he wants to stop you.

_____ Your partner physically or sexually abuses you so severely or brutally that you believe he may kill you.

_____ You think seriously about killing your partner or hiring someone to kill him, or you imagine committing suicide.

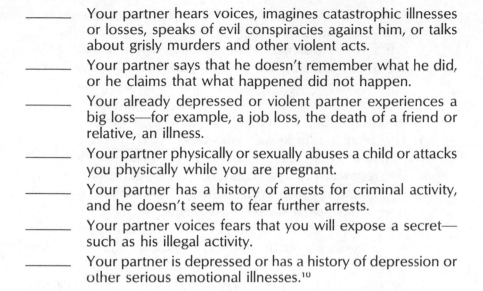

_____ Your partner hears voices, imagines catastrophic illnesses or losses, speaks of evil conspiracies against him, or talks about grisly murders and other violent acts.

_____ Your partner says that he doesn't remember what he did, or he claims that what happened did not happen.

_____ Your already depressed or violent partner experiences a big loss—for example, a job loss, the death of a friend or relative, an illness.

_____ Your partner physically or sexually abuses a child or attacks you physically while you are pregnant.

_____ Your partner has a history of arrests for criminal activity, and he doesn't seem to fear further arrests.

_____ Your partner voices fears that you will expose a secret—such as his illegal activity.

_____ Your partner is depressed or has a history of depression or other serious emotional illnesses.[10]

PLANNING FOR YOUR SAFETY

Any one or more of the reasons we've discussed—anything from your finances to your religion—might cause you to decide to stay with, or return to, a controlling partner. But if your decision is based partly on fear for yourself or your children, you should make some safety plans. If your partner threatens to hurt you, or if you are afraid he might, you may be afraid to leave him. But there are many steps you can take to protect yourself. Some of the steps we list here may or may not apply to you. Try to use those that seem appropriate and useful in your particular circumstances.

1. Find an advocate or other specialist who works with abused women and talk out your safety concerns and options confidentially with her.

2. If you continue to live with your partner, save and hide as much money as you can. Conceal a few essential items of clothing for yourself and the kids. Get an extra set of house and car keys, and hide them in a safe place. Hide a file of important documents you may need, such as bank books, birth certificates, school records, rent and other receipts, insurance papers, medical or prescription records, impor-

tant phone numbers. Include good recent photographs of your partner, in case the police have to look for him.

3. Call a shelter hotline (to find the one nearest you call 1-800-333-SAFE) and find out what help is available to you. Find a safe place to go—family, friends, a shelter—when you feel the tension escalating in the house. Memorize the phone number. Figure out how to get there.

4. Do emergency drills with your children. Help them practice calling the police. Teach them to leave your home through different exits. Before an emergency happens, identify safe places and people to run to, including a police or fire station, a hospital, a shelter, or a friend.

5. If possible, talk to neighbors about your situation and work out a signal with them so that they know when to call the police.

6. Seek medical care if you have been injured or if you experience any pain after an assault. If you go to an emergency room, ask them to photograph your injuries or give you a written report. Keep and hide any other evidence you can after an assault. Show your injuries to a friend or advocate who can photograph them and be a witness for you.

7. If you have a protection or restraining order, carry it with you, make extra copies of it (in case your partner destroys yours), and leave one with the local police and one with your advocate or other supportive person. Call the police if you are in danger.

8. If your partner has been evicted from your home, change the locks on the doors. (If there is a local victim-witness or advocacy program in town, they may provide this service free of charge.)

9. If you move to a new location and want to keep it a secret, tell the children's school, the court, your workplace, etc. not to give out your address or phone number, and tell them why.

10. If you are in danger where you live, remember that there is a network of shelters scattered throughout the United States and abroad. If you are thinking of leaving your community and you have children, speak to an attorney about your custody rights *before* you leave the state, unless this would jeopardize your safety.

Finally, although you may be in great danger, remember that escape is not impossible. Thousands of women have gotten free. In fact, many women leave controlling and violent men, not in spite of death threats, but because of them. Isabel explained to us that she left because her boyfriend became so violent she was sure he would soon kill her. She says, "It hurt to be beaten and have black eyes. I hated it, but I stayed because I was afraid he'd kill me if I tried to leave. Then toward the end he started choking me. One night he pounced on my chest and sat on me so long that I lost consciousness—and it didn't seem to bother him at all. That night I was sure I was going to die if I didn't get out of there. He said he'd kill me if I left, but it looked to me like he'd kill me for sure if I didn't leave."

IF YOU DECIDE TO STAY OR RETURN

Whatever your reasons, if you decide to stay or return to your partner, even temporarily, you may benefit from setting up some ground rules for your partner and yourself. You might insist that your partner abide by the rules as a condition for your staying with him; but if you do that, you must be prepared to follow through and leave him if he breaks the rules. If you are too frightened to make rules for your partner, or if he wouldn't listen to you anyway, then make the ground rules for yourself. Use them as guidelines to evaluate the trend of your partner's behavior.

Setting terms for your relationship (even if only in your own mind) can make you feel more in control of your life. It can help you judge whether your partner is behaving better or not. And if your partner breaks the rules, you will have clearer reasons to leave him again, or permanently. It's best to put your ground rules in writing so you don't forget them or lose track of them in the confusion of living with a controlling partner.

Ground Rules

To get you started, we've listed a few examples of ground rules women made and stuck to. Make as many ground rules as you want. You can add to the list at any time. But if you later find yourself crossing out rules, or making them easier, you are backing down under the controller's pressure. If that happens, it's time to rethink your situation, before you fall completely under the control of the controller.

> I'll stay only if my partner stops intimidating me with his temper tantrums, begins to discuss our differences calmly, and shows that he's willing to compromise.

> I'll stay only if there is no more abuse, and that includes economic threats and verbal put-downs.

> I'll stay if I can go to work and see my family and my friends without a constant battle.

Making Your Own Safety Plans

Useful as it is to set up ground rules, if your partner uses severe emotional abuse or physical force, or if he abuses substances, ground rules are not enough. If you stay with him, you must also take steps to ensure your safety and build your own strength. Again, we list some examples to guide you in figuring out the steps to take for yourself. You might also want to review the suggestions in "Planning for Your Safety" on pages 163–165. Chapters 10 and 11, on protecting yourself and your children, will give you more ideas to add to your list.

Safety Steps

I will leave home when I feel tension building up.

I will call the shelter—even if I never want to go there—and find out what they offer, just in case.

Steps to Strengthen Myself, If I Stay

For help in filling out this chart, you may want to look again at Chapter 6, "Strengthening Yourself."

I'll continue to go to a support group at the shelter and to my Al-Anon group every week.

I'll see my friends at least one night per week.

LEAVING PERMANENTLY

A final option to consider, of course, is leaving your controlling partner for good. That is what almost all of the women we interviewed eventually did. Like many other women, Ruth left her husband and returned to him several times. "My plans weren't together," she told us, "and it took me longer than I expected to get organized. He kept at me so much, there was never a moment to think." In fact, Ruth never did find the time and the mental space she needed to make plans for her escape. Like many other women, she fled suddenly—and permanently—when her partner attacked her so violently that she knew she might die.

Violence, or potential violence, is certainly not the only problem. Many women decide to leave controlling men who use no physical violence at all. "My kids meant the world to me," Karen says, "and I could see the damage he was doing to them, and I worried that it might be permanent." Inez says, "I left when I realized that my husband was a totally self-centered person who wanted a slave, not a wife." Candace explains, "For me it was the drinking. I told him I was gone if it started again, and I was."

Deena says, "I don't know what made me go. I just couldn't tolerate it any more. It took a lot to make me leave, but once I made the decision I was gone." As Deena considered ending her ten-year marriage, she faced intense feelings of grief and loss. "There were all the memories. The good times we had as a family—the vacations together and the birthdays. I kept dreaming about the wonderful times and the wonderful man I married and how I might get those back. I had to mourn the loss of my fantasies and come to terms with the fact that I would not have it the way I wanted it."

For most women making the decision to leave permanently is one of the most difficult choices in life. Lisa, who left a three-year relationship and lost her mobile home and life savings in the process, says, "If you think that leaving will be hard, you're right. But if you stay, there's almost no hope it will get better. You think you have security with him, but what you really have is headaches, and a man who uses up your life savings and makes you doubt your every word. This is not security. If you leave, believe me, some day—though maybe not right away—it will get better than what you have now."

YOUR COST-BENEFIT ANALYSIS #2

As you consider the decision to leave, we suggest that you write down the pros and cons—the benefits and the costs of leaving— just as you did when you considered staying or returning. After you fill out the chart below, consider taking it to a good friend or an advocate to talk through your ideas.

Leaving My Partner Permanently

BENEFITS	COSTS

Taking Inventory

You might also find it helpful to stop and think about your own resources. If you have lived through an emotionally or physically abusive relationship, you have many personal strengths— even if you find it hard to remember them. You probably also have more resources on hand and more sources of help than you realize. We suggest that you fill out the chart below. Consider what you will need—immediately and over time—if you leave your partner. Then write down the resources you already have. If there are gaps in your resources, don't be discouraged. You can take steps to get the help you need. In the following chapters, we'll tell you how.

In the long run, making this chart will help you see your situation and your options more clearly, particularly if you go over it with an advocate or close friend. We suggest that you fill in as much as you can now, paying particular attention to the resources you already have. As you read on, you'll want to add notes about where to get more resources to protect and help you. Then get a friend or advocate to go over the chart with you again, and take it one step at a time.

My Resources

	WHAT I'LL NEED	WHAT I HAVE	WHERE I'LL GET MORE
Emotional support			
Financial support			
Housing			
Care and support for my kids			
Protection for me and my kids			

THE ENDING IS JUST THE BEGINNING

Leaving a controlling partner doesn't end a woman's emotional ties to him. And like so much of a controlling partner's behavior, what he does after his wife or girlfriend leaves may be extreme. Nevertheless, women who've managed to get through the relationship also manage to get through the aftermath, usually getting stronger all the while.

You should be warned, however, about two different, extreme, and very disturbing patterns of behavior that we see in many controlling partners when women break off with them. Some controllers will not let a woman go, while others find a replacement almost overnight. The first are dangerous, while the second are demoralizing.

Many women who leave have trouble getting rid of their partners. The controlling partner goes on telephoning, appearing at the woman's workplace, forcing his way into the apartment, following her, perhaps coaxing, perhaps threatening. He may rape her or beat her up, even though he has never used force before. He may threaten to kill himself or her, even though he has never made such threats before. He may say that he won't let anyone else have her. Some men who behave this way give up after a while, but many don't give up until someone—either the woman or the controller—is seriously injured or dead. All men who behave in this way should be considered dangerous.

If your partner acts like this, you may be in danger and you should find a friend or advocate to help you plan for your safety. You might want to review the sections above on partners who threaten suicide (pages 159–160) or homicide (pages 160–162) and "Planning for Your Safety" (pages 163–165). We'll have much more to say about protecting yourself and your children in Chapters 10 and 11.

At the other extreme, many women are shocked to see how quickly their partner finds someone new. Because controllers have such a driving need to control, many of them waste no time in finding another person. Women may be very hurt, infuriated, and demoralized by being so quickly replaced. Often they have spent months or years agonizing about the decision to leave their partner, and when they finally leave, it doesn't seem to matter to him at all.

He just finds somebody new. In many cases, when a woman sees her former partner being his old charming self to another woman, she thinks that she must have made a mistake. Betsy told us, "Here I'd tried so hard because I thought I was so special to him, he needed me so much—and then he turns right around and inside of two months he's got another woman who looks just like me and—get this—he's already got her pregnant!" If you leave a controlling partner, you should know that you may be replaced in a very short time, and you should be prepared for your own strong emotional responses.

On the other hand, for many women, this replacement comes as a relief. As Cathy put it, "Once he got his new girlfriend, I knew he'd leave me alone. I was safe." But like a lot of other women who have been abused emotionally or physically, Cathy was troubled by another issue: should she contact her "replacement" and warn her? Some women who have been physically abused do warn the next woman, or try to. And they feel they've done the right thing, even though the woman they try to warn may brush them off, writing off their advice as "jealousy" or "lies." Cathy told us, "My husband's girlfriend told me she already knew all about me and that I just 'didn't understand' my husband. She went ahead and married him, and within a year she came and asked me if I'd help her get a divorce. We got to be real good friends—kind of like soldiers who've gone through the same war."

The experience of most women who leave controlling partners lies somewhere between these extremes. They have their ups and downs, good moments and bad, but free of the controller they feel their old strength and pride returning. Grace's experience is typical.

▪ GRACE

My absolutely worst moment was celebrating our anniversary alone. I tried to keep myself busy but I was miserable. I missed him so much. It was also hard in my new apartment. I was alone and very scared. There was nobody there to help me with the kids. I had to make all the decisions—doctors, discipline, finances—by myself. I had another horrible moment when he got married again and my kids were in the wedding.

But I made new friends—which he would never let me do—and the more time I spent with them, the more I realized that I had been making decisions and doing a good job with my kids all along. I started to feel proud of myself, independent and strong, for the first time in years. I realized I did not need a man to survive. I might want one but that was different from the desperation I used to experience. I'm in charge of my life now. And I feel so sorry for that poor young woman who married him.

A NEW BEGINNING

As we go on to the next part of this book, we'll assume that you've decided to make a new beginning in your life, under your own control. Your first step is a very practical one: gather together in a safe place all the official documents you have. These might include your birth certificate, your marriage license, your children's birth certificates, your passport, your driver's license, your voter registration card, your lease (if it has your name on it), utility bills and receipts (if you've been paying them), any current medical prescriptions for you or the children, and anything else that looks important. You may need any or all of these documents to get yourself established again. It's a good idea to make photocopies of all your official documents, too, and keep the copies in a separate safe place, or send them to your parents or a friend. Be sure to keep your bankbook or checkbook and credit cards handy, and try to put as much money as you can in your own name or in a safe hiding place. When you get ready to leave, you should have all these things ready to take with you.

In the following chapter we'll talk about the next steps: how to find a place to stay—in an emergency or on a more permanent basis. Then we'll offer some other suggestions for reclaiming your life. Even if you haven't decided to leave your partner permanently, we suggest that you gather up your documents—just in case—and read on. The information and suggestions you find in the next chapters may help you as you think through your situation again.

PART THREE

When You Choose to Leave

8

■

Finding a Place to Stay

L eaving is hard. There's just no way around that fact. But it
doesn't have to be so scary, especially if you can give yourself
the time and space to make some advance plans. And there are
people to help you. If you've already reached out for support from
friends, an advocate or counselor, or a women's group, so much the
better. If not, you may want to reach out now to get help with the
first problem every woman faces when she thinks about leaving:
where can I go? For many women, finding housing is not only the
first problem but the biggest and most difficult. Chances are that
you'll want to use all the help you can get.

In this chapter we'll describe various ways women who leave
their partners find temporary shelter and safety. We'll illustrate some
of the options women most often choose so that you can see for
yourself what some of the advantages and disadvantages might be
for you.

Since some of these options involve courts and women's shelters, you may think that they apply only to "battered women"
whose partners repeatedly beat them up. In fact, any of these options may be used by any woman who faces harassment, threats, or
possible harm from a partner or ex-partner. You will have to check

with local experts to find out how things work where you live, because laws are interpreted and enforced differently in different communities. Similarly, shelter facilities and social services available to women in need vary from one community to the next. But do *not* write off any option just because you think it doesn't legally apply to you. It may. And even if you think you won't have to face the housing problem, we suggest you look into emergency housing options in your community just in case. If you find that you really don't qualify for a shelter or public housing, give some thought to other alternatives, such as moving in with family or friends, finding a roommate, or sharing a house with another family. And one more word of caution: even if your partner has never used physical force, do not dismiss options that seem to apply mainly to physically abused women. Keep in mind that when you leave him, a partner who has not used violence before may do so.

We asked women who'd been through the experience of breaking off a relationship with a controlling partner, "Where should a woman turn when she leaves?" Molly answered, "It's probably different for everybody. I stayed with my family for a few months. It was tense, but I felt I had no other choice." Lisa described several different arrangements she tried: staying with friends, returning to her husband, moving to a shelter. She said, "I managed to leave my husband permanently only after an advocate at the shelter helped me get an order of protection and a housing subsidy. I needed that extra safety and support from the shelter to make my separation permanent." Brenda emphasized the emotional issues involved. "It really hurt my pride to reach out for help," she said, "but I did it." Once again, you'll have to evaluate your situation and do what's best for you.

We cannot emphasize often enough that any move away from a controlling person, *even one who has never been violent,* is potentially dangerous. So if you are thinking about where to go, you must think about how to get there *safely.* If you are concerned that your partner may harm you or others, you should ask a trained advocate to help you plan a safe departure before you make your move.

WHY DOESN'T HE LEAVE?
EVICTING YOUR PARTNER

Few things make women so angry as having to leave their own homes to escape from their partners. Especially when their partners are physically abusive, women rightly see themselves as the injured parties. And if they do most of the housekeeping, as most women do, they often see the home as more "mine and the kids' " than "his" anyway. It's the controller who is causing trouble—sometimes doing terrible damage to his wife and children. But usually it's the controller who gets things his way. No wonder so many women are furious.

▪ TARA

> My sister kept asking me why didn't I leave him. I said, "He's the damn criminal here. Why doesn't *he* leave?" I told him and told him to get out, but I was the one that finally had to run. So he got my apartment, my furniture, my car—that's all stuff I paid for myself. I got nothing. And when I asked the police to help me get my stuff back, they told me I should consider myself lucky I got away from him without getting hurt.

According to the law in most parts of the United States, a man who physically assaults his wife or girlfriend can be arrested, removed from the home, jailed, tried for assault, convicted, and sentenced to spend time in jail or to attend a reeducation program or counseling group for batterers. A man who harasses or threatens his partner can be restrained from doing so and evicted from the home by orders of the court. Nevertheless, in a great many places in the country, things just don't happen that way. Throughout our history, law enforcement officials have usually looked the other way when men assaulted their wives and girlfriends—and many still do. In addition, until very recently, the law regarded "a man's home" as "his castle." Law enforcement policies are changing all over the country in response to pressure from women, but they have not yet changed enough.

When the law is fairly written and fairly enforced, abused

women do *not* need to leave their own homes to find safety. Depending upon where you live and how the legal system works (or fails to work) in your community, you may be able to break with your partner and stay where you are. Your children may be able to stay in their own home and continue attending their neighborhood school. If your name is the only one on the lease, for example, or if you have obtained a restraining and vacate order (the court orders mentioned above), your partner is the one who will have to leave.

For some women this option works well. Annette told us, "I said to myself, 'Why should we have to leave when he is the one who abused us? Let him find a new house.' " She went to court for an order of protection and asked the judge to remove her husband from their home. Annette was able to take this action because, as she said, "In this town the police and the judges don't mess around. If a guy violates a restraining order, he goes to jail. My husband knew that, and it scared him to death." In addition, Annette also had supportive neighbors nearby. "Everybody was looking out for me," she said.

Most women find definite advantages in staying in their own homes. "Breaking up a marriage is hard enough on you and your kids," Annette said, "without having to worry about finding a new home." Familiar surroundings and friendly neighbors help. And children may find the difficult transition easier if they continue to attend the same school and see the same friends.

Women who voluntarily move away from their homes usually do so because they are afraid. Molly had a beautiful apartment and was very proud of the fact that she had redecorated it herself, but she gave it up because she was afraid of her boyfriend, who continued to threaten her. "I felt like a sitting duck," she said. "I felt like I was just waiting for the attack. I couldn't stand the anxiety. I had to disappear."

Many women, almost as frightened as Molly, go to court anyway to ask for vacate orders. It is so difficult for single mothers of low or moderate income to find safe and affordable housing that many women must try to stay where they are, out of necessity. Once they've got the controlling partner out of the home, they must watch anxiously for his next move, wondering whether he will step up his abuse or leave them alone. They adopt the attitude, "I'll wait and see what he does, and then I'll reevaluate my decision."

If you would like to stay in your own home and you're not too afraid to do so, you will first have to find out how the legal system works in your community. Keep in mind that it's not enough to find out what the law *says*—because very often the law is not enforced, or it is applied differently to different groups of people. You want to find out how the system actually works in your community *for women like you*. To do that you might call your local shelter, community center, or legal services office. Ask if you are legally entitled to a vacate order and if so, what you have to do to get one. And be sure to find out whether the police will look for your partner and arrest him if he violates the court order.

If you find that it *is* possible to evict your partner, and that the police will back you up, we suggest that you make a list of the advantages and disadvantages of doing so, for you and for your kids. For example, you'll want to weigh the advantage of not having to move against the disadvantage that he'll know where to find you. You'll also want to consider what other sources you can call on for moral and financial support or help in an emergency—your parents, for example, or the next-door neighbor. And if you proceed to evict your partner, you'll want to take steps to protect yourself: change the locks, alert your neighbors and your coworkers, make sure that the police have a copy of your restraining order and that your kids know how to call the police in an emergency.

LEAVING HOME: FINDING TEMPORARY HOUSING

If you can't stay in your own home, you'll be one among the thousands of women each year who leave. Like them, you'll immediately come up against a very tough problem: where to go?

Turning to Family and Friends

Most women turn first to their family, extended family, their partner's family, or their friends. Many do so reluctantly, especially if they are ashamed or aware that their family or friends have problems enough of their own. Like many other women, Laura hated to involve her parents in what she described as her "personal" problems. She says, "My parents are old, and they've lived through a lot. Why bring more trouble to them?" But one night her husband Erik punched her with his fists and told her never to talk back to him again. Laura wanted out as soon as possible, so she took the children to her parents' home. "I didn't like to do it," she says, "but I saw no other alternative. I considered staying in a motel, but it would have been way too expensive and too hard on the kids."

Before she moved, Laura asked her employer, the local telephone company, to transfer her to an office closer to her parents' home, some thirty-five miles away. "The distance made me feel a little safer," she says. When the personnel manager told her that the transfer would take a month to process (and Laura would be without income for that time) she almost changed her mind. "The idea of taking money from my parents made me cringe," she says, "but later I was grateful for the breathing space it gave me."

Laura had more to do in the next thirty days than she had ever imagined. She went to court to get a restraining order forbidding Erik to contact her or come near her. She also asked the court to award her temporary custody of the children until a permanent custody arrangement could be worked out.

▪ LAURA

I wanted temporary custody of the kids written in black and white, in case Erik tried to snatch them. I was pretty sure that he wouldn't try anything funny while I was with my parents, but better safe than sorry. The restraining order hearings were hard. I was scared to death to see Erik because I didn't know how I would feel. One minute I hated him for all he was putting us through—the move, the kids' missing their friends and school, my parents worried to death—and the next minute I felt sorry for him because he looked so pathetic and lonely. My emotions were flying all over the place, but I survived the hearings by remembering his fist in my face and by reminding myself that I would never be treated that way again. Never.

Within days of moving to her parents' house, Laura also started to look for an apartment in the area. She was shocked by the reception she received.

Several landlords asked me how I, as a single parent, could afford the rent, even though they had my income statement and a reference from my employer right in front of them. One realtor wanted to know if I had a boyfriend and if I planned to entertain men late at night or give a lot of parties. Another one came on to me and told me that he usually could locate the right apartment for a "very close friend." Those apartment-hunting days were some of the worst in my life. I'd drag myself back to my folks' house in the evening, and as I washed the dinner dishes, tears would drop into the sink. I never felt so helpless.

Laura and the children lived with her parents for two months before she met a coworker at the telephone company who had just moved into a new housing complex near work. She gave Laura the address, and Laura rushed over on her lunch hour to see the manager. Within days her lease was approved. She says, "My spirits lifted immediately. I knew there would be rough moments ahead (and there were), but at least we had a place of our own. We could spread out, invite the kids' new friends over, make popcorn any old time. We had come that far. We had a home!"

If you consider the possibility of moving in temporarily with your family or friends, one of the first things you should think about, as always, is safety—yours and theirs. Consider this question: "If I go to my family or friends, will my children and I be safe, physically and emotionally?" For some women the answer is no. Their parents' home may be violent. Their parents or other relatives may have abused them in the past, or they may be heavy drinkers or drug users. Some women fear that their own relatives will not be supportive; relatives or friends may feel divided loyalties or even take the husband's part. In other cases, women choose to stay away from relatives and friends to protect *them* from the violent partner, particularly if he has made direct threats against them. In either case—whether you're worried about your own well-being or the safety of your family and friends—you'll probably want to consider other housing arrangements.

On the other hand, for some women staying with friends or relatives seems the safest—or the only—thing to do. Sarah told us, "My husband would never go near my sister's because he was afraid of my brother-in-law." And Anna says, "I went to a friend's because my boyfriend didn't know her and would never think to look for me there."

If you plan to stay with family or friends, you may be able to make your stay easier for everyone by talking over in advance some areas of possible disagreement. If the living space is very small, for example, how do you share it? How much are you expected to contribute to the rent? And who buys the groceries? What if you don't have any income? Who disciplines the kids, and what methods do they use? Who cooks? What about guests? Bedtime? Cleaning up? Cigarettes? You'd better discuss them all, preferably before you move in. Be sure to explain the ground rules to your children, too; or if they are old enough, involve them in the discussion with your new housemates. Keep in mind that any change in living arrangements is stressful for most people. A little advance planning and thoughtfulness can ease the difficulties for everyone.

Going to a Shelter: Glenda's Story

Many people think of a women's shelter only as a place to stay for a few nights in an emergency. In fact, there are many reasons to stay as long as possible at a shelter. It provides safety, information, help, and a chance to escape the pressures of a controlling partner long enough to think for yourself. Each woman's experience in the shelter is different, and no two shelters are alike. (We'll talk more about these differences shortly.) Glenda's experience is fairly typical. Glenda is African-American and lives in a medium-sized midwestern city.

When Herbie assaulted Glenda, she felt as if she had nowhere to turn. Her parents were divorced. Her mother lived a thousand miles away, and she'd lost touch with her father. Her friends in town were poor—even less well-off than she was—and their living quarters were cramped. But Herbie got "crazier and crazier," as Glenda put it, and she knew she had to get away from him. She turned to prayer. "I kept saying, 'God, show me the way, please show me the way.'"

Glenda describes the night she left Herbie as no different from any other night.

Herbie came home and started in on me and the kids. I yelled at him to cut it out, and before I knew it, he was trying to choke me. Thank God, one of the kids called the police. By the time they got there, he'd cooled down again. All this had happened before, but this time something inside me snapped. That was the end. Period. We were leaving. I asked the police to take me away.

The police took me to the station and asked me what I wanted to do. All I could think about was Herbie. I was convinced that he would come rushing through the station door and shoot us all. I was really upset and totally unable to figure out what to do next. I remember that one officer asked me if I wanted the women's shelter to send over a volunteer to talk to me, and I said yes. To this day, I've got no idea where that yes came from.

As she waited for the woman to arrive, Glenda's fantasies about the shelter went from bad to worse. She could hardly believe it when the shelter volunteer told her, "We try to make the shelter as much like a home as possible. It's crowded and sometimes it's pretty noisy, but each family has its own bedroom, and there's a communal kitchen where everyone takes turns cooking meals." For safety's sake, the location of the shelter was a secret.

The volunteer also said that if Glenda thought she was in danger, she could go to a shelter in another town. There was a whole network of shelters around the state and throughout the country, she explained. On the other hand, if Glenda wanted to stay in town, an advocate from the shelter would help her get a protection order, if Glenda wanted one.

Glenda and her children could stay at the shelter for up to forty-five days. During that time, the volunteer explained, Glenda would be required to work with an advocate. "She'll help you apply for welfare or subsidized housing, if you need them," the volunteer said. "And there's one other requirement. You'll be expected to participate in our program by coming to regular support groups and house meetings." There were play groups for the children, too, three mornings a week, while their mothers went out to look for housing.

At that first meeting at the police station, the volunteer grilled me. She asked if I used drugs and if I could obey the house rules. She said that the shelter had strict standards about curfew and drugs, and nobody was allowed to use physical force to discipline children. I wasn't crazy about all the rules, but I realized that they had to be careful, what with so many strangers living together. Anyway, I agreed to everything the volunteer said that night. I was too scared and too tired to do anything else.

On the way to the shelter, I worried: "Who are these people and what have I gotten us into?" But I said to my daughter, "Let's give it a try. If we don't like it, we can always leave and figure out something else to do." We drove up to this nice, old brick house and I was so relieved. But then we went inside and I met the current residents—three white women who were having coffee together in the kitchen—and I thought I would die. One woman looked like a truck driver, with tattoos running up and down her arms. Of course, she turned out to be really nice and really helpful. I didn't understand the first thing about restraining orders or AFDC [Aid to Families with Dependent Children] or food stamps, and she helped me each step of the way. But that first night, I prejudged her. All I saw was the tattoos, and she scared me to death.

Living in a Shelter

Shelter workers introduced Glenda and her children to the other guests, showed them to their rooms, and offered them dinner, a change of clothes, toothbrushes, and comforting words. Although the first evening was a "blur" for Glenda and the kids, they ended it a bit more reassured than when they began.

The next morning Glenda met Shirley, her advocate. They went over the house rules again, and then they talked over Glenda's situation and made a list of priorities. Soon Glenda would apply for welfare and a certificate for subsidized housing, but, for today, Glenda wanted to get clothes and a few other things out of her house. With Shirley's help, she arranged for two police officers to escort her home and wait while she packed her belongings. For the rest of the day, she took it easy, playing with and comforting the kids.

That evening the women's support group was scheduled to

meet. "I'm definitely not a group person," Glenda told us. "In fact, I'm the kind who wants to run out of the room if I think somebody's going to call on me to say something." But the other residents encouraged Glenda to sit and listen to the guest speaker and join the discussion only if she wanted to. She sat in a corner, feeling exhausted, but during the group—much to her surprise—she started to feel better.

The speaker was a former battered woman named Nadia who worked at a social service agency in town. Her topic was the stages women go through when they leave their partners. She listed the five stages on a blackboard.

Stage 1: Still Running Scared

Stage 2: Hating the Bastard

Stage 3: Can I Be Loved?

Stage 4: Can I Really Do It?

Stage 5: Passing the Crisis[1]

Nadia asked the group, "Do you still look over your shoulder, expecting your partner to burst through the shelter security system?" Glenda saw immediately that she—and another woman who was also vigorously nodding her head—was still in Stage 1, "Running Scared." Another resident jumped in to describe her transition from Stages 2 to 3. "For weeks I hated my husband for what he did to us," she said. "I never was that angry when I was with him, but here I felt safe enough to get really mad. But then I started to miss him. I got lonelier and lonelier, needier and needier."

That loneliness is a common experience, Nadia said. Everybody in the group would go through it to one degree or another for at least another year. "Naturally, everyone wants to be loved and needed," she said. "But you'll learn that you don't need *him* to 'love' and need you. You can get these things without being abused."

"You'll enter another stage soon," Nadia continued. "You'll wonder if you can make it on your own. I went through it, too, just as every woman does. I kept worrying that my husband was right when he said (as he always did), 'You can't do anything right!' There I was searching for housing, applying for jobs, transferring my kids to a new school, paying bills, and all of a sudden I recognized that I *was* doing things—and well. That's when I made it to Stage 5."

In Stage 5, Nadia said, a woman moves on and grows strong and independent. "I left my husband two years ago and now I feel great about myself. My days are filled with people and work. I don't miss him so much anymore—except at anniversaries—and I certainly don't want him back in my life."

That night, and over the next several days, the shelter residents talked over their reactions to Nadia's visit and kidded each other about the stages they were in. During these conversations, Glenda found herself drawn to another resident, Ruby, and the two of them soon began what would remain, three years later, a solid friendship. When Glenda arrived at the shelter, Ruby had been living there for several weeks, waiting for her subsidized housing certificate. During that first month Ruby and Glenda worried and complained to each other. Glenda said, "The staff at the shelter kept saying to the residents, 'You're gaining control over your lives,' and we would joke to each other, 'Some control! No money, no housing, no direction, no plans for the future, no feet on the ground.' " But Ruby offered Glenda support and practical information when she most needed it.

> Ruby taught me the ropes about housing, and I helped her through that long search for an apartment—all those terrible times when she thought nothing would ever come through and that she'd spend the rest of her life in institutions.
>
> Ruby taught me about the shelter, too. Most of the staff was okay, but I felt like a few of them were watching me like a hawk. I was afraid if I yelled at my kids, they would call the welfare department on me. I could tell Ruby, "I can't stand my kids today," and she knew what I meant. In a shelter you are on guard because you don't want to get kicked out for breaking a rule. It's a bit like living in a room with glass windows and no curtains. The staff tried hard to be helpful, but my best support came from Ruby. I could tell her how much I missed my husband. I could say I felt guilty—for everything—and she understood immediately.

All in all, the women's shelter offered a lot to Glenda and her children. Safety, companionship, support, and a new understanding of their situation headed the list. In addition, Glenda got a lot of practical guidance and help. Shirley, Glenda's advocate, helped her apply for welfare, get legal advice, and get information about job training programs. Shirley also helped her through the difficult task of finding more permanent housing. On Glenda's list of priorities, welfare came first because she needed money to support her children even while she was staying in the shelter, and she needed assurance that she could continue to support them when she left the shelter to go out on her own. Often women apply for welfare and housing at the same time. We'll discuss welfare in the next chapter when we talk more about getting on your feet financially. Here we'll continue our discussion of the housing problem.

Using Other Shelter Services:
Housing Advocacy

In many communities, housing is extremely difficult to find—particularly low- and moderate-income housing but in Glenda's city there were a number of housing options for women with low incomes. Shirley explained them to her. All of them required that Glenda fill out a long application and wait—perhaps weeks, months, or years. But as Shirley explained, shelter residents often move quickly to the top of the list because they are homeless.

One option chosen by many low-income women at the shelter was to apply for certificates for subsidized private rental assistance, either through federal or state grants. Under the federal rental assistance program, called Section 8, a woman pays a percentage of her income—usually 30 percent—and the government pays the rest of the rent directly to the landlord each month. State-subsidized rental assistance programs work in much the same way: women pay a designated percentage of their income for rent and the rest of the rental cost is paid by the government.

Many families are trying to get Section 8 certificates, and as in the case of so many other government programs, the approval process is needlessly complicated and time-consuming and full of snags. In Glenda's city, women who qualified and were put on the priority list usually had to wait about seven weeks for approval. Like many other women faced with bureaucratic rules and regulations, Glenda doubts that she could have made it through the application process without an advocate's help. She says, "People were talking to me as if I understood, and I'm not dumb. But everything was in this technical language—like 'a Section 8'—and it was so new to me that it took a long time to absorb it."

Glenda's city offered another option: the local housing authority operated two public housing projects for low-income families. Again, women who were abused and homeless received priority on the waiting lists, but even with the priority ranking, an applicant might have to wait for two years. Glenda applied for a public housing apartment, too. She says, "Whatever they told me about, I applied for. I wasn't fixing to live in the street."

Almost two months later Glenda received the Section 8 certificate. Then she had to find a private apartment with a landlord willing to accept the certificate. (Some landlords welcome tenants with Section 8 certificates, but others slam the door in their faces.) And then she had to wait for a state inspector to check that the apartment met standards. Glenda says, "My advocate was quite helpful in this, too. She and I kept bugging the bureaucrats to get the work done." When the delays dragged on, Glenda was grateful to be living where she was. "The shelter bent the rules and extended my original stay by a few weeks," she says. "They were great and saw me through to the end. But I was one happy person the day we finally moved."

Are Shelters for Abused Women the Same Wherever You Go?

"Definitely not," Claudia told us. "The first shelter I went to in Florida was very institutional: two huge rooms with fifty beds in long rows, bars on the windows. I left, it was so depressing." It took Claudia more than a year to try a shelter again, and then only because she had to. First, she stayed at a friend's house, but she and the kids eventually wore out their welcome. "My friend told me I had to go to a shelter," Claudia explained. "She told me that I couldn't live in the car with my kids, though I almost preferred to do that."

In desperation, Claudia agreed to call a hotline in another city. The shelter they directed her to was small and cozy, with bedrooms for four families and a very large kitchen and a yard equipped for children.

▪ CLAUDIA

It was the most pleasant surprise of my life. If I hadn't gone there, I don't know where I'd be today—probably still riding around in the car with the kids. As I look back, I think it was the best thing I ever did. The staff understood what it was like to live the way I'd been living. They didn't judge me or tell me what to do, and they helped me get my life organized—housing, furniture, toys for the kids. When I moved to my new apartment, my advocate brought over two huge boxes of toys for my kids. I just sat down and cried.

It's hard to predict what your local shelter may be like. No two are exactly the same. Some are in old houses; others are more institutional: converted orphanages or remodeled motels. Most shelters house three to five families, but some are much larger. In most of them, you and your children will have a private room and share the kitchen and bathroom. But many facilities—even the best ones—are underfunded and overcrowded. In spite of these difficulties, most will make a sincere effort to help you and your children feel at home.

The staff also differs from one shelter to the next. Some shelters are run entirely by formerly battered women, others by professional social workers and mental health professionals. A few well-funded shelters have several paid professional staff members, while others are run almost entirely by volunteers. Many shelters have staff or volunteers on site twenty-four hours a day, but in others, the staff members leave for the evening and the residents take charge. In any case, you are likely to find at least one staff person who understands—firsthand—exactly what you're going through.

Shelter Life and Children

For every woman at a shelter, there may be two or three children. Women without children come to shelters too, of course, but a great many women arrive with their kids in tow. As you can imagine, the house is often far from peaceful. Children pass through "stages" during their shelter stay, just as their mothers do; and one of the great advantages of living in a shelter is that staff members who've worked with hundreds of children can often help mothers understand what their kids are going through.

At first, children are frightened of living in an unfamiliar place, so they tend to be on their best behavior. Once they know they're safe, they begin to test the limits and act out the anxiety they feel. Very often young children regress, or go backward to behavior appropriate to earlier years. They throw tantrums and demand attention. Older children may fight, insist on going home, and vow to hate their mothers forever. It's difficult for mothers to see any of this behavior as "good"—but staff members do.

"It feels horrible for the moms," one advocate told us, "but these signs indicate that the child trusts us enough to demonstrate through actions what he or she cannot put into words. The child is saying, 'I am in pain. I've been through a lot. Help me.' " Generally, advocates advise mothers to help their children by setting firm and consistent limits on their behavior and giving them extra attention, care, and reassurance—including reassurance about the new home they will make together. Children need that extra support because they have often seen their mother in a powerless position. They need to hear her say: "We'll be okay. I'll protect you. I'll take care of things."

Most shelters have special outings and activities for kids, and many offer special support groups as well. In the support groups, kids have a chance to talk about their life in the shelter—what they like about the place, and what they hate. (Many children quickly come to love living in the shelter.) They can grieve together over the many losses they're experiencing: moving to a new and secret location, changing schools, losing old friends, losing their father, adjusting to life with less money or fewer clothes and toys. And they can discuss the stigma of living in a shelter. Many children arrive at shelters withdrawn and depressed, or aggressive and hostile, but with adult support they bounce back. Often when families spend several weeks in a shelter, a mother can watch her children grow healthier and happier.

Glenda's children bounced back, and she told us that the shelter had a lot to do with it.

▪ GLENDA

I just went there for a place to stay, but the shelter staff supported me as a mother. There I was, already convinced that my son Lyle was going to become a wife beater because he was so hostile, and they said, "No, he's just hurting." The shelter workers put my kids' behavior in a context, told me what to watch for in the future, and offered practical advice when I most needed it. I felt guilty about what I'd done to my kids—staying with their father too long, and then taking them away from him—but at the shelter I realized that leaving my husband was the best thing for us all. I realized that I'm doing a pretty good job.

Going to a Shelter: Should I Do It?

No one can predict how you or your kids might react to life in a shelter, but it may help to call and talk to the staff *before* you need to leave your home. You should at least know where the nearest shelter is, just in case. (To find a shelter, phone 1-800-333-SAFE). When you call the shelter, or your local program for abused women, ask what the facility is like and what services they can provide for you and your children. If you do not speak English fluently, ask if anyone on the staff speaks your language or understands your cultural concerns. If not, ask if they can find someone to help you make your transition to living in the shelter easier. If the shelter is far away from you, or if you don't have a car, be sure to ask if they provide emergency transportation.

If you are a battered lesbian and think you may need shelter, call your local battered women's program or gay and lesbian organization and ask about your local shelter. Find out if the shelter has provided refuge for other lesbians, and if there are lesbians among the staff and volunteers. Has the staff been sensitized so that they can keep you safe, emotionally and physically? Are they aware of your need for confidentiality? If you don't feel comfortable with the answers you get, ask if the shelter can offer another housing option, such as a safe home. Although a women's shelter may not be an ideal supportive environment for lesbians, many advocates urge lesbians to use the shelter anyway, if they are in danger.

Once you are a guest in a shelter, many former residents advise that you give yourself time to adjust. "I hated it the first days I was there," Lucy told us, "and I almost bolted for my house several times. But by the end of our stay, my daughter and I loved the place." Iris told us, "I never loved it. I hated everything about it—even the food the other people cooked, and especially the constant activity. But I needed the place, and I know I wouldn't be on my feet today without that shelter."

What If the Shelter Won't Help You?

If you live in a rural area, you may have to travel a long distance to find a shelter. If you live in a small town that has no shelter facilities, you too will have to travel to another community. And even if you live in a city with several shelters, you may not find space. Because there aren't enough shelter beds for the thousands of women and children who need them, you may be turned away. Don't be surprised to hear, "We're filled. Please try again tomorrow—or next week."

If this happens to you, keep trying. If a women's hotline worker says she can't help you, keep asking, "Who can?" Some shelters also have "safe homes"—that is, backup housing in private homes or apartments. Others may be able to place you temporarily in a motel. At least they should be able to give you information about emergency facilities for the homeless in your community. Many state welfare departments are now required by law to provide ninety days of housing for homeless families in motels and hotels. Although these facilities are often inadequate and frightening places, some women flee to them to avoid further abuse at home. Once there, they request a transfer, as soon as they can get one, to a shelter for abused women.

If you are a substance abuser *in recovery,* doing your best to stay clean and sober, most shelters—though not all of them—will take you in. But if you have an active substance-abuse problem—one that requires detoxification, for example—almost all shelters will turn you away. They think that they don't have the expertise to help you. But *if you are in danger,* we suggest that you call your local shelter anyway. Explain your situation and ask them for information about detox programs and other residential substance abuse rehabilitation programs where you might find safety. Ask if they can help you make the arrangements to enter a rehab program and provide transportation.

TRANSITIONAL HOUSING

In some places, shelters for abused women have started what they call transitional or second-stage housing programs. Because affordable apartments for women and children are so hard to find, these shelters have started their own small-scale housing ventures by setting aside rehabilitated units for former shelter residents, and sometimes for nonresidents as well. In some of these new programs, families double up and share apartments. In others, each family has its own unit. Residents are permitted to stay from six months to two years—longer than in a shelter—so they have more time to get on their feet.

Unlike shelters, some transitional housing programs have very few, if any, staff members; and the job of the staff workers may be simply to provide references so women can get into school or job-training programs. Families accepted for transitional housing are expected to be able to function well on their own and, at the same time, work cooperatively as part of a community.

To find out about transitional housing in your state, call your local battered women's program, or the state or national toll-free hotline, and ask if there is transitional housing available near you. If there is, you might want to make an appointment to find out more about it.

SHARING A HOUSE WITH ANOTHER WOMAN
AND HER CHILDREN

If a woman is living in a shelter or temporarily staying with relatives, she has to answer the question "What next?" Unable to afford much rent, some women opt to share a residence with another family, usually one with children. Often they find their new roommates through a shelter or through a service that their children use, such as day care.

Renting a house or an apartment with another family has many advantages, especially for women raising children on their own. Often, by sharing the rent, two families can get more space than either could get alone. Instead of a small apartment, you might share a whole house with a yard. A good roommate can be a real partner in paying the bills, looking after the kids, sharing the chores. She can be a friend and confidante—or at least another adult in the household to talk to—and someone to rely on in case of illness or emergency.

▪ TRISHA

Things went very well for me with a roommate because I enjoyed her company and I never felt lonely. It was also a good transition for me because I was married to a man who controlled every-thing—every dime I spent—and I really needed some help to learn to manage a household again. My roommate did that for me, but I never felt useless because I was able to help her, too, in other ways.

House sharing sounds appealing, and it is when the families are a good match, but things can go wrong. Kids fight, adults fail to pay their share of the bills, chores go untouched. These problems can be avoided or solved if the potential roommates and their children sit down together, as often as necessary, and talk out differences in values and life-styles. You'll want to consider finances, sleeping and eating schedules, and expectations about housework, discipline, and child care. If you've spent time living with family or friends or staying in a shelter, you might want to think about how that experi-ence felt to you. If you were able to work out differences, compro-mise, and enjoy the company of others most of the time, the chances are good that you'll be able to do the same with another family.

RENTING YOUR OWN APARTMENT OR HOUSE

Women with Section 8 housing certificates or other sources of income (through jobs, welfare, or support payments) often prefer to rent their own apartment or house.

▪ KAY

When I moved into my own apartment, I began to get back a sense of control over my life. I was in charge. I could make my own decisions. It was hard financially, and sometimes it was very lonely, and there were times when I was just plain scared, but I needed to live by myself.

In summary, we can say that the news about housing is both good and bad. The good news is that you have several different options. The bad news is that no option is easy, especially if you have children. Every woman we spoke to told us that the search for housing was the most difficult and frustrating problem she faced, or close to it. It was so difficult in fact that many women returned to their partners—sometimes more than once—before they were finally able to make other living arrangements and a complete break from the controller. You should keep that in mind. If finding housing seems to be very hard and to take a very long time, don't blame yourself. Try to get more or better help, and keep looking.

We've emphasized the downside of the housing search in this chapter to prepare you for the worst. But the upside is this: women do get through these difficulties. We're confident that you will, too, so let's go on now to talk in the next chapter about some other steps you can take to reclaim your life.

9

Reclaiming Your Life

T his wonderful peace has come over me," Clare says. She's talking about her separation from her husband of twenty years. "I come home from work, put my feet up on the couch, cook dinner when I want to, call a friend—and nobody yells at me and calls me names. I used to be afraid to say 'good morning' to my own husband because I never knew what kind of mood he would be in. Can you imagine! I literally couldn't say 'good morning' in my own house without being afraid."

Clare describes herself as "in debt up to my neck because of him," but she insists that the last fifteen months—since her separation—have been the most peaceful time in her life. "The financial part is very hard," she says, "and I often go without. No dinners in restaurants for me. I give myself little pep talks all the time: 'Someday all the bills will be paid. You're going to make it, Clare.'"

Clare says that when she first left her husband she was scared to death. "How could I be otherwise?" she asks. "I'd been married to him almost half my life. It was hard even to imagine life on my own. But I went to see my minister about it, and he told me that God still loves me and that I was right to leave." After that conversation, Clare says, her much-needed spiritual healing could begin. "When I could forgive myself and realize that the sin was his—not mine—I could face anything. And I have."

Two years after leaving her controlling husband, Joyce looks back on what she calls "two of the best years in my life." But she also talks about the down side. "When I moved into my own apartment," she says, "I was thrilled. But I was also terrified to be on my own. I remember the first time my car broke down—I had a complete panic attack and was convinced I'd never survive the experience. But of course, I did, and I felt great when I managed that situation all by myself."

"It was so confusing that first year," Joyce says. "I was relieved to have my husband out of my life, but I also missed him. Sometimes the feeling of missing him was overwhelming. There were many times when it was all I could do to keep from calling him up." Like many other women, Joyce spent most of her first year of separation bouncing from one emotional extreme to another. She describes her feelings that year as "like one of those little silver balls that gets batted around in a pinball machine." But Joyce found new ways of looking at and understanding what she'd been doing and what she wanted to do with her life.

▪ JOYCE

> Missing him so much made me realize how much of my attention and energy had gone into *him*. I was always trying to keep him in a good mood. I was always fixing for him, helping him, escaping from him—and then suddenly he was gone, and all I had to think about was *me*. Leaving him was like giving up my life's work—like if I'd been a brain surgeon and lost the use of my hands. What do you do with yourself when your career goes away? When I thought about it that way, I had to laugh. I wasn't really longing for *him*. I was just unemployed.

As any woman who lives with a controlling partner knows, reclaiming your life is hard work. When you live with a controller, trying to assert some of your own thoughts and plans and independence can be next to impossible. But leave the controlling partner and you become responsible for *everything*. Perhaps for the first time, you may have to find money, friends, and new interests. Often you take a step forward only to fall two steps back. For example, you get a restraining order, you start to relax a little, and then, a month later, your husband threatens you again. You get your job running smoothly, the bills paid, the household organized, your kids feeling happy and doing well, and then your refrigerator dies or you find out that pushers are selling drugs in your building. Where do you turn and how will you manage?

In this chapter we'll show you the paths that some other women followed to reclaim their own lives. When we speak of reclaiming, we mean just that: to claim again what belongs to you. Or, in other words, to take back the power that you've surrendered—under pressure—to your controlling partner: specifically the power to own and take charge of your own body, thoughts, feelings, choices, and actions. This is the task of any woman whose controlling partner takes over her life, whether she stays with him or leaves, whether he stops abusing her or not. But it's a task that often can be performed only away from the controller. As Joyce says, "I couldn't have made this journey in my husband's shadow."

If you're feeling frightened, that's understandable. And if your controlling partner is extremely abusive, mentally and/or physically, and is absolutely determined to keep you or to get back at you, then you may have to go on being afraid for a long time—with good reason. But many controlling partners eventually back off. And in time many women find their fears of the partner and of the unknown lifting. Most women find that life gets better—perhaps even better than it's been in a long time—when they give themselves time to recover and fully regain strength.

GETTING ON YOUR FEET FINANCIALLY

Many women don't depend on their partners financially. They have their own income from work, welfare, inheritance, or crime—and in some cases they financially support their partner, at least in part. In those cases a woman often finds it hard to escape because the controlling and supported partner is doubly interested in hanging on to her. But once she makes the break, a woman who is used to standing on her own feet finds herself just that much farther ahead, provided her partner hasn't run off with the rent money or left her in debt. For women who *are* financially dependent upon their partners, on the other hand, the transition may be very difficult, and as we've mentioned before, it is most likely to be a transition downward to a lower standard of living.

Public Assistance

That's the situation Amy faced when she and her children left home and went to a women's shelter. She had no job skills or experience to speak of and two young children to provide for. She says, "I didn't have a clue about how I was going to make it. I don't know how I would have done it without my advocate at the shelter." Like many women, Amy had little information and many misconceptions about welfare assistance and subsidized housing. She says, "I felt like a charity case. It hurt my pride." But the shelter advocate explained to Amy that she had a legal right to receive public welfare benefits that included a small monthly cash allowance, a medical card, and food stamps.

Amy had to fill out an application form, gather all the documents required to support it (her marriage license, her social security card, and the children's birth certificates) and then go to the welfare department for an interview. The process was very complicated, and the welfare worker was not very nice, but within thirty days Amy received her first check. Because she was still living at the shelter she was able to put most of it aside for a deposit on an apartment of her own. For her own peace of mind, Amy also decided to think of welfare as temporary. She told herself, "Amy, you need this money to get your family on its feet, and then you'll get a job."

Lynn had more training and more work experience than Amy, but when she left her husband she was no better off. She had worked for many years as a licensed dental hygienist, but under her husband's subtle pressure, she let her license expire after the birth of their second child. "He told me I'd never need it again," she said, "and I was foolish enough to go for it. By the time I left him I hadn't worked in a long time and I had no valid work credentials." So after

Lynn fled to a shelter with her three children and talked with an advocate about her financial situation, she too realized that she needed welfare aid.

▪ LYNN

It was degrading to make the application. I would have given up if I'd seen any other way to get by. They made me come back time after time and bring one document after another. They treated me like some stupid, naughty child. If I asked a question, forget it. I was supposed to shut up and do whatever they told me—and they had more bureaucratic rules and regulations than the Pentagon. So I shut up and did what they said. There I was: pushing forty with three kids, and I wanted my kids to eat. But it was awful.

Lynn's experiences with welfare left her feeling demoralized. "I didn't know from food stamps, or medical cards, or managing a household on $500 a month. We did eat," she says, "but barely." As they tightened their belts toward the end of every month, Lynn and the kids made up fantasies about what they would order the next time they ate in a restaurant. "We tried to keep a sense of humor about it," Lynn says, "and we all really *like* peanut butter sandwiches. . . . But dealing with the welfare office made me feel like it was all my fault that we were in this fix—like we would have been okay if only I had a few brain cells."

Despite these oppressive feelings, both Amy and Lynn say that being on welfare was helpful. "When I look back," Lynn says, "I see the positive aspect, though I didn't understand it at the time. When I left my husband, I was totally wiped out emotionally. Getting those welfare checks gave me some time to get myself together." While she was on welfare, Lynn repeatedly went to court, first to get a restraining order, and then to work out custody arrangements. Like Amy, she also spent a lot of time with her children, who needed extra attention and love.

I needed that eighteen months on welfare—physically and emotionally—to get on my feet, to start a new life, to rest. At the beginning of the year I was a basket case. I jumped ten feet every time I heard a noise or thought someone was walking too close behind me. It took me months just to get calm again. My welfare check was my freedom from my husband, and every time I felt sorry for myself—which was often—I reminded myself of that.

Eighteen months later, when Lynn got her dental hygienist's license back and found a part-time job, welfare helped again by keeping her on a partial subsidy. On the day she switched to full-time work, she walked into the welfare department, said good-bye, and, as she described it, "felt a thousand pounds lift off my back." That night, for the first time since she and the kids fled to the women's shelter, they ate in a local diner to celebrate. Lynn remembers: "We had hot fudge sundaes for dessert—the best hot fudge sundae of my life."

Getting a Job

Like Lynn, many women dream of the day when they can walk into the welfare office and say good-bye. For most women, that means looking for work. But for many women the job search is every bit as hard as the search for housing. If you have few skills and little work experience, you may be offered only entry-level or un-skilled jobs that seem demeaning to you—or no job at all. And if you take such a job, you may find that it doesn't pay enough to cover the cost of child care. For that reason, some women take advantage of their time on welfare to learn new skills or train for higher-level jobs. They join a job-training program, take courses in English as a second language, study for their General Education Diploma, attend vocational or business school, or take college classes. Others accept entry-level jobs in companies that offer training programs leading up a job ladder.

The first thing you need is information about the possibilities in your community. To find out about jobs and job training and education programs where you live, it may help to talk to an advocate at your local women's shelter, even if you've never stayed there. Or you might ask for information and advice at a women's center, the

YWCA, a local chapter of the Coalition of Labor Union Women (CLUW), your local community college or vocational school, a program for displaced homemakers, a public or private employment office, or the welfare office. And check the classified ads in the newspaper.

Some communities have programs for displaced homemakers that are especially designed to increase the skills and confidence of women who've been out of the labor market for a long time. (To find out if there is such a program in your area, call 202-628-6767.) Some colleges and universities encourage women older than the usual college age to return to school. Promising women may qualify for admission even if they don't meet the normal admission requirements, and some receive full scholarships. A counselor at your local community college or high school may have information about these programs.

Another good source of information is word of mouth. Talk to friends and neighbors about their jobs, and let them know you're looking for opportunities. Often the best way to find out about the kind of work you'd like to do is to talk to someone who's already doing it. If you'd like to work at a bank or a TV station or a hospital, go find a woman who works there. Ask her what her job is like and how she got it. And even though you need paid work, don't rule out the possibility of volunteering in order to learn. While she was on welfare, Amy volunteered to help with playtime at her daughter's school and quickly became a paid teacher's aide.

Even searching for a job may require some special skills, and you can learn them. Look for workshops or short courses in how to prepare a resume and how to conduct yourself in a job interview. Such workshops are frequently offered for little or no cost by women's shelters, welfare centers, women's centers, and adult education programs. Some workshops are especially designed for older women reentering the job market. They can help you identify a lot of job skills you may not even know you have, such as the management skills you've used to run your home.

Maintenance, Child Support, and Property

Another source of financial help to consider is child support and compensatory or rehabilitative maintenance payments (or alimony) from the partner you're separating from. To get such payments you have to go to court, and that often necessitates finding an advocate or lawyer to help you. In Chapter 10, "Using the Police and Courts," we'll talk in greater detail about how to do it. Even if your partner has no money, or you're afraid of him, or you just want him out of your life, you should read Chapter 10 and consider these options carefully. In addition, if you and your partner accumulated any property together during your marriage, you are entitled to your fair share. An agreement dividing it up—a property settlement—is usually part of a divorce. We'll talk about this too in Chapter 10.

Money Management

Getting money is one problem, but managing it is another. Controlling partners, who like to be in charge of everything, very often deprive women of the opportunity to learn basic money management. Leaving a controlling partner who always "took care of things," a woman may not know how to balance a checkbook or plan and stick to a budget. If you feel confused about money matters or have trouble making ends meet, you and your family probably will benefit from your learning some basic money management skills. Especially if you are poor and every dollar counts, it helps to know what you're doing.

Ask your local women's shelter, women's center, or community college if they offer money management workshops. Some women's shelters offer a whole series of workshops covering such topics as making a budget, managing debts, doing your taxes, and keeping a checkbook. And some can refer you to a financial planner, a specialist who can give you individual help and advice. Or, to find out about bank accounts and keeping a checkbook or a savings passbook, you can go directly to a bank and ask an officer to explain the bank's services.

PULLING YOURSELF TOGETHER EMOTIONALLY

"Everybody in my family thought I should be happy that the 'jerk,' as they called him, was out of my life," Marcy says. "I thought I should be relieved, too. But instead I cried a lot. I was also in a constant rage. Sometimes I wondered what was wrong with me." During the year following her separation from Fred, Marcy sometimes thought she was going crazy. But in fact she was going through a normal process of getting over a relationship with a controlling partner.

Fred had put Marcy through a lot: years of intense criticism, name-calling, bad moods, threats, intimidation, sexual coercion, and economic deprivation. And Marcy had invested a lot of herself in the relationship. They'd known each other for ten years and had been married for six. He'd been her "dream man," the partner she wanted for life. With Fred, she'd pledged to work hard for the things they most wanted—children, a nice house, a garden, some wonderful vacations together when they could afford to travel. She often pictured them together in their old age.

When Marcy decided to leave, she lost those dreams and she lost a big chunk of her own history: many years of hard work and shared memories. She says, "I'd find myself thinking, 'Remember that time we took the kids to the shore . . . ?' But the only person who could remember it with me wasn't there anymore. It was like having a piece of my brain cut out."

She also had to face what she called "a profound sense of failure." She says, "I felt as if I'd blown it as a wife. I could remind myself of all the evidence that Fred's behavior was the problem— that it was Fred who blew it—but that didn't make the feeling go away." In fact, thinking about Fred's behavior made her feel worse. She saw that he was mean, and that he wasn't going to change. She had to let go of her fantasies about him. She says, "I knew that he wasn't going to walk in and say, 'Gee, honey, I'm sorry, I'll never do it again.' I had to give up my hope in him."

Letting go of that hope in Fred was the most difficult and sorrowful loss of all. Fred had been very abusive at times, but most of the time he had been fun-loving and playful—charming, witty, affectionate, sexy. Together Marcy and Fred had lived through many good and loving times. She had to put an end to the *bad* times. But the good times ended too.

In her first year away from Fred, Marcy went through dramatic emotional ups and downs, as many women do. She was angry with Fred for treating her badly and angry with herself for believing in him for so long. And she felt bitter that he'd wrecked the dreams she'd worked so hard for. At the same time, she worried about her own sanity because she had never before been an angry person. She says, "I didn't recognize myself. I was so hostile, and I took it out on other people. I'd scream at my kids. Then I'd cry and cry, trying to figure out what was happening to me. But it was pretty simple really: I was mad at Fred. All those years I'd never dared show anger toward him. But once I left him, it just poured out, like I'd been saving it up and somebody pulled the plug." And often she raged at herself. How could she have been so stupid as to waste her best years on a man like that? The best years of her life were behind her, and they had been the worst.

Marcy was going through the process of grief. She was mourning the loss of her partner, her children's father, her relationship, her history, her hopes, her dreams, everything that Fred and the relationship with him had meant in her life. And she was raging at Fred for letting her down. She felt depressed—numb, sad, irritable, vulnerable, scared, and full of rage. Her sleep was often broken. She felt tired, easily worn out, and tense around the kids. "During the first six months," she says, "it was hard to get the strength to go to the grocery store. I mean it literally. I was lucky to figure out how to get in my car and get to a supermarket. And then the job of deciding what to buy seemed overwhelming. I didn't think I'd have energy to cook anything anyway."

Generally, when people grieve, they turn to old comforts to soothe them through the most difficult moments. When a loved one dies, for example, people often like to be with family and friends and to talk about the good times they had with the person who has died. It shows love and respect, and it makes people feel better. When a woman leaves her husband, she often has the same tendency to look for comfort by recalling happy memories. But for her, this recollection can be very dangerous. It may lead a woman to think she can regain that happiness by bringing her partner back into her life again. Unfortunately, many women do go back to their partners when they're feeling this way, only to find their real troubles beginning all over again.

Marcy faced this temptation. She says, "When I was at my weakest, Fred started dropping off presents for the kids. Then he started leaving me sweet little notes, telling me how much he missed me and how much he'd changed. I felt guilty about what I was doing to him, and honestly I missed him." You'll recognize this as the kind of "nice" behavior controllers use to keep women hooked; we talked about this "on-again" phase of the controller's on-again/off-again behavior in Chapter 3. But Marcy was drawn into mistaking this show of good behavior for the "real" Fred. And as Marcy recalled more and more of the good times she'd had with Fred, she started to minimize his abusive behavior. "I found myself thinking that it really wasn't all that bad," she says. "I'd think, 'He didn't break my bones or put me in the hospital. I wasn't like a battered woman. It could have been much worse.' " Marcy's rekindled hope didn't last long, however, because Fred soon began to boss her around. Marcy says, "I could see that it was starting all over again. I just had to stay away from him—period." When Marcy refused to see Fred, he started calling her in the middle of the night to "talk." Marcy says, "He didn't pay any attention to my decisions. He thought he could ride right over any choice I made." Marcy got a new telephone, with an unlisted number.

But this incident made Marcy recognize that loneliness put her in a dangerous position, and that she would have to be on guard. Leaving Fred left a big hole in her life, and she was tempted to fill it by going back to him. Marcy says, "Somebody told me that to have a new life, you have to shut the door on the old one. But sometimes the hardest thing is just to let go and do *nothing*—to just live with the bad feelings and the loneliness and have faith that they will pass." Many women, like Marcy, feel worse before they feel better, but feeling worse may be the best sign that you are well on your way to a happier life of your own.

Finding Support

Many women who've been through sexual or physical abuse suffer from bad memories that return—sometimes when least expected—as nightmares, anxiety attacks, or deep mistrust of other people. Some women who've undergone emotional abuse also find their ability and willingness to trust others badly weakened. Consequently, some women try to tough out the difficult first year of their new life all by themselves. They usually get through, but we believe that every woman who sets out to reclaim her life is entitled to support and help. By finding support, you can make your journey easier, speedier, and much happier.

For Marcy, change began when she joined a support group at the women's shelter. "Before I went to the group," she says, "I felt sorry for myself. I was a woman alone. I'd say to myself, 'What could be worse?' " Marcy joined the women's group only because she was desperate. "I didn't like women," she says. "I didn't think they were very smart, and certainly not important. The important things in life happened around men. So I didn't really expect to get anything out of the women's group. I just couldn't think of anything else to do."

Like many of us, Marcy grew up with a cultural stereotype that distorted her sense of herself. A woman on her own conjured up horrible images in Marcy's mind: the desperate divorcee, the spinster, the old maid. She thought that women alone were lonely, miserable, hopeless creatures. They were big and fat, or old and shriveled up. Men alone, on the other hand, seemed dashing, adventurous, independent, strong—good catches. Women alone were in waiting, with their lives on hold until the handsome, exciting stranger showed up to rescue them. Then, and only then, could a woman begin the work she was destined for, the work that would fulfill her: nurturing her man and her children. Thinking about this old stereotype that she once took for granted, Marcy says, with a laugh, "Is it any wonder I felt like a failure?"

In her support group Marcy began to see things differently. At first she didn't want to talk about what Fred had done to her, for fear it would make her feel worse. But, she says, "I already felt terrible, so I gave it a try. And the more I talked, the better I felt." Marcy often found herself in tears, but she also heard herself laugh for the first time in what seemed like years. She says, "It was such a relief to realize that all these wonderful, strong women in my group were having the same problems I was. And they were telling me that *I* was special, easy to love, a good mom. I needed to hear that. I had lost my confidence, and they helped me get it back." Some of the women went out regularly for coffee after the meetings, and in that small coffee group Marcy got to know the woman who was to become her best friend. "We started to phone each other whenever we needed a boost," Marcy says. "Those calls saved me on more than one occasion."

After Marcy had been in the support group for a couple of months, it became an increasingly important check on reality. She says, "Sometimes I missed Fred, and the group would ask me, 'What do you really miss?' I'd start to say, 'Oh, he was such a good father,' and I'd watch their faces and know I was kidding myself again. They were great."

One night in the support group the women made a list of the activities that brought them the most energy and comfort. It included volunteering at a day care center, writing a journal, organizing a tenants' association, reading, going on hikes, planning a series of meetings with police officers to talk about family violence, singing in the church choir, learning to swim. The women also exchanged ideas about how they coped with moments of great loneliness. "I plan my holidays and weekends very carefully," one woman said. "I make sure I have some time scheduled with people I like." Another woman said, "I go to three Al-Anon meetings a week; and whenever I need to talk, I pick up the phone and call an Al-Anon friend." Some women who had recently begun new jobs, and two who had started courses at the community college, said they didn't have time to be lonely anymore. They were working hard at work or school, and they were starting to feel much better as a result.

During the next year, Marcy also found a job and volunteered to work at the women's shelter. And she too came to see herself in a new light. Like other women who had walked this road before, Marcy was no longer scared. She was busy and productive. She earned respect for her work on the job and at the shelter, and she felt proud of herself. She made new friendships, especially among the women of her support group. She had far fewer empty feelings to run away from. And she came to value her own company. "I love being with my kids now, and I love being alone," she says. "Life is so peaceful."

We believe that finding support by joining a group for abused women is a good choice for any woman who has been involved with a controlling partner, and it is a particularly wise choice for women whose controlling partners abused them physically or sexually. Such groups are often led by a trained facilitator experienced in working with physically and sexually abused women. Like Marcy, you may be reluctant to trust other women and talk about your problems, but does it really make sense to struggle alone with your "personal" questions when other women can help you find the answers? In a support group, the leader and the group can help you recover from harm, work through your worries, and act in positive ways to make your life better. And in a support group, you can help others do the same. And if you want to find additional sources of support as well, we suggest that you look again at Chapter 6, "Strengthening Yourself," for more suggestions.

What About Starting Another Intimate Relationship?

On this question all the experts and all the women who've been through it agree: take it slowly. Many would put it more strongly. Amy says, "Don't mess with it. Period." Marcy says, "You can't fill the hole in your life by going back to your husband. You can't fill it with another man either." Lynn says, "Take your time. You'll get what you need in a new relationship—without abuse—if you give yourself time to recover and put your life in order. If you rush, you'll grab the first loser who comes along."

Keep in mind that when you set out to reclaim your life, *you are going to change*—perhaps quite a lot. One year from today you will be different. You will have a different opinion of yourself and different goals and dreams. Most important, one year from today you will pick a different partner from the one you'd pick today. Lynn says, "I had to learn an important lesson: that my life is *my* life. It doesn't depend on a relationship. It depends on *me* to make it what I want it to be. Once I got that straight, I looked at everybody in my life a little differently."

When Lynn started going out with men again, a year after she left Mark, she felt very awkward. "I hadn't been on a date in sixteen years," Lynn told us. "What were we supposed to say to each other anyway?" Lynn felt uncomfortable with most of the men she went out with, and she often refused their further invitations. "I watched these guys like a hawk," she says, "because I was determined not to have my life taken away from me again."

When they start dating again, many women feel awkward and anxious. Many study their potential partners very, very carefully. They try to observe the new partner in many settings, with many different kinds of people, including family and children, over a long period of time. Some put them through deliberate tests. Such careful observation over a long period of time is the only way to figure out who is trustworthy, but even this method is not foolproof. For that reason, many women who've been physically abused deliberately pick fights with the potential partner to see if he will act nonviolently under trying circumstances. We don't recommend that strategy, but it's easy to see why many women use it.

It's important to pay attention to your potential partner's behavior *toward other people,* not just toward you. As we've seen, controllers are often very good at treating you well to win you over. A person who is working hard to hook you may reveal more of what he's really like in his dealings with other people. The kind, gentle person who blows up in a traffic jam may not be a kind, gentle person after all. If *in any dealings with any other people,* your potential partner becomes critical, demanding, bossy, jealous, or thoughtless, don't pass it off as a fluke or the unfortunate aftermath of a bad day at work. Instead, take it for the warning it is. Be particularly alert to how your potential partner treats and talks about other women, especially if he tells you that you are "different" or in some way "better" than other women. If you're attracted to a person who doesn't respect and like women, forget it.

As you observe the behavior of a person you're dating or thinking of dating, you might ask yourself some questions.

Who Am I Dealing With?

_____   Is this person self-centered?

_____   Does this person always want to get his way?

_____   Is this person moody, mocking, critical, bossy, or jealous?

_____   When this person gets angry, does he blow up?

_____   When this person wants sex, do you feel guilty or afraid to say no?

_____   Do you feel that you have to avoid having an argument with this person?

_____   Does this person criticize or make fun of other women?

_____   Does this person drink too much or use drugs?

_____   Does this person refuse to use condoms or take other safe sex precautions?

If you answer yes to more than one of these questions, you'd do well to follow the good advice offered years ago by Smokey Robinson and the Miracles: "You'd Better Shop Around."

Of course, there is more to a potential partner than what he's *not.* We've been talking here about the bare minimum requirements for a new noncontrolling partner. But you'll want to consider what you like about the person you're dating or thinking of dating. Lynn was drawn to a man she met through friends by the respectful attention he paid her. "He not only listened with interest when I talked about myself and the kids," Lynn says, "but he actually remembered the things I told him." For Lynn this was something new and different, and as she says, "It felt like progress."

As you reclaim your life for yourself, this is the time to consider what a really good relationship with a noncontrolling person would be like. It's time to establish some positive standards for yourself and your next relationship—and then stick to them. Participants in the Domestic Abuse Intervention Project in Duluth, Minnesota, developed the "Equality Wheel" that we reproduce here with their permission.

This wheel is designed to teach violent men what sort of behavior they must learn in order to have a good relationship with a woman, but women can learn from it too. The wheel establishes a safe circle of nonviolence, and within it EQUALITY forms the hub. Each section of the wheel names one aspect of a relationship and lists some specific actions that demonstrate it. "Responsible Parenting," for example, calls for a partner to share responsibilities and to be a nonviolent role model for children. We suggest that you spend some time studying this wheel with pencil and paper at hand. What specific behavior would you like to add to each section of the wheel? What would you like your ideal partner to do to show respect or trust and support for you?

Equality Wheel

What About Sex?

For many women trying to reclaim their lives from the effects of a controlling partner, new relationships proceed alright—until sex comes into the picture. Often when a woman has gone along with a controlling partner's sexual demands for some period of time, she loses track of her own desires and even of the boundaries of her self. She may not know (if she ever did) what her own sexuality is. Consequently, after leaving a controlling partner, some women become very active sexually with many different partners, while others—particularly those who have been subjected to sexual or physical force—can't bear to have sex at all. Some women go from one extreme to the other.

If you're troubled about your sexual desires or conduct, you should be aware that what you're going through is perfectly natural under the circumstances. It normally takes some time for a woman to come to (or come back to) her own sexuality. This may be particularly true if, even after you free yourself from your controlling partner, you are still bound by restrictive social conventions, such as the double sexual standard of male-dominated cultures. If your particular religious or cultural group believes that women should not have sex outside of marriage, for example, you may have a more difficult time sorting out what *you* think and feel.

Whatever your particular circumstances, the point remains: for veterans of controlling relationships, sexuality is often troubling and difficult. We suggest talking your concerns over with a good friend or bringing up the topic in your support group. (You'll find that everyone wants to talk about it.) And while you try to figure things out, keep in mind that no one—especially not that interesting potential partner—has a right to pressure or coerce you in any way.

There is another disturbing aspect to sex as well: the threat of illness. Every woman has to think about it. When Marcy started a new relationship and went to see her doctor about birth control, the doctor cautioned her to practice safe sex—to insist that her partner wear a condom during all of their sexual encounters. Marcy's doctor also advised her not to accept the reassurances or excuses men gave her. "Sometimes men don't know what they've been exposed to," the doctor said, "and they also lie about their sexual histories. You shouldn't take chances." The only way to prevent illness, the doctor repeated, is to practice safe-sex methods.[1]

HELPING THE KIDS ADJUST TO NEW CIRCUMSTANCES

While you're busy considering a new relationship, what about the kids? The chances are that they'll be less than enthusiastic about mom's new partner. When Lynn started seeing someone, her older daughter delivered lectures on the dangers of dating. Her son gave the new partner the cold shoulder. And her younger daughter answered the door and yelled, "Hey, Mom. Your stupid-looking friend is here again." Lynn says, "Given what my kids and I have been through together, they naturally resent anyone who takes me away from them. They've already lost one parent. They need extra attention from me right now, and they get it, but it doesn't hurt them to recognize that I have a right to go out on a Saturday night and enjoy myself, too. We're working it out."

But introducing a new potential partner is just one more jolt for your children, who probably already face quite a few problems. For example, if you move to a new home when you separate from your partner, your kids come up against a whole array of new and complicated tasks all at once. They have to get used to a different school and a different neighborhood. They may have to adjust to different styles of dress and behavior—adjustments that may seem monumental to a child or teenager. They have to make new friends. Some will face for the first time the stigma of living on welfare. They may feel a new kind of uneasiness, dreading the day their friends find out about their housing subsidy or food stamps. In short, they're put through changes every bit as big as yours, changes that may make them feel responsible and guilty, even though they didn't have a say in what happened.

As you reclaim your own life, they rely on you to help them reclaim theirs. Remember that they too were victimized by the controlling partner. (We'll have more to say about what your kids have been through and how to help them in Chapter 11.) And they too go through a grieving process, often with a good many mood swings and emotional fireworks. Their emotional difficulties may show up in falling school grades or dramatic changes in attitude, behavior, eating habits, or sleep patterns. Often children who've lived under the iron hand of a controller behave afterwards, when they feel safe, as though they've been let out of jail. They may be quarrelsome, disruptive, aggressive, hostile, and violent. They too may have bottled up a lot of rage, and now that the controller is gone they feel safe to act it out against mom.

This happened with Amy's children, especially her son, when they moved out of the shelter and into their own apartment. But the shelter advocate had predicted such behavior and helped Amy prepare to deal with it. Amy followed the shelter worker's advice to provide the kids with extra love and reassurance, a sympathetic ear, and firm but nonviolent discipline. Amy put up a sign in the kitchen, more as a reminder to herself than to the children: "No means No." Amy says, "My daughter didn't want to accept the changes at all. So for the first year, nothing was right. She didn't like the neighborhood, she hated the apartment, the kids at school were creeps." But in response to Amy's reassurance and steadiness, her children started to calm down. Amy says, "My son started talking to me about how mad he was at his father. He felt guilty about that, and he felt responsible because he'd wished so many times that his father would disappear. It seemed to help him just to talk about those things." Amy told herself that this troubled stage couldn't last forever. She was right. "By the end of the year," she says, "we'd all kind of settled down, and we were feeling pretty good."

Helping the Kids When They See Your Ex-Partner

When you leave your partner, if he is the father or legal stepfather of your children, the court may grant him partial custody or visitation rights. Or you may voluntarily agree that your ex-partner should visit with the children, if that's what the children want. (We'll have more to say about these legal matters surrounding custody and visitation in Chapter 10. Here we'll discuss some of the common emotional problems raised by visitation.) In any case, you'll face the problem of making arrangements for your children without putting yourself back in unwanted contact with your partner. And visitation leaves many women with the additional problem of protecting their kids from the self-centered behavior of the controller.

Marcy faced this problem with Fred. The children wanted to see him, and Marcy believed they should. But she wanted the visits carefully monitored, and far away from her home. When she tried to schedule the children's first meeting with Fred, he grew more surly each time they talked on the phone, and Marcy struggled to keep calm. Over time, Marcy learned not to be drawn into conversation when Fred phoned about visitation. "He would call, supposedly to talk about the children," Marcy says, "but really he would try to sweet-talk me. I learned to tell him that I had only a few minutes to discuss the kids, and I had to insist time and again that our relationship was over."

Marcy soon realized that visitation would never be the routine, smooth, and happy event she had hoped for. Fred still used it to try to intimidate and control her. He would come late, drive recklessly as he pulled out of the playground parking lot where he had picked up the kids, or cancel the visitation at the last moment, ruining her plans for the day and badly disappointing the kids. She realized that Fred could not resist paying her back through the children.

▪ MARCY

When I was on welfare, Fred would buy the kids fancy presents, and they'd think he was great. We didn't have enough food in the house, and he was buying them expensive toys. He led them to believe that if he came home, they could have toys like that all the time; so they'd start in on their "mean old mom" to let their "poor daddy" come home again. Then, of course, he'd cancel a couple of visits at the last minute and break their hearts. He makes promises and then breaks them. He'll go on and on about taking them to a ball game, and when the day comes he's forgotten all about it, or he doesn't show up at all.

For a long time I made excuses to the kids to ease their disappointments. But then I stopped. I can't protect them from reality. All I can do is listen when they need me and set some ground rules for their dad's behavior. They know I try my best to protect them from harm. I've talked to them about manipulative behavior, and I'm continually surprised at how much they've figured out for themselves. I'm afraid the world is full of people like their father, but my kids are already a lot smarter about dealing with manipulation than I was.

For now, Marcy lets the visits continue. She would have a hard time convincing a court to terminate them merely because the father is unreliable and manipulative. Like many other women who still have to deal with a controlling ex-partner, she has to make the best of a bad situation and help her kids do the same. Some women face far worse problems from former partners who sexually or physically abuse the children, or threaten to snatch them away. (We'll talk about this very serious situation when we discuss legal matters in the next chapter.) But even if your situation is no worse than Marcy's, you might want to talk it over with your support group, an advocate, or a good friend—just to get some moral support and perhaps some practical advice to help you handle it as well as possible. And in time, like many things about your former life, your hassles with your ex-partner will seem unimportant.

That may seem hard for you to believe now, but it has proved true for many, many women. By taking each day as it comes along, a lot of women gradually learn to handle with ease all the problems that look so overwhelming now, the problems we've discussed— finding housing, money, and emotional support, and helping your children through the transition.

In the next part of this book we'll consider some other resources that might be helpful to you and your children, whether or not you leave your partner. But before we move on to those subjects, let's listen again to Lynn. Three years after she left her husband and started the process of reclaiming her life, she describes some of the changes she's made. Giving yourself the opportunity to make such changes is what this chapter has been all about.

▪ LYNN

No longer do I worry about the kind of example I'm setting for my son or daughters. I know twenty years from now they will *not* say, "My mother was a doormat." I'm back to where I was before Mark started in on me. I'm strong and I'm a kind person. I wasn't strong or kind when I was living with him because I couldn't afford to be. I gave so much energy to protecting myself and my kids that I had no positive energy left. Now I can give things to myself and my children. And we enjoy each other now. I couldn't have said that three years ago because of the tension at home.

I was very hard on myself for a while because once I left Mark I couldn't understand why it had taken me so long. Today I forgive myself for the time it took me to leave. Eventually I made the right decision, and I go on making my own decisions. I go for a walk when I want. I wear the clothes I like. I say what I think. Sometimes I make mistakes—especially with my kids. But I know now that under the circumstances I did the best I could. And I still try to do that—to do the best I can.

PART FOUR

More Help for You and Your Kids

10

■

Using the Police and Courts

There's a good chance that any woman involved with a controlling partner may one day have to deal with the police or the courts. Whether you are legally married or not, whether you are emotionally abused or physically battered, whether you choose to stay with your partner or leave—you may have your day in court. The law and law enforcement are supposed to protect you and safeguard your rights. As things stand now, however, we can't predict whether the police and courts will work for or against you. You have to be prepared for anything.

The fact is that laws and law enforcement vary so greatly from state to state, from city to city, and from judge to judge that it's hard to know what to expect. If you call the police or go to court, you may get help, or you may get more abuse—not just from your partner, but from sexist police officers and judges as well. And there are some women whom the law simply may not protect: undocumented women, women involved in crime, and, in many circumstances, lesbians. In this chapter we'll try to help you answer these questions: What will keep me and my children safe? What rights do we have to safety and security? We'll talk about some of the reasons women use police and courts, how they go about it, and what they stand to gain or to lose.

But because justice is still so often blind to the rights of women, we suggest that you use this chapter merely as a general guide to issues and ideas that have concerned other women. To find out how the police and courts actually work in your community, you'll have to find a local advocate or attorney who has the knowledge and time to explain it to you. And if you then decide to use your local police or court, you'll want to find an advocate or attorney to help you navigate through the system. (You can find an advocate through your local women's shelter or women's center; and later in this chapter we'll tell you how to get a lawyer.) No two communities are alike, and any woman can benefit from specialized help. Keep in mind that you may be legally entitled to police and court protection *whether or not you leave your partner.*

No two women are alike, so you'll have to pick and choose the parts of this chapter that best apply to your situation. The chief distinction in the eyes of the law is between women who are physically abused and those who are not, but that distinction is not clear-cut. Most women who ask for protection orders, for example, are physically abused, but in many locations you can get a protection order if your partner harasses and scares you, even though he has never used physical force against you. Definitions of physical abuse or "battery" vary, too. If your partner shoves you or prevents you from leaving a room, that counts as a use of force, or physical abuse, in some courtrooms but not in others. As you can see, these legal matters are full of technicalities and inconsistencies. So if you're in doubt about exactly what procedures described in this chapter apply to you, you should take it up with your local expert.

First we'll discuss calling the police. This information applies mainly to women who are physically abused or threatened with physical violence, whether they plan to leave their partners or not. Then we'll discuss using the courts to obtain protection and vacate orders and to file criminal complaints. Again, most of this information applies to women who are physically abused or threatened with violence, whether or not they intend to leave their partners. Third, we'll discuss using the courts to resolve questions of maintenance, child custody, child support, and visitation. All of this information applies to women who are leaving their partners, whether or not they have been physically abused or are legally married. Maintenance may concern *any* woman who's leaving, while the other issues concern any woman with children. And finally we'll talk about using the courts to protect your children from kidnapping or abuse.

CALLING THE POLICE

Marilyn's live-in boyfriend Sam had always been temperamental and bossy—yelling at their kids and ordering her around—but in the eleventh year of their relationship he became much angrier and began to use violence against her. One night, he kicked her and hit her, leaving her with a bad bruise and a black eye. Marilyn was scared. She talked to her sister, who urged her to leave. She also talked to a friend at work who had gotten a restraining order from family court several months earlier. "It scared my husband," the friend said, "so at least he doesn't hit me any more. It's worth a try." But Marilyn was afraid it would make Sam furious and things between them more difficult. She couldn't figure out the best and safest thing to do.

The answer depends on a number of factors, many of them hard to predict. For example, some men become angrier and more violent when their wives call the police or go to court. Some bluster for a while but stop their assaults once the police or courts are involved. Others put on their best behavior at once. Some men ignore the authority of the criminal justice system in spite of the consequences. And too often the criminal justice system ignores *them*, effectively giving them permission to be as violent as they like. Most often women are the best judges of how their partners will respond, but they can also be surprised. And few women can predict how the police will respond the first time they're called. In the end, you have to decide what you think will work to make you safe. But many women feel like Marilyn. She says, "I was too scared to make a good plan by myself. I needed outside help and better information than I had. Sam had me more intimidated than I realized."

Marilyn was weighing what to do next when Sam brought on a crisis. He came home one evening in what Marilyn described as a "foul mood" and began to yell at her and push her around. Scared, she ran into her ten-year-old's room and told him to call the police.

As the child reached for the phone, Sam gave Marilyn a final shove that sent her flying across the room. He stormed out of the house, yelling, "Just let them try to find me!"

When the police arrived, Marilyn was shaken and embarrassed but determined to teach Sam a lesson. She asked the officers to find Sam and arrest him, but they refused. Their state had a new domestic violence law that authorized the police to arrest Sam on a misdemeanor charge if they had "probable cause" to believe an attack had taken place, even though they hadn't seen it themselves. In this case, Marilyn's son was a witness. The law even required the officers to search for Sam and make the arrest, but they said they were too busy. "If he shows up again, you can call us," one officer said, "but we haven't got the manpower to go looking for him."

The officers told Marilyn that they would file a report of the assault, however, and they said that she could request a protection order from the court in the morning. Marilyn knew that she should keep records herself, so she took down the officers' names and badge numbers. They offered to drive Marilyn and her children to the women's shelter or to the hospital emergency room to have her swollen arm checked, but she asked them to take her to her mother's house, a few blocks away. On the way there, the officers gave her a card with the phone number of the women's shelter and suggested that she call an advocate.

GETTING A RESTRAINING ORDER

Early the next morning, Marilyn had a long telephone conversation with Gail, the court advocate from the women's shelter. Gail explained that Marilyn was eligible to go to family court and ask for a "protection order." This document, valid for one year, would order Sam to refrain from hitting, threatening, or menacing Marilyn and the children. (Some people call this document a "restraining order" because it restrains the aggressive person; others call it a protection order, or order of protection, because it protects the victim. In fact, it doesn't do either one unless it's enforced—but we'll discuss that shortly.) Marilyn also had the right to ask the judge to evict Sam from the house, to give Marilyn temporary custody of the children, and to order Sam to pay child support for them. Gail explained that the whole purpose of the order was to protect Marilyn and the children. If Sam violated the provisions of the protection order by harassing or assaulting Marilyn again, he would be arrested. As long as he abided by the terms of the protection order, he would not be arrested or jailed.

Marilyn felt certain that Sam would obey the judge's orders, but she wondered if she should have him evicted from the house. What would he do? And what should she tell the kids? She talked the issues through with Gail and concluded: "Sam brought this on himself. He's getting more dangerous, and I have to do something to protect my family. He can come home when he gets help and proves to me that he's changing."

Marilyn went to the office of the court clerk and with Gail's help filled out forms, carefully describing Sam's threats and attacks against her. Two hours later, when the court officer called Marilyn's name and directed her into the judge's chambers, she was surprised at how smoothly and quickly things went. In less than ten minutes, the judge had reviewed her case, issued protection and eviction orders, and set a date for the hearing on the permanent order of protection. The judge also advised Marilyn to have the police on hand when Sam moved his things out of the house.

No woman can predict what her experience in court will be. All states have some provision for restraining orders, but laws and procedures vary widely from one locality to another. For example, in some communities you can get a restraining order in criminal court; in other communities you can go only to civil or family court. In thirty states you can ask for a protection order *pro se*—that is, by yourself—while in other states you have to have a lawyer. In some communities, there is no charge for a restraining order; in others you have to pay a fee. In some states, your minor children are entitled to a protection order; in others, they're not. In most states you can ask for a protection order, as Marilyn did, even if you are not legally married to your partner or if you have already separated from him, but in some states you can't. In twenty-four states you can request a protection order if an unrelated member of the household is endangering you.[1]

This provision in the law may be useful for lesbians who need protection from an abusive partner, but lesbians who are not "out" must proceed with caution. When a battered lesbian calls the police or goes to court, she makes her identity as a lesbian known. For some women this public exposure can lead to problems. Some women have lost their jobs as a result. And in some cases a former husband has used a lesbian's sexual preference as grounds to initiate or renew a fight for custody of children. If you are a battered lesbian, it is especially important that you speak confidentially to a knowledgeable person: a staff person in a battered women's program or a lesbian-rights organization, an attorney, or a victim-witness advocate. Ask them how you can safeguard your legal rights and your privacy.

Once you have a protection order, your partner may abide by it and leave you alone. Or he may not. And that brings us back to the police again. It's up to law enforcement—the police—to do something about it if your partner violates the restraining order. But once again, there is no guarantee that they will. In some localities, a man who goes on harassing, threatening, or assaulting his partner will be arrested and jailed, but in a great many others, he will suffer few, if any, consequences. In that case, to get the police and the court to take action against your partner, you may have to gather corroborating evidence—such as medical records, police reports, and affidavits (official statements) from witnesses—enlist the help of an advocate or attorney, and return to court again and again.

A protection, or restraining, order is issued by the court to your partner, not to you. It's the court that restrains your partner and orders him to keep away from you. Nevertheless, it's important for *you* to follow the provisions of the order, too, and keep away from him. Police and judges get understandably frustrated when a woman whose partner is under a restraining order does something that can be seen as "inviting" him to violate the order, such as letting him come home to pick up his fishing pole, or meeting him for a drink. If you get a protection order that calls for "no contact," abide by it. If you change your mind, go back to court and have it changed *legally.* That way you can impress on your partner and the court that you mean what you say. Otherwise, if you back down, you let your partner know that his control over you is even more powerful than the law. And the next time you need and ask for an order of protection, you may find that people unfairly blame you for putting up with him.

One final warning. There are some men who won't be stopped by a restraining order. It is, after all, only a piece of paper. The muscle behind it must come from your local police and courts. Every year, among the 2,000 women killed by their partners are many who hold valid restraining orders. If your partner threatens to injure or kill you or himself, and you believe he means it, you should talk with an advocate or attorney about whether a restraining order is likely to bring you protection. If the person you consult makes light of your partner's threats—if she says things like, "Oh, they all say that"—consult somebody else. Or if she pressures you to go ahead, in spite of your better judgment, "for the good of all women," as some advocates do, weigh the information she gives you very carefully. Consider following the advice only of someone who takes you and your personal circumstances seriously.

PURSUING A CRIMINAL COMPLAINT

Most often, a woman who calls the police wants immediate protection from a partner who is assaulting her or threatening to. In addition, she may want her partner arrested to discourage him from attacking her again. Louise had both these objectives in mind when she called the police during one of her husband's drunken, threatening rampages. The police didn't arrest Bruce, but Louise went to court anyway with Gail, the advocate, and got a protection order. When Bruce received the order and a summons to appear in court, he was furious. He spent the evening peeking into their house, then called Louise, described what she'd been doing for the past three hours, swore that he had her in his gun sights, and announced that now he was going to shoot her. Terrified, Louise called the police again, but it took them twenty minutes to arrive, and by then, Bruce had disappeared.

Louise told her story in court, and the judge ruled Bruce in contempt of court and fined him for violating the order of protection. For several weeks after that, to Louise's surprise, Bruce left her alone. Then, for no apparent reason, he started his telephone threats again. Louise called the police again, several times, and told them that her husband was once again violating the restraining order. The police should have arrested Bruce for the violations, but instead they told Louise, "We can't do anything until he attacks you." Louise asked, "Do I have to be carted off in an ambulance before you'll take this seriously?"

In fact, one night, that's what happened. Bruce jumped Louise in the driveway of their home when she got out of her car. A neighbor called the police, and this time they arrived in time to catch Bruce still punching his unconscious wife. An ambulance took Louise to the hospital, where she was checked for internal injuries and released. The police finally took Bruce to jail.

This time he was charged with assault, a felony. His case would not go to family court, where Louise had gotten her order of protection, but to criminal court. Like most people, Louise found the criminal justice process confusing, so she talked to Gail to find out what might happen next. She felt that she was in great danger, particularly when Gail told her that Bruce might be released on bail or with something called a "desk appearance ticket," a notice to appear in court at a later date. Even if a man is charged with a serious felony offense, such as assault or battery with a weapon or with the intent to kill, he may be released on bail in the morning. It's up to the judge.

That made Louise angry. Maybe he would try to assault her again. How could she get protection? Gail advised her that all she could do was go to court when Bruce was brought in to be arraigned, or officially charged with the crime. At the hearing, Louise could tell the judge about Bruce's threats and ask the judge to keep Bruce in jail. If the judge decided to let him out on bail anyway, Louise could ask the judge to make it a condition of Bruce's bail that he stay away from her and stop harassing her. Then, if Bruce violated that bail agreement, he could be arrested and fined or held in jail.

Gail also warned Louise that the criminal justice process was usually long, complicated, and frustrating. "An arrest and criminal charges may not even lead to a trial," she said. She explained that Bruce's case might be postponed for a long time. It might be "diverted" and handed over to a mediator to settle out of court without ever going to trial. That was up to the judge. (We'll have more to say about mediation shortly.) Bruce might also settle his case by plea bargaining—that is, he would agree to plead guilty to some crime, perhaps one *less* serious than the crime he was charged with, and because he cooperated and saved the trouble and expense of a trial, the judge would let him off with probation.

Louise was outraged and scared. It looked as though there was nothing to stop Bruce from walking out of jail and beating her up again, but together Gail and Louise convinced the prosecutor not to divert or mediate Bruce's case. "He is too dangerous to bargain with," Gail argued to the prosecutor. "He must get the point that there will be negative consequences for his violence." But Bruce, free on bail, began to call Louise again. He'd plead for one more chance and then say angrily, "You better drop those charges if you know what's good for you." Louise was afraid, but she knew she'd be in greater danger if she backed off now.

Louise and Gail met with the victim-witness advocate in the prosecutor's office—a special advocate, assigned to serious assault cases, to keep victims like Louise informed of hearing dates and new developments in their cases. Several months later this advocate informed Louise that her husband's case was going to be plea-bargained.

Bruce pleaded guilty to the original charges against him and was placed on probation. But thanks to Gail and Louise, he was given probation *only* on the condition that he stay away from Louise. Both Gail and Louise talked with Bruce's probation officer, and as a result both the probation officer and the judge warned Bruce on the day of his sentencing that if he so much as telephoned Louise he would serve his sentence in jail.

After that Bruce left Louise alone, and she's convinced that her persistence paid off. She says, "He won't try anything because he knows that he won't get by with it again. The whole process was a hassle, and it took forever, but for my peace of mind, it was worth it."

Unfortunately, many other women who live where police and courts take domestic violence even less seriously have almost nothing good to say about the criminal courts. Their cases are dropped, plea-bargained, or lost in the system. Overworked prosecutors—representing the interests of the state, not the victim—commonly ignore women's requests for restraining orders or special conditions to be placed on bail or probation. Prosecutors' offices forget to notify women of hearings, and when women fail to appear, drop charges against their partners. Many women see their cases diverted to mediation, where they are asked to work out an agreement face to face with the partner who has assaulted them. Later, when their partners predictably break the terms of the agreement by assaulting them again, the women are shocked to find out that, after referring the case to mediation, the prosecutor drops all charges. Consequently, the court won't punish the additional assault. In fact, to have any control placed on a partner's behavior, the women have to start the entire process—arrest, filing charges, preliminary hearings—all over again. And during all these procedures, they still have no protection. This is why so many women who've been through the process say, "Find an advocate when you deal with the courts."

SEPARATION AND MAINTENANCE

When you separate from your partner you can ask the court to give you temporary custody of the children and direct your partner to make monthly payments to you for their support. When you divorce your husband you can ask that the court direct him to pay you compensatory maintenance—that is, monthly money payments to repay you for the services you've performed as homemaker that kept you from developing a career of your own. (Some people refer to such payments as "rehabilitative maintenance," because they supposedly help "rehabilitate" women so they can be self-sufficient again. And some people still refer to such payments as "alimony.") When you divorce, you should also be entitled to a substantial part of the property that you and your partner accumulated during your marriage. That, too, is decided by the court.

Both Louise and Marilyn, however, wanted to keep their partners as far away as possible. Marilyn and Sam were not married, but they had children together, and Marilyn believed that any property or custody agreement that forced her to rely on Sam for anything would only give him additional opportunities to harass her. Although she needed money, she didn't want to be financially tied to him. Thus, when Marilyn requested custody of the children, she decided not to ask for maintenance or child support. This decision made sense for her because she and Sam didn't own any property together and he rarely held a job for long. "Even if the court ordered him to help support the kids," Marilyn says, "I knew I'd never see a dime." Louise waited two years to start divorce proceedings against Bruce, for fear of giving him an excuse to assault her again, and she also decided not to ask for maintenance or child support. She says, "I'd have paid *him,* just to get him out of my life." For similar reasons, many women are prepared to do without financial help from their husbands. But for many others, giving up legitimate claims to property, maintenance, or child support is not a wise choice.

Maintenance is awarded in only a small percentage of divorce cases—14 to 17 percent of all divorces, to be exact—and the awards are often extremely small and next to impossible to collect. Nevertheless, if you think you are entitled to it, you should consult a lawyer. Some circumstances increase the possibility that the court will award you maintenance. If you worked to put your husband through school, for example, or postponed your career for his, or helped him in his business, the court may recognize your contribution to his financial success. Similarly, if you gave up your work to raise your children, or if you want to continue to stay at home with your preschoolers, you may be entitled to temporary maintenance, at least for the time it takes you to get on your feet, or as the courts put it, to "rehabilitate yourself to economic self-sufficiency."[2]

A good lawyer can advise you about the customary attitude of the courts in your area and your chances of being awarded maintenance. A lawyer can also tell you how aggressively the courts enforce maintenance awards, and together you can assess your chances of actually collecting money from your husband. A lawyer may also warn you of another very common problem: when a divorcing wife asks for maintenance, many husbands counter by fighting for custody of the children. In many cases the men do not actually want custody, but they and their lawyers use this tactic to threaten women and make them give up their money claims. When that happens, the wife may end up with the children to support and no financial help from the husband—just as he wanted. This tactic is exactly the kind of manipulative, coercive behavior that controllers are particularly good at. If your partner tries this on you, you will need a lawyer to fight back.[3]

PROPERTY

Apart from maintenance and child support, there may be property to consider. Most divorces include a property settlement: an agreement spelling out how the wife and husband will divide up any property they acquired together during marriage. If you and your husband have any joint property, such as a home, a car, furniture, a boat, stocks, bonds, or savings, you are entitled to your fair share, or a money settlement, at the time of your divorce. Again, you will need the advice of a lawyer who is an expert in family law and divorce matters.

Your lawyer should also understand the kinds of threats, ploys, and violence your husband might resort to during a divorce. The lawyer should stand up for your rights, but at the same time respect your judgment of the potential danger of fighting your husband over legal issues. It's up to you to evaluate very carefully your husband's behavior. Is he merely trying to intimidate you so that you'll give up your just claims, or is he truly dangerous? The chances are that after the divorce you and your kids will be worse off financially, while your ex-husband will be better off, so you shouldn't give up your legitimate claims. But you shouldn't risk your safety. Finding the balance between these two objectives is up to you.

DETERMINING CUSTODY

"I was right to be worried about what Sam might do," Marilyn says. "When he was served with the protection and vacate orders, he went nuts. He said he'd fight for the kids and claim I was unfit." After Sam's threats, Marilyn realized that she needed additional protection for her children.

Married women often obtain temporary custody of their children in family court. Later their cases may move to the divorce court where final determination of custody (along with property settlement, maintenance, and support) is made. Because Marilyn and Sam were not legally married, their custody proceedings took place in family court. Each jurisdiction handles things differently, and remedies vary from state to state. Thus, before you do anything about custody—including leaving your home state—you should talk to a good local attorney who practices family law. (If you have to move to a different state before you have a chance to talk to an attorney, find one immediately in your new community.)

You may need that lawyer to represent you because, unfortunately, abused women often look "bad" in court. Some women have to flee in the middle of the night, leaving their children behind. Some change residences several times, perhaps to escape a persistent abuser, or perhaps to keep a step ahead of the landlord if they have no money for rent. Some have lost their jobs, or more than one job, often because they've been too injured or upset to go to work. Some have turned to boyfriends for help. Some have tried to get money by shoplifting or prostitution and have ended up with a criminal record. Often the instability in a woman's life is caused by the violent partner she's trying to leave, but to the court she looks like an "unfit" mother. As a result, some women lose temporary custody of their children, and if they do, they have a much harder time getting them back later. If for any reason you think you may look "bad" in court, you need an attorney.

FINDING AN ATTORNEY

To find a good attorney you might contact any of the places listed below. When you do, explain your circumstances and financial situation briefly, and state what you want the lawyer to help you with. Say, for example, that you have been emotionally or physically abused and that your husband is fighting for custody. Explain that you are looking for an attorney who specializes in family law. Ask for the names of several different attorneys. If you have a limited income, say so. The phone numbers of many of the national organizations and agencies named here are listed in the Resources section at the back of this book.

1. Call your local Legal Services or Legal Aid Society office to find out if you qualify for free services. (Your income has to fit within certain guidelines. Make sure that the legal service does not count your partner's income in determining your eligibility.) Even if you don't qualify, or their waiting list is

too long, you can ask them to refer you to a competent attorney.

2. Call your local battered women's hotline, women's center, YWCA, state domestic violence hotline, or the National Center on Women and Family Law, and ask them to refer you to a lawyer or legal service.

3. Your local or state chapter of the National Organization for Women (NOW) may be able to make a referral. Call the NOW national office to find the number of your local chapter.

4. A local child support advocacy group, chapter of the American Civil Liberties Union, or displaced homemaker program may also be able to recommend attorneys.

5. If all else fails, contact the local women's bar association or the city or county bar association and ask for the names of three attorneys who specialize in family law.[4]

Interviewing an Attorney

After you find three or four attorneys who specialize in family law, make an appointment to interview each of them briefly about their experience and practice. About an hour or less should be time enough for you to discuss some issues and get a sense of what each person is like. Keep in mind that you don't have to tell your whole story to gather information about the attorney and the law. (Ask in advance if there will be any charge for the interview.) Remember that this is *your* case—and your children's future—so you should feel comfortable with the person who represents you. Most legal experts advise that you keep looking for an attorney until you find a good one, even if you have to borrow money to pay the fees.

We offer here some questions you might want to ask in an interview. But don't hesitate to follow your instincts. You may have to work with your attorney for a long time, so pick someone you like. Above all, if the lawyer doesn't listen, talks over your head, and makes you feel too intimidated to ask for clarification, this person is not for you.

1. How much experience in contested custody or divorce cases do you have? How many cases have you worked on?

2. In what situations do you recommend mediation? Do you ever advise against it? Do you think it's appropriate in cases where a man has physically abused his partner?

3. What kinds of custody awards do local judges make in cases like mine? What do you think of joint custody? Do you think it's appropriate in cases where a man has physically abused his partner?

4. If I am entitled to child support, a property settlement, or a money settlement, what do you think I can reasonably ask for?

5. What are your fees? What work do these fees cover? What other expenses might I incur? Would you charge me by the hour (and, if so, how much) or a flat fee for your service? Do you charge extra for court appearances or negotiating sessions? Do you have a fee based on ability to pay? Would you expect full payment right away, or would you work out a payment plan with me?

6. If new circumstances occur, will you go back to court with me? If that happens, or if my case gets more complicated, are you going to ask for additional fees *before* you continue working with me? (Reader, beware: this is often what happens.)

7. Will you put our agreement, for fees and for work promised, in writing?

8. Will you handle this case differently from others, knowing that my partner is dangerous?

9. What should I do to assist you with my case? Will you work closely with me so that I can be involved?[5]

At their first working meeting, Marilyn's new attorney explained to her that because Sam was the father of her children, he had a legal right to request custody. (If your partner is *not* the father of your children, he has no right to their custody, except in very extraordinary circumstances, and rarely does he have an obligation to support them, even if you are legally married to him.) In determining custody, courts use a standard called "in the best interests of the child." In many states, if both parents are "emotionally fit," the court is supposed to give preference to the parent who has been the children's primary caretaker, regardless of her financial resources, but in contested custody cases it doesn't always work out that way.

In Marilyn's case, as in most cases, any one of several different arrangements was possible. Courts can award sole legal and physical custody to one parent and visitation rights to the other, or they can award custody to both parents jointly. Joint physical custody can be worked out in various ways: the children may shift between their parents' homes, or they may live in one. When parents share legal custody, all major decisions about the children—medical care, education, religion, and where they live—must be made by both.

Joint custody often works well in families where parents have relatively equal power and can work things out smoothly, where the woman is free from intimidation and the man is not trying to control her through the children. Many judges, and many women, feel that joint custody makes the most sense for the children and is fairest to everyone concerned. But when one partner is a controller and the other is intimidated, joint custody often merely extends the controller's domination of his wife and children. In addition, a joint custody arrangement can work to a woman's disadvantage by reducing her partner's support payments, making her ineligible for welfare, or preventing her move to another state.

Marilyn's attorney advised her that some women fight for sole custody out of concern for their children's emotional or physical safety. When a man is physically abusive to his wife, children learn both to disrespect women and to accept violence. Marilyn's attorney was prepared to argue that because her children had witnessed Sam's violence (even though they were not the targets of it) they were very frightened and would be emotionally harmed by being placed, even partially, in Sam's custody. After considering Sam's close relationship with the children, Marilyn decided that she didn't want to end it, but she wanted to put some limits on it. And she didn't want to put herself or the children back under Sam's control by giving him a major say in their affairs. She told her attorney, "I'm willing to give him generous visitation, but if he tries to get custody, I'll fight him for it."

To Marilyn's relief, Sam did back down in court. He merely requested visitation with the children, and he agreed to attend a weekly counseling program at the local mental health center. Nevertheless, Marilyn followed her attorney's advice to go on the offensive and petition for custody, just in case Sam changed his mind later when he finally realized that she wasn't ever going to take him back.

WHAT IF YOU ARE ORDERED INTO MEDIATION IN A CUSTODY OR CHILD SUPPORT DISPUTE?

If a man and woman can't agree about custody arrangements, the judge often will insist that they meet with a mediator to try to work things out. A mediator is a kind of referee—officially neutral—who is supposed to help the parties in a legal dispute resolve their differences. Mediators can be assigned or suggested for cases that originate in family, civil, criminal, or divorce courts. Unlike an attorney, a mediator is not there to speak on behalf of any person or to give anyone legal advice. His goal is to negotiate an agreement that both disputing parties can live with, so that the issue does not have to take up the judge's time. The mediator works by give and take. He may, for example, suggest that you compromise on one issue, such as custody, and encourage your partner to bend on another, such as support.

Attorneys and advocates for physically and emotionally abused women, however, strongly object to mediation in custody and support disputes. Mediation may work well for disagreements between equal partners, but a controlling partner and his wife are not equals. In addition, the supposedly "neutral" mediator often has an agenda of his own. One mediator may believe that the traditional family is ideal, while another may value equal parenting; but both mediators, by virtue of these beliefs, are likely to be biased in favor of joint custody. Consequently, as attorney Laurie Woods, director of the National Center on Women and Family Law, points out, they may pressure women into agreements that are not in the best interests of their children or themselves. "Often," Woods explains, "a woman is so frightened of her partner that when she has to sit in a room with him and a mediator, she agrees to anything—and later she regrets it."[6] If a woman is intimidated by her partner, mediation is not for her. In addition, because the mediator's job is to reach a settlement, he may begin to see her as a troublemaker if she does not agree to what he recommends, and he may describe her to the judge as a "problem."

According to a publication of the National Center on Women and Family Law, "Studies show that women, in general, are not as happy with mediated property and support settlements as men are."[7] In a mediation session, a man may lie or hide information about his assets, and because he is not under oath, as he would be in court, he faces no legal penalties for lying. Thus, if you don't know much about your family's financial affairs (property, bank accounts, your partner's salary, pensions, insurance, and other assets) you can easily lose out in a mediated support settlement.[8]

But what if, despite these warnings, you want to try mediation? Or what if the court *orders* you to go to a mediator? Attorney Woods says, "Remember that you can be ordered to mediation, but you cannot be ordered to come to an agreement."[9] If you are ordered to mediate and you are intimidated by your partner, you can ask the mediator to take special precautions. Ask to meet privately with the mediator and explain your concerns. Once a good mediator hears that your partner intimidates you, particularly if your partner has assaulted you, the mediator should stop the negotiations and suggest that you see an attorney. If the mediator still insists on mediating, ask him to schedule separate sessions for you and your partner. Another warning: remember that what you reveal to a mediator is *not* confidential and may be disclosed in court; this includes your address, phone number, and place of employment.[10]

SECURING SUPPORT

All states now have legal guidelines that specify the amount of child support that should be awarded by the court. Usually the award is based on a percentage of each parent's income. But a judge is free to adjust the amount up or down. That's where your attorney comes in. The attorney can help you develop legal arguments to persuade the judge to increase the amount of your award. (Of course, your partner's attorney may be figuring out reasons to decrease it.) As you work with your lawyer, you must think carefully about your current expenses, as well as your future needs.

Even with good legal representation, however, the amount of your child support may be disappointingly low. One Colorado study found that two-thirds of the awards amounted to less than the father's monthly payment on his car loan. In fact, because of the hassles involved in getting a child support order and then enforcing it, fewer than half of all parents entitled to receive child support actually get the full amount.[11]

Many women forgo child support altogether. Some decide that the only thing they really want from their partner is his disappearance. They give up child support just so they and their children won't have to deal with him anymore. Many other women, however, give up child support because they fear their partner. If you are afraid of your partner and can afford to carry on without child support, that may be the right decision for you. But many women simply can't afford to make that choice. If you are afraid of your partner and in need of child support, you must find ways to get the support and protect yourself at the same time. In any case, you should request at least a token payment of child support—say, ten dollars a month. Once a court awards you a sum, you can always go back to court later, when circumstances change, and have the amount raised; but if you pass up child support at first, you may not be permitted to ask for it later on.

Many women who are afraid of their partner want to conceal their address, and so have the child support paid through the court or through their local Office of Child Support Enforcement (OCSE). Many women move with their children to another state and then ask for support collection under the Uniform Reciprocal Enforcement of Support Act (URESA). Under this law, you can request that a URESA office file your case without disclosing your new address.[12] (If they refuse, however, your partner may find your new address through them.) In any case, as we mentioned before, if you decide to move to a new state, you should talk with an attorney about custody and support before you go, if possible, or immediately after you arrive.

Once you get a child support order, you may need help enforcing it. But according to Laurie Woods, women everywhere in the United States have more options today than they had ten years ago for collecting child support awards, although it may not be easy to use them. Options now include automatic wage withholding, contempt of court procedures, liens, and legal interceptions of state and federal tax refunds.[13] In some areas, for example, if your partner misses a payment, the court can order the money automatically deducted from his paycheck.[14] To find the enforcement method best suited to your needs, contact your state child support commission or enforcement office, your state commission on the status of women, or your local legal services or legal aid office.

If you are on (or applying for) welfare, the state will expect you to cooperate in its effort to get child support from your partner, unless you can show good cause not to. If you or your children have been assaulted, or if you believe that your partner is a danger to you or your children, this legally constitutes a "good cause" not to name the father or sue him for child support. However, as with other problems that involve the welfare office, you may need to find a good advocate or legal services attorney to help you enforce your right to be safe. The women's shelter is probably the best place to start looking for an advocate.

If the state does sue your partner for support, he may countersue for custody. The judge then has the right to rule on custody as well as support matters. Because you cannot predict what your partner may do, legal experts advise that you ask to be notified of the child support hearings and attend them. If your partner petitions the court for custody, you can ask the court to adjourn and get yourself an attorney.[15]

SCHEDULING VISITATION

Unlike many other women we talked to, Marilyn describes visitation as "relatively easy to work out." In her case, visitation rights were first spelled out in her order of protection and later specified in her custody agreement. This process, of course, varies from state to state.

The children wanted to see Sam, and Marilyn believed that he would treat them decently. "If he didn't," Marilyn told us, "I was prepared to cut off the visits. As far as I'm concerned, his right to see the children depends on how he behaves." But Marilyn was afraid for herself. If visitation were to take place in her own home, she feared that Sam would push her around again. On the other hand, he might be sweet and seductive, coaxing her to take him back. Or he might make her feel guilty by suggesting that the kids weren't behaving very well without him. Marilyn had heard enough stories from her advocate and other women to know that unless visitation rights were carefully spelled out, Sam would start dropping by to fix the plumbing, check on a sick child, or bring them gifts. Slowly he would work his way back into the house, and maybe into her heart. Marilyn was too frightened and had already gone through too much to let that happen.

She also knew that the moment when children are transferred from one parent to another is dangerous. That's when threats are made and violence breaks out. With the help of her attorney and her family, Marilyn was able to work out a way for Sam to see the children without seeing her. Sam agreed to visit the kids at his mother's home every Wednesday night and on alternate weekends. Marilyn's sister drove the children to their grandparents' house and picked them up. And it was Marilyn's sister that Sam was to notify of any unforeseen change in the plan—if, for example, he was ill or kept late at work.

Marilyn was luckier than many women. She had relatives in town to help her, a comfortable place for the visitation, former in-laws she trusted, and an ex-partner who did not abuse the children. But what if this were not the case? What does a woman do if she believes, as many do, that children are endangered when they visit their father?

Experts in family law tell us that it is almost inevitable that a father will receive some kind of court-ordered visitation privileges. To deny or severely restrict his privileges, you will have to offer very good reasons—such as the sexual abuse of a child. And you will have to convince a judge of the accuracy of your charges, a task that may be difficult, time-consuming, and often impossible. If you try to deny your partner visitation, you will need reputable medical and mental health professionals on your side: people who are both qualified and willing to testify that it is not in the best interest of the children to see their father. (If you seek help from professionals, look for someone in your community who specializes in child abuse and who is sympathetic to abused women.)

Although common sense might tell you—as many psychologists do—that it is damaging for a child to see his mother being abused or to visit with a father who threatens to kill his mother, many courts disagree. Wife abuse, they often hold, has nothing to do with being a good father. Courts have even awarded custody of young children to men who murdered the children's mother. Thus, the chances are that even if the father of your children has been extremely violent toward you, the court will not restrict his visitation rights. You have the right, however, to ask for a visitation plan that will keep you and your children as safe as possible.

Possible Visitation Options

Remember that visitation is often arranged as part of a divorce and custody proceeding, but in many localities you can request specific conditions—the hours and place of visits, for example—as a part of your protection order.

1. You can ask that visitation take place at a child protective agency or social service agency under supervision. A few communities have established visitation centers specifically for this purpose. You or someone else drops the child off at the agency office, and a staff member watches your child and husband while they visit. Some agencies provide this service free; some charge a fee.
2. You can ask that your partner visit the children in the home of relatives or friends. Make sure these people do not minimize or discount your concerns about safety. Friends or relatives can pick the children up for you or bring them back home. In this way you avoid contact with your partner.
3. You can ask that all visits be brief and that they take place during the day in a public place.
4. You can ask that visitation be contingent on your partner's participation in a batterer's treatment or substance abuse

program. If your partner drives recklessly or drinks excessively, you can ask that he not be allowed to drive or drink with the children present.

Before you enter into any court-ordered visitation agreement, speak to an advocate or attorney about judicial practice in your community. When a man violates a visitation agreement, what do the courts do? Are some judges firmer than others? Be prepared, if necessary, to return to court if your partner fails to keep the agreement; and be prepared for him to raise other issues when you try to charge him with a violation. Most legal experts advise: have your attorney with you. As one weary but proud mother told us, "Every time I tried to enforce the visitation agreement, he tried to reduce the amount of support he gave the kids and change our custody order. But I held firm and was lucky enough to get a judge who refused to put up with my husband's nonsense."

CHILD SNATCHING AND CHILD ABUSE

A number of men who abuse their female partners also threaten to kidnap the children. Often the threat is simply a way to harass and punish the mother, or, in other words, a way to continue the abuse. But some men do carry out their kidnap threats. "I lived a waking nightmare for ten months until I found my daughter," one mother told us. According to attorney Joanne Schulman, formerly of the National Center on Women and Family Law, even if the kidnapping parent is located, there is still no guarantee that a child will be returned. Schulman cautions, "The best solution to the problem is to avoid it in the first place."[16]

Most legal experts recommend that, if you fear a kidnapping, you get a court custody order as quickly as you can—preferably not for joint custody.[17] With your attorney you can discuss other options to lessen the likelihood of your partner's kidnapping a child. These might include court orders that allow him to see the child only under supervision, or prevent him from relocating or getting a passport for the child.[18] (Remember, however, that such restrictions can be imposed on both parents, limiting your safety and mobility, too.) Once you have a custody order, it's a good idea to leave a copy at your child's school or day care center and inform teachers of your concerns and legal rights.

If you don't have a custody order and your partner has already taken your child out of state, it is not too late to seek custody. According to the Women's Legal Defense Fund, you should get an attorney and apply for custody even if you don't know where your child is. If you file within six months of your partner's leaving, you can block his ability to obtain custody in another state. If you believe that your child has been moved across state lines, the Women's Legal Defense Fund recommends that you find an attorney who is familiar with the Uniform Child Custody Jurisdiction Act (UCCJA).[19]

If your partner takes the children *after* you have legal custody of them, then he has broken the law. It's a crime in many places to take a child from a custodial parent.[20] In this case, experts advise that you use every legal means possible to find your child. You may file a criminal complaint with local authorities. You may petition the court to secure the help of the Federal Parent Locator Service (FPLS), an agency of the United States Department of Health and Human Services that uses computerized files to track down parents and missing children. In some communities there are organizations of parents who have lived through abductions; they can give you moral support and ideas. The National Center on Women and Family Law, listed in the Resource Directory at the back of this book, publishes helpful material on locating abducted children.

Child Sexual Abuse

Some women who try to free themselves from controlling partners find that their partners continue to exercise control in a terribly disturbing and tragic way—by sexually abusing the children. In many cases, these assaults begin after the parents separate, and they take place during visitation.[21] If this happens to your child, you can ask the court to cut off your husband's visitation rights or place severe restrictions on them; you'll need your attorney's help. Or you can make a criminal complaint against him. Either case is very difficult to win. In the next chapter, "Protecting Your Kids," we'll discuss this problem in greater detail as we consider child sexual abuse, how to recognize it, and what to do about it.

*   *   *

The legal matters we've discussed in this chapter are complicated, arbitrary, and, for many women, quite depressing. For a strong woman it can be very disheartening to learn that even though you thought you could handle your own troubles, it may in fact take an advocate, a lawyer, a judge, and a bunch of police to help you out of them. But keep in mind that this chapter, like all the others in this book, is based on the experiences of a great many women who were able to use the police and courts to help safeguard themselves and their kids. And although many of them did not get the help they needed (the help that all women deserve), there are signs that under increasing public pressure some police departments and courts are learning to do a better job. They are *supposed* to protect you and your kids, and if you push hard enough you just might be able to make them do it.

11

Protecting Your Kids

Sometimes women who are determined to cope with a controlling partner overlook or minimize the damage he does to the most innocent victims: the children. Iris says, "Glen never started in on me until after I put Elaine to bed. I thought she never knew. Then one morning—she must have been six or seven—she looked up at me at the breakfast table and asked, 'Did daddy kill you this time?' I stood right there and watched my own denial system crumble. I always thought, 'He's good to her. She needs him. I'm staying for her.' But it was a lot more complicated and terrifying for her than I had seen."

Sometimes, it seems, we take abusive behavior almost for granted. Perhaps we've seen too much of it on TV. Darlene, for example, watched her second husband abuse her children emotionally, but she thought such behavior was "natural." She says, "He started by screaming, calling the kids dummies and idiots every morning at breakfast. My youngest son threw up every day before school. I dismissed it at the time because I thought that my husband and the kids just needed some time to adjust to each other." Six years later, he beat one of the children with his belt. Darlene knew immediately that she had to get her children away; she made plans and left soon after. Looking back, having learned something about emotional child abuse, Darlene says, "He beat my kids up with his mouth for six years and I knew they hated it, but I couldn't see it as child abuse. My kids paid a high price. We may never get it straightened out."

Women in controlling relationships usually try to protect their kids as best they can. They constantly monitor their children's behavior—keeping them quiet, sending them outside—in order to shield them from the controlling partner. Often they intervene and take a tongue lashing or even a beating rather than let their children be scolded or harmed. Some sit silently, knowing that if they say a word in a child's defense the child will be in for worse treatment. And most finally get their kids away, as both Iris and Darlene did. But like Darlene, some women don't recognize abuse for what it is. Some, like Iris, minimize or deny its effects. Many don't realize that children are harmed merely by seeing their mothers harmed. And some mothers become abusive themselves, treating their children in much the same way a controlling partner treats them. One way or another, the children suffer.

In this chapter we'll describe some of the effects on children of emotional, physical, and sexual abuse directed at them or at their mothers. We'll give you some guidelines to help you recognize child abuse, and some suggestions to help you protect your children. We'll speak mainly about the physical abuse and sexual abuse of children in this chapter, both because more is known about these types than about emotional abuse, and because kids are dying from them every day. We'll also talk about the emotional damage done to children by seeing their mothers abused.

CHILDREN AS WITNESSES TO VIOLENCE

For many years, it was commonly believed that children were spared the trauma of verbal and physical abuse when it was directed only against their mothers. Even today some experts still hold to this opinion, especially if the violence is sporadic and "hidden" from the child. In fact, some children of abused mothers perform well in school and show few signs of distress, but there may be more to their story than meets the eye.

Olivia says, "The children know, even if you are convinced that they don't. After I left Clark, my kids repeated gory details that stunned me." Olivia believes that her children adjusted—all too well—to the violence in the house. "My daughters became super-kids. Although they were never hit, they were sure that sooner or later they would be if they did anything wrong. So they were perfect."

Olivia's daughters also worried a lot, at a very young age. "Jo-anna, my oldest, was frightened whenever I was home by myself," Olivia said. "She would call me at her lunch hour to make sure I was okay. She was in third grade when this started. It began with a nightmare she had of my falling down the stairs."

Seeing their mothers humiliated and hurt, many children become like Olivia's daughters: concerned, hard-working, scared overachievers. Just like their mothers, many children are over-whelmed by confusion and guilt; and just like their mothers, they blame themselves. "Did I make Daddy do this to Mommy?" they wonder. "Why can't I make him stop?"

Annette knows exactly why her children felt this way. She says, "He never hit the kids, but he would yell at me and hit me whenever they misbehaved. The children felt responsible for what was happening to me. They were miserable because they could not protect their mother."

Annette's husband also threatened the children with statements like, "If you tell anyone that I punched your mother, I'm out of here."

• ANNETTE

The kids were carrying a dreadful secret. If they talked, they would lose their dad, and they would be responsible for "break-ing up" the family. If they didn't talk, they felt like they were taking part in my abuse. The kids were torn to pieces by the time we left him. And even that didn't end it. Every time he had visitation he'd grill them about me, and he was always trying to make them choose between him and me. He'd coach them on things he wanted them to say to me, and then they'd have to decide: "Should I say it to her or not?" He tried to turn them into weapons in his war on me. It was horrible for them.

In response to such stress some children "space out," while others begin to imitate what they have observed.

▪ JOCELYN

One morning after my husband left for work, my sons were in their room and as I cleaned up the kitchen, I realized that they were role playing one of our fights. My youngest called his brother a "rotten cunt," and I wanted to die. Over the years the imitation continued. The older one wanted to beat up his dad for me and tried on a few occasions. But the younger one walked around the house calling me a fat pig. Eventually he started to hit me. That was too much. It opened my eyes. I wouldn't tolerate this behavior from an eight-year-old, so why was I tolerating it from my husband? I realized that my kids were growing up with a totally distorted image of what a family is, what a normal mom is, what a normal dad is, what love is. They'd already learned to disrespect women—to disrespect me.

▪ CHERYL

One day my husband laid into me because I was delayed at the church and I wasn't home with dinner on the table when he came in from work. He cursed me out and carried on, and afterwards my son said to me, "I'd be mad too if I came home and my wife wasn't there." He was only nine years old. I hated the way he thought about women and the way he talked to me, and I realized that if we stayed there he was going to wind up thinking and acting just like his father.

Many women have observed in their own children this tendency to identify with and imitate the attitudes and actions of the controlling partner. But the effects on kids of watching their moms pushed around (literally or figuratively) seem to run deeper than that. Although research on this issue is scanty and contradictory, it suggests that some children who witness violence against their mothers develop symptoms like those of their peers who are actually physically and sexually abused. Sometimes these categories, created for research purposes, blur in real life; the child who is a witness to emotional or physical abuse may also become the victim. Amanda says, "My husband never punished my children when they were young. They just watched what he did to me. But as they got older, they couldn't stand his bossiness and mean streak. So they started talking back and defying him. Wouldn't you know it? He went after them with the same restrictions and punishments he put on me."

Some children who are witnesses to their mother's abuse may become victims by accident.

▪ LUCY

I came home from the store with the baby, and I started unloading the groceries from the bag. Out of the clear blue sky—we hadn't even exchanged a word—Tom started screaming at me that it wasn't his responsibility to unpack groceries, that the baby should shut up and grow up. He went to put a can of green beans away, it was one of those sixteen-ouncers, and he turned around and threw the can at me, but it missed and hit my daughter on the side of the head. At that moment I knew I was leaving. It took me three years to get out and although he never struck my daughter again, I knew I was going.

Although many children who witness abuse do remarkably well and display none of the behavior we describe below, others are more deeply affected. They require more help and support. Many of their symptoms are transitory; that is, they will disappear over time, especially once the children are safe and settled away from the abuser. But other symptoms may persist, and they may lead you to seek more specialized advice. If you feel guilty as you read this list of symptoms, remember that you can do something positive for your child's future. Even severely traumatized children can recover if they have good support.

Symptoms in Children Who Witness Their Mother's Abuse

_____ Sleeplessness, fears of going to sleep, nightmares, dreams of danger.

_____ Headaches, stomachaches.

_____ Anxiety about being hurt or killed.

_____ Fighting with others; hurting other children or animals.

_____ Temper tantrums.

_____ Withdrawal from other people and activities.

_____ Listlessness, depression, little energy for life.

_____ Feelings of loneliness and isolation.

_____ Substance abuse.

_____ Talk about suicide or suicide attempts.

_____ Fears of going to school or of leaving mother alone, truancy.

_____ Stealing.

_____ Frozen watchfulness or excessive fear around the abusive person.

_____ Acting perfect, overachieving, looking like small adults.

_____ Worrying, difficulties in concentrating and paying attention.

_____ Bed-wetting.

_____ Eating problems.

_____ Medical problems like asthma, arthritis, and ulcers.[1]

WHAT IF YOUR PARTNER IS PHYSICALLY OR SEXUALLY ASSAULTING YOUR CHILDREN?

In her interviews with 400 battered women, Lenore Walker found that over half of their male partners (53 percent) also abused their children.[2] These numbers terrify most of us. The thought that her children might be abused left Lucille sleepless. She says, "I kept asking myself, 'How can I save my children if I can't save myself?' " Lucille worried most about the fact that her husband often spanked their daughters. Her worry led to more intense feelings of guilt and self-blame. She asked herself, "What's wrong with me that I let this happen to my children?"

Lucille's questions were important for her to answer, but they may have been slightly misdirected. She wasn't responsible for her husband's abuse. She didn't "let" it happen to her children. She objected to her husband's use of force, fought with him over it, and eventually separated from him because of it. She tried her best to protect her children, but sometimes she was caught up in circumstances beyond her control.

▪ LUCILLE

My three-month-old woke up in the middle of the night with an ear infection and temperature. My husband screamed, "Shut the baby up, I'm trying to sleep!" I was trying to comfort her, but nothing worked. He got up, took her from my arms, and whacked her. She had a black-and-blue rear end. Now what should I do? I thought, "If I take her to the doctor, they'll take her away from me because I'm the mother and I allowed this." My husband told me, too, "No matter what you say, I'm going to tell them that you did it."

As Lucille's children got older, they were subjected to other forms of her husband's controlling behavior. Lucille says, "I had to leave my daughters with my mother so that they would get a candy bar or a McDonald's like other kids. He had money but he was so tight with it that he wouldn't let me buy them treats or presents." His emotional neglect of the children and his demands on Lucille's time were constant.

At night he used to come home from work and go right to bed—at 6:00 at night. He expected me to go with him and leave the kids in their room playing. It was so stressful for me. He showed the kids no attention, and when he was home I was supposed to show attention only to him. I kept worrying that the kids had no good father figure. And half the time they didn't have a mom either.

Penny had left her husband Greg and was fighting him in court for custody of their daughter when she discovered that Greg was sexually abusing the child. Advocates and medical professionals alike report increasing numbers of such cases of sexual abuse.

Sometimes these assaults begin after the parents separate and occur during visitation. It seems that some fathers sexually abuse their children to punish women for leaving them.[3] Penny believes that's exactly what happened to her.

▪ PENNY

When my daughter came home from a weekend visitation with her father, I noticed a discharge on her underwear; and when I asked her about it, she said, "Daddy and me played a game." When I confronted my husband, he said, "Kids always make these things up." Later he switched tactics and threatened me. He said he'd accuse a man I was going out with. I told him, "Just try it and see how far you get." He tried it and we're still fighting in court. He's trying to say that I'm not fit to have custody because I let my boyfriend abuse *his* child. It's a nightmare. And he's done it all just to get back at me for leaving.

When they suspect that something is wrong, many women do as Penny did: they talk to their children, listen carefully, and believe them right away. Acknowledging what's happening to children is the necessary first step toward protecting them. But if you suspect that your partner is hurting your child—emotionally, physically, or sexually—you may not want to believe it. Some women shrink from looking at what their partner is doing. And some respond to what the controller does to the children in the same ways they respond to what the controller has been doing to *them*. They minimize and deny and place the blame elsewhere. Sometimes they put the blame, and their anger, on a child, saying, "If you weren't so bad, daddy wouldn't have to do this to you." Or, they fall into the explanation trap again, making allowances for the controller's behavior. They say things like, "My husband's had a tough time lately," or "He's been under a lot of stress at work."

Some women see no way to protect their children, and because they don't want to face up to their own powerlessness, they shut their eyes to the abuse. Or at least they try to. Geneen says, "In my heart I knew something was wrong. I had to learn to listen to myself and my kids again." When she did, Geneen saw what she most feared: "terror in my children's eyes."

Although Geneen's husband never left black-and-blue marks on the children, and a child abuse investigation probably would have turned up no evidence, Geneen held to her conviction that something was wrong. She applied her own test to the situation. She asked herself, "Has my husband damaged my children because of the way he behaves?" In her opinion the answer was yes. Geneen's question is one that each woman must answer for herself.

To help you answer that question, we offer here some definitions of child abuse and neglect drawn largely from very helpful pamphlets published by the National Committee for Prevention of Child Abuse. We name a number of actions that are abusive or neglectful. *It's important to recognize that many acts often called "play" or "discipline" are in fact acts of physical force and violence—child abuse.* And we present some lists of the signs and symptoms considered by professionals—doctors, nurses, teachers, social service workers—when they look for child abuse and neglect.

Physical Child Abuse

Physical abuse is nonaccidental injury or a pattern of injuries to a child.

It includes spanking, shaking, slapping, punching, hitting, kicking, grabbing, choking, pushing, restraining, pulling hair, pulling ears, poking, boxing, squeezing, tripping, banging head against an object, tossing or swinging violently, intentionally dropping, pinching, dragging or pulling by the arm, twisting arm, throwing, throwing objects at, beating, holding head under water, forcing into very hot or very cold water, smothering, tying up, cutting, burning, biting, hitting with a weapon such as a belt, broom, or paddle.

Physical signs and symptoms:

1. Bruises, broken bones, lacerations, puncture marks, swollen areas, missing hair, or marks that might have been made by bites or cigarette burns.
2. Frequent signs of minor or severe injuries.
3. Numerous injuries in various stages of healing, indicating that they could not all have occurred at the same time.

4. Neglected injuries, or evidence of delayed or inappropriate treatment.

Behavioral signs and symptoms:

1. Bizarre or impossible explanations of injuries offered by the child.
2. Inadequate or conflicting explanations of the child's injury offered by the child's parent(s).
3. Habitual lateness or absence from school. (Parents may keep the child at home until physical evidence of abuse disappears).[4]

Child Neglect

Neglect is depriving a child of the physical care and protection that normal human growth requires.

It includes failing to feed or clothe adequately or appropriately, failing to ensure adequate sleep, failing to maintain cleanliness and good hygiene, failing to attend to medical needs.

Physical signs and symptoms:

1. Hunger, dehydration, bloating, or malnutrition.
2. Dirtiness, disheveled appearance.
3. Sleepiness, inability to stay awake in school.
4. Frequent illnesses or obvious unattended injuries.

Parents' behavioral signs and symptoms:

1. Parent provides little or no routine in the child's life.
2. Parent may appear indifferent to the child.
3. Parent may leave child unattended for hours or days.[5]

Child Sexual Abuse

Child sexual abuse is sexual contact between a child and an adult or older child for the sexual gratification of the offender.[6] It may be physical (such as handling the child or inducing the child to handle the offender) or nonphysical (such as compelling the child to see or hear sexually explicit material or behavior). Sexual abuse is always coerced. The coercion may be achieved through physical force or nonphysical, psychological pressures such as bribery and intimidation.

It includes commenting on child's body, talking to a child in a sexually explicit manner, kissing or fondling inappropriately or against the child's will, encouraging sexual contact between children, exposing adult genitals to a child, exposing the child's genitals, coercing a child to touch adult sexual parts, tickling inappropriately or other touching of child's sexual parts under the guise of a game, exposing child to pornography, exposing child to sexual assault on mother or adult sexual relations, penetrating with fingers or objects, intercourse.

Physical signs and symptoms:

1. Irritated or reddened genitals, itching of genitals or anus.
2. Pain or injury to the genital area or the mouth.
3. Vaginal or penile discharge.
4. Urinary infection, difficulty with urination.
5. Unusual and offensive odors.
6. Venereal disease.
7. Pregnancy.[7]

Child's behavioral signs and symptoms:

1. Fear of a person or of certain places, such as showers or washrooms. (If the offender is a parent or loved person, the child may show no fear in his presence.)
2. Clinging, anxious, irritable behavior.
3. Regression to babyish habits, such as thumb-sucking.
4. Sudden self-consciousness about genitals; sudden interest in genitals of others, sexual acts, and sexual terminology.
5. Fearful behavior toward examination of the mouth.
6. Sexual behavior that is inappropriate for the child's age, such as a young child "French kissing."
7. Increase or decrease in appetite.
8. Drawings that are scary.
9. Vehement overreaction when questioned about whether he or she was touched.[8]

10. Relating to a parent in a significantly different way from the other children in the family.
11. Arriving early at school and leaving late.
12. Nervous, aggressive, hostile, or disruptive behavior toward adults, especially toward the parents.
13. Running away.
14. Alcohol or drug use.
15. Sexual promiscuity.
16. Withdrawal from social relationships, or into a fantasy world.
17. Appearance of mental retardation.
18. Nightmares, bed-wetting, fear of the dark, difficulty falling asleep, new fears, excessive crying.
19. Acting out sexual, abusive, or aggressive behavior with toys, animals, or people, sometimes including stealing, bribing other children with trinkets to form friendships, and assaults.
20. Poor peer relationships and inability to make friends.
21. Indirect statements about abuse, such as: "I don't like to be alone with John," "Mrs. Smith acts funny with me," "He fooled around with me," "I'm afraid to go home tonight," "Can I stay with you tonight?"[9]

Psychological Abuse

Psychological or emotional abuse is a form of child abuse that results in impaired psychological growth and development. It frequently occurs as verbal abuse or excessive demands on a child's performance and results in a negative self-image on the part of the child and disturbed child behavior. It may occur with or without physical abuse.[10] Experts cite five forms of emotional maltreatment: rejecting, ignoring, terrorizing, isolating, and corrupting.[11]

It includes yelling, swearing, using angry or frightening gestures, being lewd, ignoring, criticizing, mocking, name-calling, blaming, having only negative interactions with the child, manipulating to take sides in adult disputes, twisting words, locking in closet or room, harassing, badgering, embarrassing in public, depriving of money or essential items, destroying possessions or pets, giving alcohol or drugs, exposing to reckless or drunk driving, scaring, threatening with violence or abandonment.

Parents' behavioral signs and symptoms:

1. Penalizing the child for positive, normal behavior such as smiling, exploring, lively play, vocalizing, and manipulating objects.
2. Discouraging the child's attachments, for example, to the other parent or to friends outside the family.
3. Penalizing the child for showing signs of positive self-esteem.
4. Ignoring the child; pushing or sending the child away.
5. Creating a climate of fear; bullying; attacking or destroying possessions, pets, people, and things the child loves.
6. Inappropriately rewarding the child's aggression, delinquency, or sexually precocious behavior.[12]

Child's behavioral signs and symptoms:

1. Fear, withdrawal, excessive shyness and isolation.
2. Excessive showing off and demanding attention.
3. Temper tantrums, dramatic displays of anger, hostility.
4. Nightmares, sleep disturbances.
5. Running away.
6. Substance abuse.
7. Perfectionism.

IF YOUR CHILD HAS BEEN ABUSED

If your child actually tells you that your partner has physically or sexually abused her or him, there are a number of steps you should take. Experts generally agree that while these actions may be very difficult, they will help both your child and you.

1. Believe your child. It is extremely rare for children to lie about abuse.
2. Keep cool. Overreacting may doubly traumatize the child and lead you to rash actions that can jeopardize your case for custody.

3. Protect your child immediately from the suspected offender.
4. Reassure your child that it is not his or her fault, and that you're glad the child told you.
5. Get a medical exam at once for your child even if he or she appears to be unhurt, but keep in mind that the doctor may not be able to find medical evidence of abuse.
6. Report the suspected abuse to the state agency responsible for investigating abuse. If you are a poor woman, a woman of color, a lesbian, or if you don't know English well, we strongly urge you to talk to an advocate *first*.
7. Help your child work with the professional who will handle the case.

It is particularly important that you seek medical treatment for the child. When you do, however, remember that your doctor is required by law to report signs of child abuse to your state child protective agency (usually called the Department of Social Services, Department of Youth Services, or Department of Children and Family Services). This agency is required by law to investigate the situation and determine if children are at such risk that they should be removed from their home. The agency may offer services to your family, such as day care or visiting nurses, which may make it possible for the child to remain in the home safely.

Many women are afraid of child protective authorities. They believe that the authorities will blame them for abuse they did not commit and could not prevent, and they fear that the authorities will take their children away. A number of women have friends and relatives who have lost children to the state foster care system. Others are less afraid of the "system," but terrified by their partners. "If Bill found out I talked to DSS, I was dead," Sarabeth told us.

Sarabeth faced the agonizing dilemma of many women involved with controlling partners. If they reveal the child abuse, they get in terrible trouble at home with the abuser—and maybe with the authorities, as well. On the other hand, if they conceal the abuse, the child may be badly harmed or even killed. If the child is injured, the authorities (child protective agencies, doctors, and mental health professionals) probably will label them mothers who "fail to protect." If a mother who "fails to protect" then decides to remain with her partner or reunite with him after a temporary separation, she may find her children removed and placed in foster care, sometimes for years.

If this is the dilemma you face, we suggest that you turn to organizations that will guard your rights and help you explain yourself to the child protective authorities in your community. If you must go through a child abuse investigation, you'll need support from people who know the system. And keep in mind that if you're poor or a woman of color you are particularly at risk to lose your children to foster care. Resources vary from one locality to another, but you might begin by talking to an advocate at a women's shelter, a Legal Services office or a law school legal clinic, or Parents Anonymous. (An advocate for abused women is most likely to understand the bind you're in and the danger you face if your partner decides that you're turning against him, but bear in mind that if you tell her about child abuse, she is legally required to report it.) If they can't help you, ask them to refer you to organizations that can.

Jocelyn Tilsen, Executive Director of Parents Anonymous of Minnesota, offers this advice to women who take a child to a doctor, a school counselor, or a shelter and suddenly face a child abuse investigation: "Although your instincts tell you to avoid the investigation, it may be more helpful to present yourself as a person who is willing to cooperate. In fact, it may be better if you call in the complaint yourself. If not, the agency thinks you have something to hide. Get help from other services and tell your investigator what you are doing. If you are afraid of your partner, explain why and ask that the investigator conduct his assessment in a way that will protect you—away from your home, for example. If there is a program for abused women in your community, find an advocate there who will support you through this process."[13]

Many incidents of child abuse reported to authorities cannot be substantiated. There isn't enough evidence to make a finding of abuse, and the agency closes the case. Women frequently report that when this happens, their partner becomes more violent. He pays her back for telling on him and tries to make sure that she won't do it again. It is at this point that many women flee with their children.

To those who can't get away, people who serve as advocates for children offer this advice: "You need to be an advocate and protector of your children. Develop safety plans with them. Figure out places they can hide or flee to, such as a neighbor's, a friend's, or a grandparent's home. Teach kids to call the police or to tell their teachers about what is happening. It might be best for the kids to live elsewhere temporarily—with relatives or friends— while you figure out what to do. In this way they can be safe."

Marian planned and saved money for three years before she was able to escape. During that time she worked overtime to protect her kids. She says, "For three years I wouldn't leave them alone with him, ever. They went with me wherever I went. He put up a stink about it, but it was too bad." Marian sent her kids to visit friends and grandparents when "trouble was brewing." She took them for long rides, put them to bed early, and kept things calm.

Marian also found ways to help her kids emotionally, even while they continued to live with her controlling husband. She says, "Most of all I tried to keep tabs on their emotions and listen to them, even though I would have preferred to avoid the pain they shared with me." Marian talked to her children a lot in those three years. "I told them that they would be safe, that I wouldn't let anyone hurt them. In reality, for those three years, that was hard to do, but I kept trying to protect them. I also told them that their father had a problem, that he was wrong and it wasn't their fault. None of it was."

Child advocates suggest that you listen to your kids' concerns and try not to let your feelings get in the way. Although it's hard to do, put your defensiveness aside and *listen*. Then *validate* the child's feelings. For example, if a child says, "I hate what Daddy does to us," you may want to defend your husband. You might say, "He doesn't mean to lose his temper." Or, in your anxiety to keep your husband calmed down, you might tell the child, "You have to learn to be quiet when Daddy's tired." Either way, you leave the child unsupported and ashamed. Children need to know that it's okay to feel what they feel. In this case, the child needs to know that hating what Daddy does is a healthy response, that Daddy *is* wrong to behave as he does, and that the child is in no way responsible for what the father does. In addition, letting the child talk and listening carefully may be very good for *you*—especially if the child is saying things you'd rather not hear. If you're still denying and minimizing your partner's behavior, the child may see it much more clearly than you do.

WHAT IF YOU WANT TO TAKE LEGAL ACTION?

As we said earlier, some cases of child sexual abuse begin after the parents have separated. In many cases, it appears that the father abuses the child to extend his control over the mother and to punish her for leaving. If this is your situation, you may want to take legal action against your ex-partner to restrict or stop his visits with the child, or perhaps to punish him for his crime.

Unfortunately, when mothers complain to the police and courts that they suspect sexual abuse, they are often dismissed as vindictive wives, making false accusations in order to deny their husbands visitation or custody. Many judges view such charges merely as part of an ongoing fight between wife and husband. If this is the situation you face, it is important to get good legal advice and support from advocates and professionals. (You might follow the suggestions in Chapters 6 and 10 on finding an advocate and an attorney.)

Despite the failure of the criminal justice system in many communities to uphold the law, it *is* a crime to sexually abuse a child. If you suspect sexual abuse, you should take your child to a good doctor, preferably one who specializes in sexual abuse cases. You should also call your attorney and a local rape crisis center and ask them for help. A good rape crisis center should be able to explain the legal procedures in your community and advise you what to do next. In fact, sexual assault programs often provide free legal advocacy, counseling, and support.

If you consider taking any legal action against your partner, you'll need documentation of abuse from reputable sources, such as police and hospital records. It is vitally important for you to keep a record of your partner's abuse, both against yourself and against the children, and to gather supporting documents from official sources whenever possible. You can use the record in any proceeding to demonstrate to the judge that your partner has a long and serious history of threats, sexual abuse, or physical violence. This may make it easier for you to get protection orders for you or your children, to limit his custody rights or visitation, and to have him sent to treatment. It will also be important evidence if you decide to bring criminal charges against him. If you want to keep a record, the following charts may be helpful.

Incidents of Abuse

DATE/ TIME	DESCRIPTION	WITNESSES

Calls To Police

If you call the police, write down the officers' names and badge numbers, and ask for a copy of the incident report.

DATE/ TIME	INCIDENT	OFFICER/ BADGE #	WITNESSES

Medical Treatment

If you or the children require medical care as a result of abuse, keep a record of the incident and the treatment you received. If you feel safe doing it, tell the doctor or nurse exactly how you or your child were injured, and ask that they officially record your injuries as the result of an assault.

DATE/ TIME	INCIDENT/INJURIES	DOCTOR/ HOSPITAL

One reminder: if you keep a record of your partner's abusive behavior, keep in mind that in a few states a mother can be prosecuted if she fails to report her husband's abuse of a child. Whether you have left your partner or are still with him, if child abuse is occurring in your family, we urge you to talk to an attorney right away.

WHAT IF YOU ARE NEGLECTING OR ABUSING YOUR CHILDREN?

Lenore Walker found that 28 percent of the 400 abused women she interviewed also abused their children. A number of the women reported that they abused their children less or not at all once they were safe from abuse themselves. Walker concluded: "Our mothers were eight times more likely to hurt their children while they were being battered than when they were safe from violence."[14] It would seem that women who are dominated by a controller may try to dominate their children in similar ways.

Many women say that the way they treat their children reflects the strain of living with a controlling partner.

▪ MARTHA

My husband was always exploding at me, and I had to keep my anger in or else he got worse. So the children were the closest thing to take my feelings out on. I never hit them. I would just pick, pick, pick, nag, nag, nag. I had no patience with them. I would say, "Go to your room and play. Get out of my sight. Leave me alone." I was never like that before.

Allyce says she was so preoccupied with worry that she started "throwing together meals for the kids and sticking them in front of the TV." She says, "I just didn't have anything left inside me." Eventually, when the children wanted more attention from her, she says, "I started hitting them to get them to leave me alone."

If Walker is correct (and most experts believe she is), then leaving a controlling husband might be the best way for Martha and Allyce to help themselves and their children. For other women who have always belittled or neglected their children, punished them severely, or hit them, or used them as a weapon against their partner, the solution isn't so clear. In any event, every woman *chooses* the way she treats her children (just as her partner *chooses* the way he treats her), and she must take responsibility for it.

▪ ALLYCE

When I was in a shelter for battered women, they told me it was a rule that I couldn't hit my kids. One woman said to me, "Think about how you felt when your husband hit you, and then consider how your kids might feel when you do it to them." Boy, was I mad at her. Who did she think she was? I almost left. But when I started to think about it, I knew she was right and I needed help. I had never learned how to discipline them—except to hit them.

Allyce started to attend a Parents Anonymous (PA) group that met regularly in a church near the shelter. In the group, she heard other parents talk about the guilt and self-hatred they experienced when they hurt their children and the new methods of discipline they were using, often successfully. Through PA, Allyce found that she could change her behavior if she chose to and have more fun with her kids. She could forgive herself for some of her past abusive behavior, without making excuses for it. She came to understand that she was handling her children in the same ways she had been handled when she was a child. She remembered how much she had hated that treatment, and she decided that she could and would do things differently. With that, her parenting, and her sense of self-worth, improved dramatically.

The first step to end abusive behavior is to overcome your fear and denial. The second is to build a support system that helps you face the problem in constructive ways. There are various places to start, depending on your needs and resources.

1. Parents Anonymous is a self-help group, with chapters around the country holding regularly scheduled meetings. The group focuses on helping you stop behavior that damages your relationship with your children.

2. Crisis Nursery and Respite Care Programs are places where you can leave your young children for a few hours or days when you feel overwhelmed. In some places a trained nurse or other professional may come to your home and relieve you from the pressures of child care for a few hours. Although not every community has such services, if yours does, we recommend using them. Many mothers find them invaluable. You can call the Visiting Nurses Association or Public Health Department for more information.

3. Early Childhood and Family Education Programs provide information about what to expect from children at each stage of their development and how to respond appropriately. You might find such programs in a public school, hospital, or college in your community.

4. Programs for abused women in many parts of the country have children's and women's advocates on staff. They have helped many women who abuse their children to find assistance. Some shelters offer parenting groups as well.

5. Crisis hotlines, public health nurses, and school social workers also should be able to provide you with information about the services in your local area.

When you seek help, remember that if you talk about any action that fits your state's legal definition of child abuse, neglect, or emotional maltreatment, the professionals you're talking to (including the staff of the organizations listed above) are legally bound to report it to child protective services. You may want to telephone the agency or organization first, without giving your name, to make sure you understand what might happen if you pay them a visit and ask them to intervene. You may be very frightened of losing your children, but if you are motivated and make use of the services listed above, child protection agencies are more likely to view your case favorably.

But there are exceptions. For example, suppose that as you separate from your partner, you reveal to a hospital social worker that the two of you harmed a child. The hospital will either report the abuse to the authorities or ask you to report it. If you take the opportunity to report the abuse yourself, the authorities are more likely to see you as a responsible and cooperative person. Then the child protective agency will design a service plan for you, probably requiring you to attend a parenting group. If you do well in the group and in your relationships with your children, the agency may close your case.

If you reunite with a violent partner, however, the authorities are likely to reenter the picture. They may even intervene to place your child in foster care. In spite of your efforts and because of your partner's abuse, the child protective agency may decide that your child is at too great a risk to remain with you. If you face this dilemma, we urge you to find good support so that you can decide what is best for you and your child.

Some women who are not able to get help to protect their children from an abusive husband decide to "disappear" with their children. Disappearing is risky and difficult, and it means that the mother and children will give up a lot: family, friends, job, schools, familiar surroundings. If a woman flees in defiance of a court order—such as an order giving her husband custody or visitation rights—she risks heavy penalties. If she is caught she may be fined or put in jail, and she may permanently lose custody of the child.

If you consider disappearing, we urge you to see a good lawyer first to make sure you fully understand the possible consequences and how to protect yourself. It's a good idea to talk things over with more than one advocate, too, to explore any other options that might not have occurred to you.

WHEN PROTECTING A CHILD BACKFIRES

Women in abusive relationships sometimes find themselves in a terrible bind with their kids.

▪ LAUREN

> I was harder on the children than I needed to be because if they misbehaved in the slightest, Keith would get furious at them. So I was always shushing them up. Or Keith would make ridiculous demands on them, like telling them to clean up their rooms and be in bed by 6:30. I had to go along with it. The kids were furious at me. I knew it was wrong, but it only got worse for them and me if I objected.

Yolanda says that she would side with her husband in his arguments with the children, even though she almost never thought he was right. "If I agreed with him," she says, "I got to choose the punishments, and I would make them small—much smaller than he would." When her husband's abuse escalated, Yolanda's way of taking care of her children was to send them to a sister who lived hundreds of miles away. There, Yolanda's children started misbehaving and running away, and only later could they tell her why.

▪ YOLANDA

> They thought they were being punished—again—by being sent away. Here I was trying to protect them, and they thought I'd sent them away because I didn't care about them. It broke my

heart. I could see how I'd even got out of the habit of talking to them. I just assumed they must know how much I love them, but I'd been siding with my husband for so long that—well, how could they know?

A lot of women tell stories like Yolanda's. Renee says that she stayed with her upper-middle-class husband at the urging of her son's psychiatrist. In that way, the psychiatrist told her, Brian could be protected by his mother and continue to go to the good schools his father was paying for. When his father broke Brian's arm and the child abuse investigator suggested that Renee was "failing to protect her son by staying with a violent man," Renee realized that Brian's safety was far more important than his school. She turned to her parents and her sister for help in getting away and starting over with her son.

In our society mothers are almost always held accountable for everything that happens to their children, whether they actually have any control over it or not, while fathers (especially abusive ones) are seldom called to account. The result of this injustice is that many women are placed in impossible situations. Doris told us that after she separated from her husband, he kidnapped the children at gunpoint and threatened to kill them if she did not return to their rural farmhouse. She went back home. Three weeks later, her husband allowed her to replace the phone he had ripped out of the wall. When he became violent again, Doris called the police, who then phoned for a child protective worker. You might expect the police to arrest Doris's husband for his violence and his use of dangerous weapons, but they didn't. After the police left, the child protective worker turned to Doris and asked accusingly, "Why did you wait so long to phone us? Your kids could have died, you know."

Today, in some parts of the country, Doris and her children would be helped to find safety and her husband arrested. In other places, however, abusive men still get away with violent behavior. Until the law is enforced more consistently, and family violence treated as the crime it is, women like Doris will continue to face this difficult dilemma. They must protect their children from harm even when they are denied the resources and the legal means to do so.

But for many women, help is available. And when it comes to

helping your children, remember that you yourself have the ability to help them a great deal merely by listening to them, validating their feelings, and talking with them. You also have some ability to protect them from your partner by facing up to your situation, seeking help, and taking action to change it. And if you have mistreated your children yourself, you can choose instead to treat them with love and respect. That power, at least, you have in your own hands.

12

■

Finding Help for Your Alcohol and Drug Problems

Many, many women survive life with a controller without turning to alcohol and drugs. We certainly hope you're one of them—and if you are, you can skip this chapter. But there is no doubt in our minds, after our extensive interviews over many years, that women who live with controlling partners, and particularly with partners who use force, may be especially vulnerable to the pull of alcohol and drugs.

If you're having a problem with these substances—or if you consider them your "friends"—this chapter is for you. Whether you are still in a relationship with a controlling partner, trying to leave your partner, or trying to start over on your own, if you have a problem with alcohol or drugs, your first task is to get sober and "clean" (drug-free).

First, you should know that you're not alone. It's estimated that between two and four million American women are addicted to *legal* drugs.[1] Doctors in the United States write more than 200 million prescriptions for mood-altering drugs every year, two-thirds of them to women[2]—often women who seek help for the emotional and/or physical abuse their controlling partners inflict. In addition, at least three million American women are alcoholics today, and the number is growing. A number of women alcoholics report that they started drinking either at the insistence of a controlling partner or to ease the strain of living with him. Many other women, under the pressure of living with a controlling partner, turn for relief to illegal drugs.

Alcohol and drugs seem to offer survival. Rather than face the full force of a verbal or physical attack, many women drink before their partners come home. And after a blowup, they numb their feelings again with pills. Some say that their partners won't let them get medical treatment for illnesses or for injuries the partners inflict, so they medicate themselves with alcohol. Some say that alcohol and drugs ease the depression and dull the shame they feel living with a controlling partner. Some say they drink to blunt their anger. "If I hadn't been drunk," Ruth says, "I probably would have killed him."

The problems of women in controlling relationships may be intensified if they grew up in families made dysfunctional by drugs or alcohol, as millions of Americans do. Addiction disrupts the household and affects every member of the family, no matter which one is the active addict. (Most often it's the father.) Children brought up in such families often carry with them into adulthood an immense burden of shame, confusion, and insecurity. To function in the world, they may take on the family's powerful habit of denial. Like their parents, they deal with problems by pretending the problems don't exist.

Obviously, a habit of denial is dangerous for a woman involved with an abusive partner. The longer she denies what her partner does, the harder it becomes to change the relationship or to leave it. (In Chapter 2 we mentioned that women often respond to abuse by disbelieving or minimizing it.) And if she becomes addicted to alcohol or drugs herself, her old habit of denial will make it hard for her to seek help or to accept it if it's offered. In the short run, denial may help a woman feel that she can cope with things, but in the long run, it traps her because it prevents change.

Some women are already in trouble with alcohol or drugs when they enter a relationship, but many start using them to calm down a hostile partner. Often they feel guilty about what they've done, while their partner's hostile moods increase. Some manage to escape from their partner, but others grow more dependent on the booze and drugs he provides. Trapped by drugs and threats, some women are too scared to make a move until they hit bottom. Some lose their children. Some get too sick to function. Some die of alcoholism, overdose, or accidents that happen when they're high. And many, we're happy to say, find the right help.

Most women caught in the double bind of abuse and addiction face a set of no-win choices. As a result of living in a controlling relationship, women feel scared and trapped. Their sense of self-worth plummets. At first, alcohol, pills, marijuana, or crack/cocaine eases the pain. But as time goes on, abuse, violence, blackouts, and chemicals combine to make them shakier, more confused, and less sure of themselves. They lose whatever good judgment and confidence they once had. "I should have known I was in trouble," Sherry says, "when I told myself that my boyfriend—violent as he was—and my drugs were keeping me together, making life normal." Only now, after two years in treatment and recovery programs, can Sherry see things more clearly. "Drugs totally clouded my thinking," she says. "I had to learn to think straight again."

WHAT IS ADDICTION?

There are many different definitions of addiction, or chemical dependency. The First Step of Alcoholics Anonymous suggests the simplest definition: "We admitted we were powerless over alcohol—that our lives had become unmanageable." Vernon Johnson, an authority on substance abuse, defines chemical dependency in a similar way. He writes, "If the use of alcohol or other drugs is causing any continuing disruption in an individual's personal, social, spiritual, or economic life and the individual *does not stop using,* he or she is chemically dependent."[3]

Addicts come from all walks of life. And they use whatever is available to them, legally or illegally. In this chapter we'll focus on the substances most frequently used by women we talked to, namely: alcohol, tranquilizers, sedatives, marijuana, and crack/cocaine. Other women in similar circumstances may turn to other drugs in widespread use—anything from over-the-counter diet pills and antidepressants to heroin. Many addicts regularly use two or more substances.

Eventually, many of the women we interviewed went into detox programs or joined Alcoholics Anonymous, Narcotics Anonymous, Women in Sobriety, or other self-help groups that aided their recovery. Some women turned first to clergy, doctors, or therapists who in turn referred the women to such programs. Most women in recovery say that the hardest step is the first: breaking through denial, facing the problem, and reaching out for help. That's what we'd like to help you do here.

ARLENE'S STORY: ALCOHOL, TRANQUILIZERS, AND SEDATIVES

For the first eleven years of her marriage to a corporate executive, Arlene never touched alcohol. She says, "I knew only too well what it did to my husband. He got violent whenever he went near the stuff." In fact, Doug was extremely abusive to Arlene. Many times he punched her, choked her, and raped her, and three or four times he threw her down the stairs. Two of her four children were conceived during sexual attacks. Doug often hit the children, too.

Although a few family members and outsiders knew about Doug's violence, no one offered Arlene a way out. "This was twenty years ago," she says, "when everybody acted as if the problem would go away if they closed their eyes, and there was no such thing as a shelter." In her own way, Arlene kept trying to get help. Many times she sent her youngest child to school dressed so his bruises showed, in hopes that teachers would notice, report the abuse, and offer help, but no one ever did. She confided in the family doctor, too. She says, "I thought I was going crazy so I went to the doctor. I told him that Doug attacked me and that I couldn't sleep at night. I would toss and turn and want to cry but I couldn't. The doctor gave me sleeping pills." Over the next several years, Arlene went back to the doctor many times and told him that she was getting more nervous as Doug grew more violent. The doctor gave her more pills: stronger sedatives and increasingly powerful tranquilizers.

"I felt trapped," Arlene says. "My parents were dead. I had four kids and no money. Doug told me I'd never get a cent from him. So what was I to do?" One morning she filled a glass with bourbon.

I started to sip, and my stomach stopped jumping around. That sick feeling went away. I drank all day long, and nothing seemed to matter anymore. At night I fell asleep—actually I passed out, but I called it "sleep." Anyway, it didn't hurt as much when Doug yelled at me or hit me because I would be anesthetized. I started to get a little bit of courage—from the alcohol. I wasn't afraid. That was the main thing: I wasn't afraid of Doug anymore.

But even then Arlene knew that alcohol was a mixed blessing.

There was no time during the day when I felt safe without it. So I had to drink more and more. Eventually I had trouble functioning. And then I started to worry, "What are people going to think of me?" I knew they'd say, "She's a drunk who neglects her kids. Doug really has a reason to hit her. She deserves what she gets." I felt I had no credibility left. I was caught in a catch-22. I drank to cope with Doug, but because I drank, nobody wanted anything to do with me. That's when I tried to kill myself.

Arlene was hospitalized, and then sent home to Doug. She tried again to kill herself, and again she was hospitalized, and then sent home to Doug. Arlene tried for a third time to take her life. This time, at the hospital, she met a sympathetic, experienced counselor who persuaded her to join an in-patient alcohol treatment program. She began her recovery in that program, and with the ongoing support of Alcoholics Anonymous, she found the sober courage to leave Doug.

But Arlene's problems were far from over. Because of her alcoholism and suicide attempts, Doug was awarded custody of the children. She says, "While I went through the court battle trying to get my kids back from Doug, I relapsed several times." The first time was the morning after Doug showed up at her apartment door, threatening to kill her and then the children. Badly shaken, Arlene called her attorney and went to court with him to get a restraining order. The attorney saw how upset she was as they waited for her turn to see the judge, and he gave her a tranquilizer. At lunch he bought her a drink and gave her a second tranquilizer. "Of course, it was a disaster," Arlene says. "We went into court after lunch, and my wealthy, well-dressed, alcoholic husband looked like a prince—

and I couldn't get a sentence out of my mouth. Not only did I not get my restraining order but I had to fight for years to win the right even to see my kids. They said I was an unfit mother. Doug laughed at me through it all."

Five years later—poor, recovering from her addiction, and rebuilding relationships with her children, who continued to live with their father—Arlene got a job as a counselor in a women's drug treatment program. "I know what it means to hit bottom," she says. "I even lived on the streets for a while. So I have a lot to give others." Today Arlene is very clear about the advice she offers to women who live with controlling men.

> First, I tell them, "You might die—physically or spiritually—staying there." Secondly, I tell them, "You might lose your kids forever." And third, I tell them, "The relationship is not worth the pain." I really badger them. "Do yourself and your kids a favor," I say. "Find help and leave before you get as sick as I was."

ASSESSING YOUR ALCOHOL AND DRUG USE

Today's women begin drinking early. Three out of four high school girls and eight out of ten college women use alcohol. Experts believe that one-third of all these young women may develop a problem with drinking.[4] And after they develop drinking problems, women develop alcohol-related disabilities (such as liver disorders, high blood pressure, malnutrition, and memory loss) more quickly than their male counterparts do.[5] And, to make a bad picture worse, female alcoholics are frequently addicted to at least one other drug—sedatives, barbiturates, painkillers, diet pills, tranquilizers, speed, crack, heroin—which, in combination with alcohol, can be deadly.

How do you know if you have an alcohol or drug problem? Later in this chapter we'll give you a quick test to help you decide. But for now, consider the following summary of the stages of alcohol addiction, drawn up by Katherine Ketcham and Ginny Lyford Gustafson in their book *Living on the Edge.* Do any of these signs sound familiar to you? If so, be fearlessly honest with yourself, and check them off.

Early-Stage Signs of Alcohol Addiction

_____ Social events without alcohol are a disappointment, a waste of your time. Drinking is the most important reason to have a party. You seem to enjoy drinking more than most people do—unless, of course, you've chosen your friends among a hard-drinking, alcoholic crowd.

_____ You drink more than you used to, and more often. You gulp drinks, make stronger drinks, and find more occasions and reasons for drinking.

_____ You may have hangovers or tremors, and sometimes you may feel sorry or guilty about your drinking, or about things you've done while you were drinking.

Middle-Stage Signs of Alcohol Addiction

_____ Symptoms may appear in your behavior. You rationalize and deny your alcohol use. You make promises to yourself or others that you'll quit or cut down, and you break the promises. You decide to limit your drinks, and then you drink more than you intended. You limit yourself to beer or wine instead of "real" alcohol. You hide bottles. You steal alcohol.

_____ You may have psychological symptoms, such as moodiness, irritability, depression, nervousness, anxiety, guilt, despair, self-pity, loss of self-respect, and resentment when other people criticize your behavior.

_____ You may have physical symptoms as well, such as increased tolerance for alcohol, blackouts, tremors, high blood pressure, ulcers, gastritis, nausea, and diarrhea.

Late-Stage Signs of Alcohol Addiction

_____ You feel intense cravings for alcohol, even though your drinking may be leading to the loss of friends, job, family—everything important in your life.

_____ You try to quit, but you feel that you have to drink to control your withdrawal symptoms. You find that your body can no longer tolerate the large amounts of alcohol you seem to need to manage withdrawal.

_____ You may drink in the morning, binge, lose interest in hygiene, fall down stairs, or have other kinds of accidents.

_____ You may require frequent hospitalizations for medical care.

_____ You may have intense and unreasonable fears, and thoughts of suicide.

_____ You may go through life-threatening withdrawal symptoms like convulsions and delirium tremens, or "the shakes."[6]

TRANQUILIZERS, SEDATIVES, AND BARBITURATES

Each year Americans consume over five billion medically approved doses of Valium and Valium-like tranquilizers known by a variety of names, such as: Ativan, Centrax, Dalmane, Halcion, Librium, Paxipam, Restoril, Serax, Sereen, Tranxene, Verstran, and Xanax. Many of these drugs are also sold on the street. Of the 1.5 million Americans hooked on these "downers," most are women. Most of them believe that the "tranqs" are nonaddictive. Doctors prescribe them to relieve symptoms of anxiety, tension, depression, and insomnia, but the drugs can produce the very problems they're supposed to remedy. Very often, when women take tranquilizers and suffer these troubling effects, they think they haven't taken enough medication. So they take more.[7] Or, they have a drink along with their pills and begin a dangerous and potentially fatal habit.

Many experts who've studied the effects of tranquilizers now believe that they _are_ addictive. In their book _Women and Drugs,_ for example, Emanuel Peluso and Lucy Silvay Peluso point out that after a woman stops taking tranquilizers, she may suffer severe withdrawal symptoms: pain, headaches, muscle tremors, anxiety, nausea, depression, convulsions, and memory loss. Withdrawal from tranquilizers, they advise, requires expert medical help and guidance.[8]

Doctors also often prescribe barbiturates and barbiturate-like compounds ("downers") to relieve anxiety. They're sold under names such as Luminal, Seconal, Tuinal, Placidyl, and Doriden. They're highly addictive. So, too, are sedative and hypnotic drugs, such as Quaalude, or "ludes." At first, barbiturates and sedatives create effects much like those of alcohol. They numb pain and produce a mellow feeling. But the user quickly builds up a tolerance and feels the need to take more and more. And that's dangerous. With barbiturates, the line between a "safe" dose and a fatal one is thin and unpredictable. Barbiturates are one of the most frequently cited causes of death in women's suicides, and it's often hard to tell whether a death is a suicide or an accident.[9]

Experts agree that women should never take barbiturates, sedatives, or tranquilizers for long periods of time or in doses larger than prescribed.[10] In fact, because doctors prescribe these drugs to women much too freely, many women's health advocates suggest that women shouldn't take them at all, even under prescription. If you're already taking them, you'll probably go through some severe withdrawal symptoms when you quit, such as agitation, itching and "crawling" skin, general discomfort, headaches, stomachaches, sleeplessness, and jitters. You should have medical care to help you through.

The experts also point out that alcohol, painkillers, sedatives, and tranquilizers all produce similar effects on the central nervous system. Thus, taking one of these drugs gives you a head start on the next. For example, an alcoholic who starts to take tranquilizers can develop a tolerance to the tranquilizers very fast, because her central nervous system has already been affected by alcohol. (To "develop a tolerance" means that your body gets used to the drug, and you have to take more pills more often to get the effect you want.) The woman who combines alcohol and one or more other drugs in this way will have to go through a particularly intense and unpredictable withdrawal that may include seizures and hallucinations. She will need medical help.[11]

MERYL'S STORY: PAINKILLERS

As a young teenager, Meryl experimented with drinking and smoking dope. She says, "I just liked to change the way I felt. Home was a pretty sad and depressing place." At nineteen, when she met and married Paul, Meryl thought her luck had changed. "He was exciting," she says. "He was a bit wild—but he had a good job. And we had great times together." But after they married, Paul began to get angry a lot. It seemed to Meryl that he was constantly blowing up over little things. He would scare her periodically by disappearing for hours or driving at dangerously high speeds.

One night, as they headed home from a friend's house, Paul started an argument with Meryl. The louder it got, the faster he drove. Meryl asked him to slow down, but he laughed and stepped on the gas. He lost control of the car, and it crashed into a tree. Paul wasn't hurt, but Meryl had to be hospitalized for observation and treatment for severe back pains. While she was in the hospital, Paul visited her only once. He said he had to go out of town on business. "That's when I found Demerol," Meryl says, "and the empty feeling inside disappeared."

Over the next few years, Meryl went from one doctor to another with her back complaints, asking for more painkillers. One doctor would prescribe Percocet, another codeine, and yet, in Meryl's eyes, no doctor did enough for her. She says, "I'd tell myself that none of them fully appreciated the pain I was in." Every time she changed doctors, Meryl held on to the pills she already had, and added more. "One part of me knew I was in trouble because I started to take pills to get through the work day," she says. "But for a long time I rationalized by saying, 'I'm in pain and taking a prescription the doctor gave me.'"

Paul's behavior only added to Meryl's troubles. He drank more and more, and he became more abusive. Several times he managed to injure Meryl's back again. She says, "I went to a chiropractor for my back, and after every visit, Paul would give me what he called a 'love pat' right across my shoulder. He would swat me hard, but not hard enough so you could say he was really hitting me. I couldn't tell my chiropractor, and she couldn't figure out why I didn't get better." Depressed, Meryl spent more and more of her time looking for drugs, and she took whatever she could find.

A nurse in a pain clinic was the first person to talk to Meryl about her drug addiction and her marriage. "I was miserable and ready to die," Meryl says, "but when that nurse first tried to take my drug history and tell me I had a problem, I was furious." Only after Meryl was diagnosed with a liver disease did she begin to listen to the nurse. Then she checked herself into a detox program at the hospital.

"I had to start from scratch," Meryl says. "Detox was so hard— physically and spiritually—but there were a lot of people to help me. I was forced to look at why I was so unhappy and what was happening in my marriage." After she successfully completed her in-patient treatment program, Meryl joined Narcotics Anonymous and a support group for abused women. She knew she had to stay away from Paul for her recovery to work. "This struggle was a hard one, too," she says, "and I needed a lot of support to do it. But I did."

Painkillers

In their research in a pain clinic, Dr. Joel Haber and his colleagues found that 50 percent of their female patients had a history of physical abuse, but only 20 percent had ever been asked about the violence in their lives by the doctors and nurses taking down the history of their ailments. Haber believes that these patients turned to painkillers to cope with the stress of ongoing or past abuse, but the professionals handing out the pills often failed to see the connections between abuse and pain—and painkillers.[12]

The most common painkillers are narcotics: Demerol, methadone, codeine, morphine, and heroin. In small doses, they produce pleasure, and at the same time, they dull pain, fear, and anxiety. They bring on sleep and create apathy. Larger doses can produce nausea, vomiting, breathing difficulties, convulsions, coma, and death. With these drugs, addiction comes fast and hard. An alcoholic may drink for years before she shows any withdrawal symptoms when she goes without a drink, but a narcotics user will show symptoms of withdrawal only a few weeks or months after she becomes addicted. And many narcotics addicts die. Heroin addicts, for example, between the ages of twenty-five and forty-four die at a rate ten times greater than that of the general population.[13] And these days, they die not just from heroin but from dirty needles, too. An addict needs medical help to detoxify—and the sooner the better.

DONNA'S STORY: MARIJUANA AND COCAINE

Donna began to smoke marijuana as a way of keeping the peace with a controlling partner. "He liked to smoke socially," she says, "and if I passed, he'd say I was trying to embarrass him in front of his friends. He said I wasn't any fun. When I smoked with him, he was nicer to me."

Often Donna and Gordie went out on Saturday nights to drink beer and smoke dope with Gordie's friends and their wives. Occasionally, one of the men would bring out some cocaine, and they'd all get high. "It was no big deal," Donna says. "Just every once in a while somebody would drop fifty bucks for some coke and we'd all do a little, just for fun. I could take it or leave it, but Gordie decided to make coke his thing."

At first, when Gordie began to buy coke and smoke it at home, Donna did it too, and she enjoyed it. But Gordie began to use more coke more often, and he became harder to live with. "He'd always been bossy," Donna says, "but when he smoked, he thought he was king. He started giving orders and literally pushing me around, and when I complained about his spending all our money on coke, he started telling me how boring I was, and how stupid." Donna and Gordie fought more and more. Gordie started going off for days at a time with other women who were, as he told Donna, "more fun." He kept the coke for himself. Donna told us, "I was real mad and real hurt, but when he went off was when I found out how much I missed the coke."

For the first time, Donna went looking for cocaine, and she knew where to find it—among Gordie's friends drinking beer in the clubs. She had no money to buy cocaine, so she took up with Gordie's supplier, a man called Curtis. He often hit her, but she kept going back to him because he was generous with cocaine. One night, when she couldn't find Curtis, she went home with one of his friends.

Everybody got to know me as a woman who would sleep around in exchange for coke. I told myself that these men were my good friends—sex was just another way of showing my friendship. But in fact I was a coke whore. A lot of men really got into doing the most sexually degrading things, but I kept going back. The tricks and the coke got all mixed up in my mind. Curtis told me that I was a true masochist. He said I had a deep craving for sexual abuse and pain, and I believed him. He said I'd *chosen* this exciting life, and I thought he was right. But of course it was the drug I was craving. I couldn't "choose" anything. I was a total addict.

Donna spent her time looking for drugs, turning tricks, doing drugs, and patching up the injuries she got at the hands of her husband and other violent men. She lost interest in her two young daughters and no longer had time to care for them. She dropped them off at her mother's house—and didn't pick them up.

One day Donna couldn't make a connection for cocaine. She kept drinking beer and taking diet pills (as she had been doing all along) but she couldn't stop crying. When she had been twenty hours without cocaine, she fell from the second-story balcony of a club and broke her leg. In the hospital, doctors recognized her withdrawal symptoms and put her into a detoxification program. When she was released, she joined Narcotics Anonymous and went to live with her mother and her children. Three years later, she is still there.

I keep up my recovery program religiously. But addiction is so evil and so sneaky. I still need my mother's support. The thing that still scares me the most is how fast it all happened. In less than two months, I was totally hooked. In less than two years, I not only lost everything, including my girls, but I thought I was giving it all up voluntarily so I could live a better, more exciting life. That idea died fast too, and then the whole last year was like being in hell. Everything I did, I did for cocaine. I've been clean for more than three years now, but it's going to take me a long time to feel good about myself and safe again.

Marijuana

Many marijuana users cling to the notion that it is harmless and nonaddictive, but experts disagree. Most researchers now consider marijuana psychologically addictive, and in heavy users it produces physical addiction as well. Heavy users feel a constant urge to use the drug, and they can't cut down or give it up. Chronic marijuana smokers need the drug to get by.[14]

Katherine Ketcham and Ginny Lyford Gustafson describe three kinds of symptoms of marijuana addiction:

1. **Psychological symptoms:** The user gets depressed and feels inadequate. She may be disoriented and fearful and have hallucinations. She may get irritable and have mood swings and suicidal thoughts.

2. **Behavioral symptoms:** The user promises to cut down or quit, but she doesn't. She may be aggressive and "hyper." Or she may lose interest in things, including personal hygiene, and become passive and isolated. She may think of suicide or attempt it. She may lie, and she'll almost certainly deny that dope is having any bad effects on her life.

3. **Physical symptoms:** She may have headaches and feel fatigued. She may not be able to concentrate or remember things or do anything very complicated. And her sense of time may get very distorted.[15]

Cocaine

Cocaine belongs to a class of drugs known as stimulants, or "uppers." It creates a feeling of limitless energy and power—at least while the high lasts. But it doesn't last long. When cocaine is snorted, the user gets a high that is followed, about half an hour later, by a letdown. When cocaine is injected, the crash comes more quickly; and when cocaine is smoked as freebase or crack, the good feelings disappear in a few minutes.[16] Consequently, cocaine addicts find themselves using it more and more often, just to feel "normal" or to hold off the fatigue and depression that always set in after its use.[17] Or else they dull the pain of cocaine withdrawal with other drugs—such as alcohol, tranquilizers, and marijuana.

Addiction to crack (the smokeable form of cocaine) can occur within weeks and produce an overwhelming need for the drug. It's also associated with sudden heart attacks, seizures, strokes, and malnutrition. Like Donna, cocaine addicts may seem very eager for sex, but in fact they're interested only in the drug. The sex drive actually diminishes. Chronic cocaine users may also undergo mood swings and personality changes. Most often, addicts become short-tempered, suspicious, confused, anxious, paranoid, and potentially dangerous. Those who share needles to inject cocaine risk hepatitis and AIDS, and a pregnant woman may pass these diseases and her drug addiction to her unborn child.[18]

DO YOU DESERVE TO BE HIT BECAUSE YOU USE ALCOHOL OR DRUGS?

Even if she isn't addicted, a woman who uses alcohol or drugs is at a disadvantage in a relationship with a controlling partner. Remember that he's always ready to blame her for whatever goes wrong in his life. Her use of alcohol or drugs gives him a perfect excuse. In the first place, her alcohol or drug use probably does disrupt family life, and she may feel guilty. So when he blames family problems (or even his own problems) on her alcohol or drug use, she may accept the blame. Edith says, "We went to marriage counseling, and I was so brainwashed that I told the counselor exactly what my husband was always telling me: that he would never hit me if *I* didn't drink. I really believed that alcohol was making me so irritable that I provoked Larry to hit me." Although alcohol made Edith irritable and snappish, it did not *make* Larry assault her. In fact, Edith says, "Larry abused me for years—long before I drank. Besides, I couldn't even make him carry out the trash. How could I *make* him hit me?"

Like Edith, Delores found her partner's excuses for his violence confusing. She refused to believe it was her fault that Phil hit her, but when he accused her of "neglecting the kids" because of her drug problem, she agreed with him. Delores says, "For a long time I thought I deserved what I got." Her ideas changed when she found out that Phil had assaulted his previous girlfriend, who never touched drugs or alcohol. Delores says, "I realized that no matter what I did—or whatever anyone did—he would find a reason to hurt a woman and blame her for it."

Most women are taught to solve problems, mend differences, keep their families together, be responsible—for everything—and above all, maintain self-control. All women are expected to be good mothers, whether they've been taught how to parent or not. If women "fail" by losing control of their lives to drugs and alcohol, they're often labeled "bad wives" or "bad mothers" and rejected by family, friends, and helping agencies alike. Controlling partners use this evaluation to their own advantage. They say things like, "You can't do anything right. You can't even take care of your own kids." What's left of a woman's pride may crumble under attacks like this. Ashamed, she may try harder to hide her substance abuse problem. Hemmed in by violence and chemical dependency, she will isolate herself more and more, and fall more firmly under the control of an abusive partner.

Only now, as more women courageously come forward to seek treatment, are some substance abuse programs learning to respond to the client who is fleeing two problems: addiction *and* abuse. As a counselor in one of these programs told us, "We say over and over again to women, 'You were living in an impossible situation, and you did the best you could to survive in the circumstances. It's time to forgive yourself and move on. No one had the right to abuse you *no matter what you did.*' "

Assessing Your Alcohol and Drug Use

The following questions will help you evaluate your own use of alcohol and drugs. Answer yes or no.

_____ Do you make promises to yourself or to others about cutting down on your use of alcohol or drugs?

_____ Do you have trouble keeping those promises?

_____ Do you feel guilty about your drinking or drug use?

_____ Do you ever feel bad about what you did while you were drunk or high?

_____ Have you lost time from school or work or missed appointments or social engagements because you were using drugs or alcohol?

_____ Do you need more and more to get drunk or high?

_____ Do you eat or sleep poorly when you are drinking or using drugs?

_____ Do you use alcohol or drugs to help you get to sleep, or to wake up and "get going"?

_____ Have family members or friends ever objected to your drug or alcohol use?

_____ Do you feel annoyed when family members or friends mention your alcohol or drug use?

_____ Do you crave or "need" alcohol or drugs?

_____ Do you often think about your next drink or drug?

_____ Do you try to hide your alcohol and drug use—or at least part of it—from family members and friends?

_____ Have you ever suffered a partial or complete loss of memory while using drugs or alcohol?

_____ Are you worried about your drug or alcohol use?

_____ Do you drink or use drugs to build up your confidence or to numb pain?

_____ Are you more alone than you were before?

_____ Do most of the people you like to spend time with use drugs or alcohol just as much as you do?

_____ Do you dread spending time with people in situations where you may not be able to use alcohol or drugs?

_____ Before going to an important meeting or social gathering, do you sometimes fortify yourself with a drink or drug?[19]

If you answered yes to several questions, you would be wise to look for help now.

WHAT TO DO IF YOU SUSPECT YOU HAVE A PROBLEM WITH ALCOHOL OR DRUGS

If you answered yes to several questions, you may be thinking: "I don't have a problem." "I certainly don't need *treatment*!" "I know what I'm doing." "Why are they making a big deal out of nothing?" or, "I can handle myself." Do we seem too concerned about a little harmless pleasure? Do other people sometimes get after you about your little highs? Are you convinced that everyone else is wrong? If so, it may be time to face the fact that all substance abusers think the same thing. All the alcoholics and drug addicts in the world began by thinking they could control what they were doing, and many died of their addictions, still saying the same thing.

You may very well have other problems right now that seem

bigger or more important than your alcohol or drug use. Living with a controlling partner is an enormous problem in itself, especially if he is violent or potentially violent. And having a controlling partner is bound to worsen any other problems you may have, like money worries, or tension at work, or difficulties with your children. If that's your situation, alcohol and drugs may not seem to be problems at all. Like Edith, you may believe that a bottle of booze or tranquilizers is your best friend: the only thing that gets you through.

That reasoning makes a certain kind of sense, but it's backwards. Even though alcohol and drugs may seem helpful, they actually stand in the way of solving other problems. Especially when they seem like "friends," they offer you only temporary escape—like little naps in the middle of real life, only far more dangerous. In fact, they prevent you from taking action, or even thinking clearly. And they can sink you in trouble deeper than you can imagine. So whatever other problems you may have, it makes good sense to deal with your alcohol and drug use *first*.

If you're unsure whether you're getting into trouble with alcohol or drugs, people with professional training and experience can help you answer the question. Your first step is to find the right helpers. Many cities and towns have a community drug and alcohol treatment center that will set up an evaluation appointment for you. You'll probably find it listed along with the names of other licensed treatment facilities in the yellow pages of your phone book under Alcoholism Treatment. You can also telephone the National Council on Alcoholism for a list of the detoxification programs and licensed substance abuse counselors who provide alcohol and drug treatment in your area. Or telephone your local Alcoholics Anonymous (AA) or Narcotics Anonymous (NA) chapter and ask them to refer you to the nearest substance abuse center. Or you can call the National Institute on Drug Abuse Information and Treatment Referral Hotline, 1-800-662-HELP.

If your community doesn't have such a center (or if you don't like the center in your community), you can attend some open meetings of AA or NA, listen to what other people say about their addiction, and see if you identify with the feelings they express. Both AA and NA recommend that you attend many different meetings before you decide whether you are or are not an alcoholic or addict. You can call AA or NA to find out the time and place of meetings in your area. Be sure to ask specifically for "open meetings"—that is, meetings open to the general public. And keep in mind, everything that happens in AA or NA meetings is confidential. If you want to talk over what you hear in meetings, the best thing to do is ask someone from the group to have coffee with you or give you her phone number. If possible, pick someone who said things in the meeting that you liked or admired. If you're confused, don't pick someone who seems just as confused as you are. Often you'll find that there's a whole group going directly from the meeting to the nearest coffee shop, and you'll be welcome.

Some women feel uncomfortable going to a public agency or a public meeting. You may think it would be easier to talk to your doctor or minister or therapist; but we don't recommend it. Many doctors, ministers, and therapists know little about addiction. The doctor may minimize or misunderstand the problem, or worse— prescribe more medication. The minister may be moralistic and judgmental. And unless the therapist is a specialist in substance abuse counseling, she may keep you for months, or even years, vainly examining your childhood for the source of your problems. Any of them may blame you for drinking or drugging. And if they don't know much about controlling partners either, they may blame you for your partner's behavior as well. In any case, a good doctor, minister, or therapist (one who *is* well informed about addiction) will send you to a detoxification program or specialized counseling center for addiction, or to AA or NA. You might as well go directly to people who specialize in the kind of help you need.

BEGINNING RECOVERY

If you visit a community alcohol or drug abuse center, a counselor will ask you about the history and pattern of your alcohol or drug use: when you started, what you use, and when. The counselor will ask about your behavior and your general health, and perhaps about your family. After evaluating this information, the counselor will make recommendations to you about treatment.

For some people, treatment starts with detoxification, a gradual process of ridding the body of "toxic" (poisonous) substances accumulated during heavy alcohol and drug use. This process takes from two to four weeks and requires careful medical monitoring. (If you are pregnant, it's especially important to have medical supervision.) It is usually carried out in a hospital or special center, commonly referred to as a "rehab" or "detox" center. (We can already hear you saying, "What am I going to do with my kids for a month?" We'll get to that.) You may have seen movies in which an actor locks himself in a room, goes "cold turkey," and thrashes about in horribly painful and crazed withdrawal seizures. But don't let that scare you. These days detoxification is designed to cause you as little physical and mental discomfort as possible.[20]

After a hospital stay, some patients go on to residential treatment for several more weeks or months. That is, they live in a group residence with other recovering addicts and go through a program of individual and/or group therapy. Others live at home and continue individual or group therapy at the hospital, returning for sessions several times a week. Many people in the early stages of recovery find the supportive atmosphere of the residential center or hospital out-patient program very helpful.

Many women in the early stages of alcoholism or drug addiction don't need detoxification, residential treatment, or hospital out-patient treatment. After your evaluation, the substance abuse counselor may recommend that you begin individual or group counseling at the community substance abuse center, or that you join AA or NA—or that you take part in both the center program and AA/NA meetings. The counselor will help you sort out what's best for you.

Whether the counselor recommends detox, residential treatment, counseling, or AA/NA, your recovery will take time. In fact, many women choose to participate in a recovery program for the rest of their lives. Recovery is a step by step process. Its goal is to help you live a healthy, happy, and productive life—one day at a time.

YOUR SPECIAL NEEDS IN RECOVERY

Alcoholics Anonymous and most substance abuse programs were originally designed by men to help men. Over the years, they have helped many women recover, but substance abuse research, literature, and services are still based largely on male experience. That means that some parts of AA, NA, and community substance abuse programs may be inappropriate for women in general, and for abused women in particular. For example, most recovery programs try first to break down the addict's denial. Step One of AA, as we mentioned, calls for the addict to admit that her life is unmanageable. But if you have been struggling to keep your partner calm and your family together, it may be doubly hard to admit that you are not successfully "managing." Similarly, Step Four calls for the addict to make a "searching and fearless moral inventory" of her wrongs, and Steps Eight and Nine tell her to "make amends" to all the people she has "harmed." Members of AA and NA are expected to think about their "shortcomings" and their "defects of character." But if you have a controlling partner, you hear all about your shortcomings and defects all the time. These steps are helpful to most addicts because it is vitally important to recovery that they take responsibility for their own behavior; but if you are abused at home, all this talk about your shortcomings may seem like more of the same. It is rarely helpful to abused women. And unfortunately, many communities still do not have specialized services for the woman alcoholic or drug user.

In some localities, however, you can find AA and NA meetings especially for women or for lesbians. You may find the discussions in these groups more helpful and supportive. And acceptance and support are exactly what you need. As one expert on recovery told us, "An abused woman must feel comfortable and accepted and encouraged and liked in order to recover from alcoholism and drug addiction. Women who have the best chance of recovery are those who find another person or group to literally love and support them back to health as they try out new nonaddicted behavior."[21]

Incidentally, being "loved" back to health is not a prescription for a new relationship. Many women in early recovery find a distraction in a relationship with a new partner, or a series of new relationships. But substituting love affairs for alcohol or drugs prevents real change, and often leads to worse problems. Most experienced substance abuse counselors give this good advice: spend one year working on your recovery before you even think about looking for a new partner. And when you choose a sponsor to guide you in AA or NA, choose a person who is *not* a potential sex partner, either from your point of view or the sponsor's. That is, if you're a straight woman, choose another straight woman. If you're a lesbian, choose a gay man.

FINDING TREATMENT AND RECOVERY GROUPS FOR WOMEN

Where specialized treatment and counseling facilities for women alcoholics and drug users do exist, they provide invaluable service. Alison found a women's treatment program at her local hospital. The staff understood that her use of alcohol and drugs was different from her husband's, and that her needs were different. Like so many other women addicts, Alison had been unable to go to a detox program because she had to look after her children. (Rehab and detox centers, like so many other parts of substance abuse programs, were designed for men who simply leave their kids at home with their wives.) Alison says, "The women's program cared about my kids when nobody else did. They helped me get some financial help from welfare and one month's foster care for the kids, so I was able to go into the hospital for treatment."

Marcia found that, like many other women who have been abused by men, she couldn't speak freely until she joined a women's group at her community alcoholism and drug treatment center and an all-women's AA group. "I needed that kind of environment to feel safe enough to talk," she says. "When I was in detox I couldn't talk about what my husband did to me, and I'd never bring it up in a regular AA meeting. I've had enough of abusive men. But talking about it was really important to my recovery."

To find a women's treatment or recovery program where you live, call the National Council on Alcoholism, your local substance abuse program, a women's shelter, hospital, or mental health center. But keep in mind that some staff members at these agencies may still hold out-of-date and hostile attitudes toward female alcoholics and drug users. Marcia says, "I was stunned when the battered women's hotline worker I first called practically hung up on me. She told me, 'We don't serve women with drug and alcohol problems.' " More and more women's shelters, however, have special counselors in substance abuse, often women who are recovering from abuse and addiction themselves. Help is there, but you may have to search for it.

This is especially true for mothers like Alison who require in-patient care. Where does she place her children while she is in treatment, and if she temporarily relies on foster care, she wonders, will she ever get the kids back? There are no easy answers to these questions. But if you search, as Alison did, you may find a counselor or an AA or NA member who understands your problem and will help.

Sometimes, even in a women's substance abuse program, coun-selors may have little understanding of controlling partners. As a result, they may minimize the difficulty and danger you face. They may even suggest that your legitimate fear of your partner is a "paranoid" symptom of alcoholism or drug abuse, a symptom you must "let go." If this is the case, turn to a program for abused women in your community and ask for help.

Jennifer says, "My recovery from an alcohol and pill addiction began the night I went to a support group for abused women at the women's shelter. I never said a word to them about my drug habit, but there I started to understand why I drank." In retrospect, Jen-nifer believes that to survive and recover successfully, she needed to find help for two problems: her addiction and her violent mar-riage. She was lucky enough to find both. The leader of the support group for abused women referred her to the women's alcohol and drug program at her local hospital. After she completed that pro-gram, Jennifer joined AA and returned to the abused women's support group. She says, "In the support group I could talk about my pattern of alcohol use—how I drank whenever I got scared of my husband, or too near my father who had sexually abused me as a kid. There were other women in the abused women's group who were struggling to stay sober, too—so I found great support. I couldn't have done it without them."

A number of women also turn for help to Al-Anon. Al-Anon was designed many years ago as a self-help group for the partners of alcoholics, but since most of the alcoholics were men, Al-Anon became mostly an organization of women. Today, its membership is still largely female. And its members understand what it's like to live with an abusive and violent man. In most cases that's what brought them into the organization.

Some Al-Anon members, however, identify themselves as "codependent." Broadly speaking, a codependent person is someone who places the needs of another person before her/his own and tries very hard to win approval. Unfortunately, some experts suggest that codependency, like alcoholism, is a kind of disease, and that codependents bring their problems on themselves by being too dependent. We disagree; we believe that codependency is merely a description of the things people do to survive with controlling and abusive partners. As we discussed in Chapters 1 and 2, women involved with controlling partners cater to and appease their partners to keep the peace, and in many cases to save themselves from serious injury or even death. In other words, being involved with a controlling partner may prompt a woman to act "codependent"—not the other way around. Nevertheless, women coming out of relationships with controlling partners often want to rid themselves of the habit of putting the other person first, and for that purpose they may find the Al-Anon program very helpful. In any case, it's easy to see why some abused women addicts might feel more at home with the abused wives of addicts than with male addicts—and why they might get more support in Al-Anon, Adult Children of Alcoholics, or Co-dependents Anonymous than in AA or NA.

Every community is different. Search your community for the right kind of help for you. Keep in mind that you are entitled to seek help for your alcoholism or drug addiction on your own terms, with people you identify with and trust, with women who have gone through similar problems and accept you as you are and want you to be happy. And when you find help, use it. When you find a safe place, talk about your fear of your partner, if he is dangerous. Talk about your grief and anger. Talk about your children and your fears of losing custody of them. Talk about your nightmares and your dreams. Alison says, "My treatment and recovery depended on my sharing those things that most bothered me. It took me a while, but I found both a counselor and an AA sponsor who understood." And Marcia advised us: "Tell your readers that if they survived their partners, they will survive this. And they will go on to do a lot better."

13

■

For Family, Friends, and Helpers

What can I do to help?" That's the question asked again and again by the family members and friends of a woman involved with a controlling partner. Often family and close friends see her unhappiness, even before she is ready to see it herself. But for one reason or another, most of us hesitate to intervene in the personal relationships of others. And when we do offer an opinion or suggestion, we often find that it's not welcome. Professional helpers—social workers, advocates, therapists, doctors, clergy—often have the same experience. Many of us do our best only to be rejected. We're left baffled and perhaps hurt or angry, still wondering, "What *can* I do to help?"

In this chapter we'll look at some of the reasons why offering help to a woman with a controlling partner sometimes proves to be a frustrating experience. We'll offer a new perspective on the problem of intervening in her situation. And we'll suggest some ways to offer help more effectively.

Like so many other people, Tracy felt totally frustrated when she tried to talk to her sister Robin about her boyfriend. Tracy says, "I tried and tried, but I never got through to her. Or, at least that's what I thought. Then one night she called and asked if my offer still stood:

could she move in with me? I was so relieved." Robin herself says, "When Wayne started in on me that last time, listing all my many faults one more time at the top of his voice, I could just hear Tracy's voice in my head saying, 'You don't have to put up with this. You can make it on your own.' I got out of there—and stayed out—by repeating my sister's words over and over in my head."

Many women involved with controlling partners need and use the help of an outsider to leave the relationship. Yet most of those outsiders never know how much they help. Many helpers believe, as Robin's sister did, that they're not getting through. And many abused women aren't able to let helpers know that they made a difference.

The problem is the lag between the time a woman receives helpful information or support and the time she feels ready to act on it. Kerry says, "A social worker at the hospital gave me a card with my legal rights and a shelter phone number, and I carried it around for months before I was able to call." Today Kerry wishes she could thank that worried social worker. (She tried, but the woman had moved away.) Kerry says, "When I left her office that day, I told her I didn't need any help. I told her I was fine. I told her I loved my boyfriend! I'm sure she was totally frustrated. The sad thing is, she has no idea that she saved my life."

Unfortunately, this time lag leaves a false impression. How often have we heard the would-be helper's side of the story, or voiced it ourselves? "I tried to help her, but she wouldn't listen." "I told her what to do, and she told me to mind my own business." "How can you help a woman who won't help herself?" These are the voices of understandable frustration. They contribute to the widespread belief that abused women are too masochistic or too passive or too stupid to help themselves, and that what they go through must not be so bad after all.

In fact, control *is* as bad as women say. Many women and their children are seriously hurt by emotional or physical abuse. And women with controlling partners do want information, support, and help. Your first task as a helper is to believe, despite evidence to the contrary, that the help you offer, as a concerned relative, friend, neighbor, coworker, or professional, *will* make a difference.

Signs of Abuse

Do you suspect that a woman you know is being emotionally or physically abused? If you answer yes to several of the following questions, it is very likely that you are right.

_____ Do you see or hear about repeated bruises, broken bones, or other injuries, the result of "falls" or "accidents"?

_____ Does she complain about anxiety, depression, or vague fears? Does she seem frightened, withdrawn, isolated, unusually quiet, reluctant to speak?

_____ Do you feel uncomfortable when her partner is present? Does he criticize her in front of you, or make "joking" remarks that belittle her? Does he tell her what to do and not to do? Does she seem significantly different—perhaps unusually cheery or exceptionally quiet? Does he appear charming and solicitous while she is withdrawn, quiet, and tense?

_____ Is her partner so "attentive," jealous, or demanding of her time that you can never see her alone? If you leave messages for her with him, does she get the messages?

_____ Are you ever afraid of her partner?

_____ Does she refer to his bad moods, anger, temper, or short fuse? Does she refer to obnoxious things he does when he drinks? Does she hint that there is trouble or conflict at home?

_____ Does she scurry around to avoid upsetting him, or does she ask you not to discuss certain topics in his presence?

_____ Does he ignore the children or abuse them emotionally, physically, or sexually? (See pages 256–60 for signs of child abuse.) Do they seem timid, frightened, or angelic in his presence? Do the children abuse her, verbally or physically?

_____ Have there been suicide or homicide attempts or threats in this family?

_____ Is he accusing her of having affairs with other men or women? Does he try to control her every move? Must she account for her time?

_____ Is there alcohol or drug use in the family?

_____ Does she constantly defer to him? Does she speak of him as though he is a far better or more important person than she is? Does she seldom speak of activities, events, or people that are *her* interests?

_____ Is she often unwell? Is she often late or absent from work, or has she quit her job altogether? Does she break appointments at the last moment or fail to show up? Does she often have to leave work or social engagements early because her partner is expecting her?

_____ In warm weather, does she sometimes wear inappropriate clothes with long sleeves, turtlenecks, or neck scarves? Does she sometimes wear unusually heavy makeup, or at inappropriate times, hats, head scarves, or sunglasses?[1]

TRYING TO HELP: GIVE IT TIME

If you conclude that your relative, friend, neighbor or coworker probably is emotionally or physically abused, and that you want to help, keep in mind two fundamental principles. First, give yourself and the woman you care about some *time* to make changes. And second, remember that there is no single correct way to help. The important thing is that you try.

During the eighteen months Robin lived with Wayne, her sister Tracy zigzagged between sorrow and anger.

▪ TRACY

Things would get bad between them and Robin would say, "I'm leaving," and then things would get better and she would say, "Everything is fine." I thought Robin had lost her mind. She'd certainly lost her good judgment. I thought she was throwing away her life, and sometimes it made *me* feel guilty. I wondered what our family had done to make her like this. What made me mad was that I knew she was covering up for Wayne and lying to me about their relationship. I could see for myself how domineering and critical and mean he was, so I knew that in private things must be much worse, and certainly worse than she let on. I couldn't stand that. We'd always been so honest with each other.

Many would-be helpers are troubled by the same behaviors that Tracy complains of in her sister: first, that the woman can't make up her mind, and second, that she covers up for her partner. But both these behaviors are a *direct result* of living with a controlling partner. It may be helpful to you to read Part One of this book to get a better understanding of the dynamics of a relationship with a controller. That may help you to see that her apparent indecisiveness and loyalty to her partner are essential tactics she uses to survive. They don't mean that she doesn't need and value your help. In fact, just the opposite is probably true. Her indecisiveness and loyalty to her partner are additional signs—and big ones—that she probably is being emotionally and/or physically abused.

Emotionally or physically abused women often make decisions about their relationship that are difficult for outsiders to understand. Perhaps most difficult of all is a woman's apparent reluctance to leave a controlling partner. We hear the question repeatedly asked about battered women: why do they stay? Many women say, as Robin did, "I'm leaving," and then they change their minds. And many helpers say, as Tracy did, "It drives me crazy."

SEE IT HER WAY

From the perspective of the abused woman, this apparent indecisiveness makes sense. As we explained in Chapter 1, most women, abused or not, don't give up on relationships easily. Most see it as their responsibility to make relationships work.[2] And if the abusive partner blames the woman for every problem (as most controlling men do) the woman may try harder, at least for a while. All relationships, even abusive ones, presumably started well and continue to have good moments. What women seek, both by staying and by temporarily leaving, is to recapture that good relationship.

She has many other things to think about: emotional, economic, social, and religious concerns, and her own safety as well. Any of us might give a spouse a second, third, or fourth chance if we were afraid of living in poverty, depriving our children, spending eternity in Hell, or being seriously injured or killed. Nevertheless, when the relationship is bad, a woman fights back with one of the few weapons she has: the threat of her absence. She leaves. By doing so, she issues a warning to her partner: change your ways, or else. Under that threat, most men do behave better, at least temporarily. When the partner promises to reform, and the relationship improves, she may go back to try again.[5] Her tactic has been successful, for the time being. If the partner reverts to his old controlling ways, as most do, she may leave again to issue another warning.

But a woman's apparent indecisiveness may have another dimension as well. If the controlling partner is dangerous, a woman may draw *closer* to him, trying to appease him in order to survive. Many controlling men stalk, attack, rape, mutilate, and/or murder wives and girlfriends who are trying to get away. A terrorized woman may well make a reasonable decision to stay put. She may not be able to flee until she feels safe enough to try.[4] Consider all the dimensions of her decision, then, and you find that a woman may decide to stay with a controlling partner because the relationship is improving, or because it's terrible; and she may leave because the relationship is bad, or because it's better than usual. In short, the situation of the woman with a controlling partner is very complex and difficult to second-guess.

Your next task as a would-be helper, then, is to step back and try to see the situation from the perspective of the woman you'd like to help—even though you may not be able to make sense of it. Keep in mind that what may seem crazy or hopelessly indecisive by your standards can seem very reasonable or necessary to a woman caught in the daily craziness of living with a controlling partner.

HOW BAD CAN IT BE?

Women who have been repeatedly abused emotionally often experience some severe emotional reactions: fear, shock, shame, sadness, and a sense of helplessness. But the situation becomes even more complicated if the woman you want to help is undergoing physical or sexual abuse, for that is likely to leave a woman even more severely traumatized. Like other trauma survivors—survivors of crimes, accidents, disasters—physically or sexually abused women are left feeling powerless and ashamed, but they carry on as best they can. Some feel paranoid and crazy, others depressed or sad. Some "numb out," medicating themselves with alcohol and pills. Many proceed with daily life in a manner so flat and unemotional that you wouldn't know they felt anything at all. All violence leaves victims feeling helpless, vulnerable, immobilized, and overwhelmed.

If you suspect that the woman you want to help is suffering physical or sexual abuse, you must make an even greater effort to understand the complexity and the difficulty of her situation. But in any case, patience often pays off, as Tracy found when her sister Robin finally left her boyfriend and took up Tracy's offer of a place to stay. If you offer help and a woman turns you down too many times, you may give up. But by withdrawing you stop short of giving her something she very much needs: assurance of your continuing support whenever—in the future—she is ready to use it. You can't "save" her. Why get mad at *her* because you can't? What you can do, by offering your ongoing support and whatever help she needs, whenever she needs it, is be an essential part of her process of saving herself.

WHAT IF YOU'RE RELUCTANT TO GET INVOLVED?

Many people are sympathetic to women in trouble, but for one reason or another, they hesitate to get involved. If that's the case with you, we suggest that you read Chapters 1–5 and then reevaluate your reasons. If you still feel sympathetic but reluctant to intervene, you'll want to consider ways to limit your involvement without making a woman who seeks your help feel judged and rejected. Let's look first at some common reasons why people hesitate.

Like women with controlling partners, outsiders—relatives, friends, coworkers, helping professionals—tend to minimize and deny what the controlling partner does. They may say things like, "He would never do *that,*" or, "It's only happened a few times." And just as wives do, outsiders may make excuses for the controlling partner and explain away his behavior. They may say things like, "He's been working too hard," or, "He'll settle down when he finds a job." If this sounds like you, it might be helpful to read about minimizing and explaining in Chapters 2 and 3.

Some outsiders stress that there are two sides to every story. You may be sympathetic to a woman, but you want to be fair; you believe that her partner must have grievances too—as every controlling partner certainly does. It may occur to you that this woman is probably very difficult to live with. She may be very nervous. Maybe she drinks or yells at her kids or nags her partner. Maybe her house is a wreck. Maybe you wouldn't want to be married to her for five minutes. You're entitled to these feelings, but before you blame the abused woman for her partner's actions, we suggest you look at Chapters 3 and 5. And we remind you that no one, no matter what she does, deserves to be hurt.

If you are religious and hold the marriage vow sacred, you may overlook abuse or consider it merely a trial that a good woman must endure. In the view of many religious people, it's a woman's duty to keep her marriage vows, no matter what. If you are among them, you may find it harder to recognize that she also has a duty to protect herself and her children. And you may forget altogether about the controlling partner's duty to love and honor his wife.

You may be frightened. If a woman confides in you that she is physically abused, you may not want to come up against her violent partner for fear that he might turn against you or your family. That's certainly a legitimate fear, and one that you must weigh carefully as you decide how to proceed. But if you're afraid of the man, imagine how his partner must feel.

Hearing all about someone else's bad relationship can be more than we're prepared for. (Many women will come right out and tell you about the emotional abuse they're undergoing, and some will talk openly of physical abuse as well.) A woman may ask you for advice or help, but because you see what a terrible problem she has, you may feel saddled with a responsibility you hadn't bargained for. You'd like to help—but then again, you wouldn't. You understand that her problem seems overwhelming to her because it seems overwhelming to you, too—and you're afraid to touch it. Carefully setting some limits for yourself will enable you to give help.

But what seems to make most people reluctant to intervene is the belief we all share that adults ought to be able to look after themselves. We say things like, "She made her bed, she has to lie in it." Women, in particular, often say, "I wouldn't stand for that. Why doesn't she leave him?" And often we hear people say, "It's a private matter, between consenting adults." Until very recently, in fact, that was the official attitude of our police and courts: marital "disputes"—even violent ones—were considered private matters. If our official institutions won't get involved, why should we?

Many of us hope that in time the problem will simply go away. But that is highly unlikely. Experts agree that emotional and physical abuse usually become more frequent and more severe over time. Without outside help, we can almost guarantee that an emotionally or physically abused woman will be abused again. The more a woman is coerced and assaulted, the more she will want to get out. But—and here is the paradox—the more she is coerced or assaulted or threatened, the more difficult it may become for her to do so.

Thus, even if you try to be helpful, she may reject your offer, leaving you hurt, frustrated, and more reluctant than ever to get involved. Consider, however, that a woman with a controlling partner may have good reasons for keeping her distance from you, reasons she can't tell you. Controlling partners usually see to it that their victims have little contact with family and friends. It's easier for the controller to keep control when he isolates his victim from other people. Very often, to achieve that end, the controller makes it so unpleasant for a woman to see her friends and family that she "voluntarily" drops them. He may stage an emotional scene. He may beat her up. He may attack the children. He may threaten harm to family members or friends or even professionals (lawyers, counselors, or shelter workers) who might be a "bad influence" on his victim. An abused woman, then, may keep her distance from you to make things easier on herself and her kids. If she doesn't talk to you, he'll have one less reason to blow up. Or she may avoid you in order to protect *you*.

WHAT TO SAY TO A WOMAN YOU THINK IS BEING ABUSED

The hardest part of talking to an abused woman is getting started. One well-meaning friend told us, "Every day I'd resolve to talk to my secretary about what was happening to her. But I couldn't figure out the right questions." Because a controlling partner lays all the blame on her, a woman is likely to hear any questions about her actions or her background or her personal life as accusations. Such questions will silence her. Many women feel particularly blamed when outsiders ask probing questions about their childhoods. Julia says, "I was afraid my husband might kill me any day, and everybody wanted to ask me a million questions about me and my parents—as if there was something wrong with *us.*"

The first conversation with an abuse victim may not be easy, but to be of help, you must begin. First you must have (or create) the conditions necessary for a conversation: privacy, and enough time for her to talk at length, if she feels like it. Then it's often most helpful to say the obvious: "You seem so unhappy. Do you want to talk about it? I'd like to listen, and I'll keep it between us."[5] Even if she rejects the offer, your observation about her unhappiness supports her by affirming some of her feelings. And you've left the door open for a confidential conversation in the future.

If that approach doesn't work, or if she wants to talk but can't get started, any of the following questions might help. Notice that these questions do *not* imply that you are psychoanalyzing her, looking for explanations of her behavior, challenging her, or passing judgment. Instead, they invite the woman to talk about what the controlling partner *does* and what she *feels* about it. Begin with a broad question, such as 1, 2, or 3. Ask more specific and direct questions, such as 9, 10, or 11, when she seems ready and willing to talk about these things.

1. What's it like at home for you?
2. What happens when you and your partner disagree or argue?
3. How does your partner handle things when he doesn't get his way? What does he do?
4. Are you ever scared of him? Does he threaten you?
5. Does he ever prevent you from doing things you want to do?
6. Does he ever follow you?
7. Do you have to account to him for your time?
8. Is he jealous, hard to please, irritable, demanding, critical?
9. Does he put you down, call you names, yell at you, punish you in any way?

10. Does he ever push you around or hit you?

11. Does he ever make you have sex? Does he ever make you do sexual things that you don't like?[6]

Many women will be eager to talk, if they feel safe. You can help a woman feel safe by assuring her that you'll keep her story confidential—and doing so. When she tells you her story, listen attentively. Don't interrupt. And don't let your facial expression or body language convey doubt or judgment of what she's saying. If she has trouble talking, you can ask another question—but be very careful of the kind of question you ask. When she finishes talking, ask, "How can I help?" Let her know that you care and that there are people and agencies who want to assist her. She may not know (and it is important to tell her) that thousands of other women experience such abuse and that, over the last fifteen years, special shelters, services, and laws have been created to help them. Make clear that her partner has a problem, and that she cannot fix it, no matter how much she wants to or how hard she tries.

And remember: if she refuses to talk to you today or says "no" to your offer of additional help, she has her reasons. Express your concern for her anyway. Tell her that emotional abuse and physical abuse are wrong and that she deserves better. Assure her that you will stand by, ready to talk or help, if she asks. Then give her time.

WHAT TO DO WHEN A WOMAN CONFIDES IN YOU

When a woman talks to you about her problems with a controlling partner, your reaction is vitally important. Here are some recommendations:

1. Believe her. She will not lie about abuse. Many controllers are so charming and gracious to outsiders that what you see of his behavior may deceive you. Even if the incidents she describes seem incredible, listen to her story and respect the way she tells it. Because abuse is so painful to experience, she may recall details slowly and in disjointed fragments. The pieces may not seem to fit together or make much sense. Remember that violence itself is arbitrary and irratio-nal. So, no matter what she tells you, *believe her*—and let her know that you do.

2. Acknowledge and support her for talking to you. She has taken a risk: her partner could hurt her or you could reject her. Let her know that you appreciate what she has done.

3. Let her know that you consider her feelings reasonable and normal. It is common for her to feel frightened, confused, angry, sad, guilty, numb, hopeless.

4. Let her lead the conversation. You can ask questions like, "How can I help you?" but don't expect her to have answers the first time she talks. She needs you to be a good listener. And if she asks you to do anything within reason, do it.

5. If she asks you to do something you can't or don't want to do, say so. Talk it over with her, and try to find both *(a)* another way of meeting the particular need she presented, and *(b)* another thing that you can do to help. Be careful not to impose your ideas of help on her.

6. Tell her you care about her and her safety. Take her fears seriously. Feel free to express your genuine feelings of con-cern with statements like, "I think you are in danger. I'm worried about your safety."

7. Don't blame her for the abuse. Let her know that the abuse is not her fault. But remember that her feelings about her partner probably are confused and mixed. If you express too much anger at her partner, she may feel the need to defend him.

8. Offer your help to find resources in the community for protection, advocacy, or support—that is, if you are actually prepared to follow through. (Don't ever offer things you can't deliver.) If she wants to go to an agency or battered women's program, volunteer to go with her. If she is in immediate danger, call the police. Always encourage her to get more support and information. Give her newspaper articles, books, and pamphlets produced by your local shel-ter for abused women.

9. Respect her pace and be patient. No one decides to give up a relationship overnight. She may also face threats and es-

calating assaults. So help her make plans, but let her make the decisions. As you plan, seek the advice of experts about abuse in your local community.

10. Remind her of her strengths, accomplishments, and positive attributes. Avoid treating her like a child or a helpless victim.

11. Always support her when she acts on her own behalf.

12. Remind yourself that many communities still don't protect women's rights. Don't assume that police, courts, and public agencies will protect and help her. And don't be surprised if she feels safer taking no action. Do not mistake her strategy of doing nothing for passivity or indifference. Instead, find out what help actually is available for her in your community, and offer to take her side with agencies, family, and friends. Try to find her a legal advocate from a program for abused women.

13. With the permission of the woman you're trying to help, work on expanding her circle of support. Find out if there is a support group for abused women at your local shelter or women's center, and encourage her to join. With her permission, enlist other coworkers or friends to help with child care or go along to court. (You can support one another in your efforts to help the woman in trouble.) The more supporters she has, the stronger she may become.

Women who've left controlling partners with help from others say that every bit of help, every expression of support, matters. Most are extremely appreciative of concrete help: a place to stay, a loan, a ride to court, an offer to go with her to the police or to court or to see a lawyer, or to look after the kids while she takes care of these matters. And most understand and appreciate it when a helper sets clear limits—when a helper says, for example, "I don't think I can give you as much support as you may want, but I'd like to make some calls and find out about advocacy and counseling services for you, if that's okay with you." Women who are afraid of their partners also understand that helpers must look out for their own safety. Before you undertake any practical help for a woman who confides in you, ask her if her partner is violent or threatening. If so, call a local domestic violence program or shelter to talk over the situation, assess the danger, and plan for safety. You might suggest that you and the woman make this call together.

WHAT ABOUT HER PARTNER?

As we discussed in Chapters 3 and 5, the heart of the woman's problem is her controlling partner. In theory, the best way to help her is to make her partner stop his controlling behavior. But as we pointed out in Chapter 5, that is not easily done. If she can't make him change, there's no reason to think that you might be able to. Nevertheless, unless you think that confronting the controlling partner would place the woman, yourself, or others in danger, we think it's worth a try. We suggest that you ask the woman first, "Do you want me to confront him? Is that a safe thing to do?"

Often in social gatherings of family and friends, we overlook squabbles between partners. Forced to sit in on a couple's argument, we pretend it's not happening and try to change the subject. But when you repeatedly hear a controller criticizing and abusing his wife or girlfriend, we suggest you confront him or take him aside and let him know that you disapprove of the way he acts. As we mentioned in Chapter 5, the more people there are who voice their disapproval of a controller's behavior, the more likely he is to reconsider it.

SPECIAL ADVICE FOR HELPING PROFESSIONALS

Many professional helpers receive little, if any, training about emotional abuse and domestic violence, even though battering is now the single most common cause of injury to women in the United States.[7] Although former Surgeon General C. Everett Koop labeled family violence a "national public health epidemic," schools of medicine, social work, nursing, and counseling are only just beginning to recognize the problem. As a result, you may be completely at a loss when a woman tells you that she is emotionally or physically abused. It can be very distressing, when you think of yourself as a skilled professional, to suddenly come upon a gap in your own training.

In the first five chapters of this book, we provide a new way of understanding the dilemma of women emotionally and/or physically abused by controlling partners. We see at the heart of the problem the controlling partner, trained by a male-dominated culture to think himself entitled to a woman's service, and supported in that belief by our cultural and social institutions. Changing his worldview and his behavior is a job probably too big for any single helping professional, and certainly too big for the woman unlucky enough to be his partner.

But since controllers seldom feel the need to change, it's the emotionally or physically abused woman who's likely to come to you for help and bring to your attention that blank page in your training. A great number of women in controlling relationships report that some helping professionals still subject them to views long ago repudiated by specialists in emotional and physical abuse. These professionals have good intentions but inadequate information. To spare you—and your clients—from such mistakes, we'll review here the most common misconceptions about relationships with controlling partners. (You'll find most of these topics covered in greater detail in Chapters 1–5.) We'll focus primarily on battered women here, but keep in mind that physical force is only one tactic used by controlling partners. Emotionally abused women suffer from many of the same problems and the same misconceptions. You'll note that some of these misconceptions have important implications for the form as well as the substance of appropriate professional help.

Misconception 1: The problem is spouse abuse. These are violent couples who assault each other. She gives as good as she gets.

In fact, the problem is woman abuse. The controlling person consistently harms his partner emotionally or physically, and should be held accountable for that harm. It's true that some women may hit back in frustration, anger, or self-defense. They may even throw the first punch. But when it comes to serious assault, the kind that causes real injury, women are almost invariably the victims. And while the controller's aim is to intimidate, dominate, terrorize, and control his victim, women who fight back rarely inspire terror. In any case, whether a woman strikes back or not, when she is abused, she is entitled to protection and help.

Many professionals try to see couples together to "negotiate about the violence," but such mediation is totally inappropriate when one partner dominates the other. Couples counseling inadvertently affirms the abuser, damages the emotional well-being of the abuse victim, and may place her life at risk. Even if a woman requests couples counseling, the conscientious professional, balancing her request against the professional duty to protect clients, will have to say no.

Misconception 2: *Violence is associated with substance abuse. It will disappear when the substance abuse is treated.*

As a matter of fact, there is a high correlation between substance abuse and domestic violence, but many batterers do not use alcohol or drugs, nor do their victims. And many extremely emotionally abusive controllers do not use either substances or violence. The professional must ask every client about both emotional and physical abuse.

Studies suggest that between 30 and 60 percent of all batterers abuse substances.[8] But many men who have successfully participated in drug and alcohol treatment programs continue to use violence to get their way. And many who have participated in batterers' programs continue to use nonviolent control to get their way. As we discussed in Chapter 5, the addicted batterer has two obvious problems —his chemical dependence and his violence— and he must be treated for both of them. But even if he is successfully treated and gives up both chemical addiction and violence, he may still be a controller.

As we discussed in Chapter 12, the addicted abused woman also has two problems: her chemical dependency and her controlling partner. In a great many cases, she becomes addicted by using alcohol and drugs to cope with the abuse she experiences. Professionals often misdiagnose the problem, defining her as an addict while overlooking or minimizing the emotional and physical violence she endures. The abused woman who is an addict should receive two kinds of services: substance abuse treatment and the support of a battered women's group.

Misconception 3: A woman chooses a relationship like this, so there isn't much I can do to help her.

The fact is that each woman originally chooses a partner who professes to love her. Once the controlling partner begins to exercise his control, she continuously makes choices and evaluates options, but her options are circumscribed. If she leaves her partner, she stands to lose a relationship, a home, her standard of living, perhaps her children, perhaps even her life. It shouldn't surprise us if a woman repeatedly changes her mind or decides to stay put. When our choices may have negative, life-threatening consequences, we too feel ambivalent about our decisions and procrastinate. But even if a woman decides to stay with her controlling partner, you can help her a great deal. Keep in mind that change is a process. By sticking with her, you play a crucial part in that long-term process.

Misconception 4: Why should I waste my time? She'll go back to her partner anyway.

It's true that some abused women come and go in their relationships; they are looking for ways to maintain the relationship but end the abuse.[9] Some women leave five or six times before they make a final break. Leaving and then going back is not a failure on the woman's part (nor on the part of the helping professional). It is a woman's first courageous step away from danger and if it happens once, it can happen again. The help you give an abused woman today—help that may seem to do no good—might enable her to act decisively in her own behalf next month, or next year.

Misconception 5: Battered women are masochists who like abuse and provoke it. They have such low self-esteem that they pick partners who'll beat them up. They come from such dysfunctional families that they naturally fall into this self-destructive pattern.

In fact, every year 1.8 million American wives are beaten by their husbands, and several million single, divorced, and separated women are also abused. (The number of emotionally abused women cannot be calculated.) Far too many women are beaten for us to subscribe to the idea that the personality of the victim explains the abuser's behavior. In fact, after reviewing fifty-two research studies about the characteristics of victims and victimizers, sociologists Gerald Hotaling and David Sugarman conclude: "The search for characteristics of women that contribute to their own victimization appears futile. There is no consistent evidence, after 15 years of research, that any behaviors, attitudes, demographic characteristics, or personality traits can predict what types of women will become victimized by husband or male partner violence." The authors continue, "This review of victim characteristics makes it clear that the most influential victim precipitant is being female. The victimization of women may be better understood as the outcome of male behavior."[10]

Despite these findings, old myths such as female masochism and up-to-date theories such as the "intergenerational transmission of violence" locate the cause of the problem in the woman's pathology. The truth is that any woman may become the victim of a controlling and violent partner, whether or not she comes from a dysfunctional family, has low self-esteem, or delights in masochistic sexuality. The truth is that women find physical and sexual assaults humiliating, painful, and terrifying.

Misconception 6: *Help is available, but women don't use it.*

In fact, most women make many efforts to stop abuse or to seek help. When they do, they often meet hostility, disbelief, denial, or self-righteous lectures about a wife's duty. A study at Yale-New Haven Hospital found that one out of four battered women leaves the hospital with the label neurotic, hysteric, hypochondriac, or "well-known patient with multiple complaints."[11] This study found that the real issue—violence—is hidden, and the woman herself is labeled the problem.

In addition, many people urge abused women to change themselves or to help their mate by enduring his beatings. In a survey of conservative Protestant clergy, 21 percent believed that no amount of abuse would justify a wife leaving her husband *ever,* and 26 percent agreed with the statement that "a wife should submit to her husband and trust that God would honor her action by either stopping the abuse or giving her the strength to endure it."[12] The failure of police and courts to protect battered women is well known. Some more enlightened communities have made dramatic progress against woman abuse, but it is still generally true that even the most elementary help is unavailable to many—perhaps most—women who are victimized.

Misconception 7: *Abused women fail to show up for appointments, they lie about their relationships, and they don't follow through with what they promise to do.*

The fact is that one of the main tactics of controlling partners is isolating their victims. The controller knows that the more contact the woman has with others, the more likely she is to defy him or to leave. To isolate her, he may try many different things: He may punch her in the face, bruising it, so that she is too embarrassed to go out for an appointment. He may take her car keys or remove the battery from her car. He may promise to babysit and come home so drunk that she is afraid to leave the kids alone with him. So she misses more appointments. After several of these incidents, her shame—already intense—is constant.

Shame, however, is only one reason for the failure of some women to follow through. Hope for the relationship is another. So is fear. If, for example, a woman believes that her partner will retaliate after she secures a protection order, and that the police will not enforce the order, she may decide not to go to court again. Or if she obtains a temporary restraining order and her partner backs off, she may decide to leave well enough alone rather than set him off by returning to court. In short, the behavior that often looks to professionals like irresponsibility or "complicity in her own victimization" is further evidence that a woman is abused and that she is struggling to cope. The reality is that her partner controls her life.

Many other abused women, it must be said, do keep appointments, do speak out, and do follow through. For example, in some cities, such as San Francisco, where a special unit of the prosecutor's office handles charges made by abused women, the women follow through with their cases to conviction. We find that whenever agencies and institutions back up abused women, most of the women work hard in their own behalf. We believe that most often, when an abused woman fails to follow through as professionals require, the problem lies with the partner who controls her. And sometimes the problem lies with the professional or with the institutions that fail to help and protect her. There are many reasons why an abused women misses appointments, but a conscientious professional must ask herself: "What help was I offering her? What did she have to come back *for?*"

Misconception 8: *My professional role is strictly limited. It's not my job to work with other agencies to secure my client's rights to restraining orders, police protection, and shelter.*

Just the opposite is true. Because many criminal justice agencies have failed to enforce the rights of abused women, professionals must be doubly careful to see that their clients are protected. Men who batter are dangerous. Every year approximately 2,000 women in the United States die at the hands of their husbands or male companions.[13] Many of these women are in the process of separating when they are murdered. If they took the risk to come and see you, they need your help.

If a client wants to get a restraining order or press charges against her husband, professionals must be prepared to offer information, support, and safety planning. Workers for mental health facilities, child protective services, criminal justice agencies, and shelters must cooperate fully to protect clients.

If you treat abusers, it is important that you cooperate with local services for abused women and with the criminal justice system to hold them accountable for their behavior. In general, abusers change only when they face consequences, such as jail time or court-mandated treatment, for their criminal violence. (See Chapter 5.) If you subscribe to the theory that one shouldn't force clients to change, you give them permission to continue to harm others. Keep in mind that the behavior you tacitly approve—assault—is a criminal offense.

In addition, some widely accepted professional theories are so inappropriate to abused women as to be positively harmful. Professionals whose primary mission is to keep the family together, for example, are likely to minimize abuse or disregard it. This stance is again a silent approval of assaultive behavior and thus guarantees that it will continue. The abused woman is doubly victimized, by her partner's acts and the professional's theories and practice.

Misconception 9: *She provokes him. She needs to learn and practice better interpersonal skills so she can handle him.*

In fact, it is a terrible mistake to suggest that the woman is to blame, or that she can change her partner's behavior. Ruth's counselor kept asking her questions that sounded like accusations: "What do you do to make him so angry? Couldn't you try something else?" The counselor worked with Ruth on developing "better communication" with her partner. She clearly believed that women set off their abusive partners and could learn to calm them down instead. But anger is not the heart of the problem; it is merely a tactic the abuser uses to intimidate and gain *control* over the victim. Thus, anger control is not the solution, and in any case it is not the responsibility of the target. The professional's job is to help the client—not to help the client help somebody else.

Misconception 10:   *Abused women are not rational. They refuse to help themselves.*

As a matter of fact, professionals often think they know best and grow impatient for change the client is not ready to make. But there are many financial, logistical, and emotional reasons why a woman might need time to make the choice to leave her partner. Thus it's a big mistake for a counselor to plan the client's life and then get mad at her when she doesn't carry out the plan. Many battered women tell of therapists who decide the client should leave her partner and go to a shelter—but the client refuses. In anger and frustration, the therapist terminates services. One such professional told Phuong, "If you refuse to help yourself, there's nothing more I can do for you." Joyce, who had a similar experience, says, "Counselors should treat us like grown-ups. We're not helpless victims, and we're not stupid. We're in trouble, but most of us can still make up our own minds."

We hope that this review of common misconceptions about women with controlling partners has prompted you to reconsider your views, for no matter how skilled you are in your professional practice, if you maintain any of these beliefs or theories, you will not be able to provide adequate help to women emotionally and physically abused by controlling partners. In that case, no matter how good your intentions, you are bound by professional ethics to refer these clients to professionals who can provide the help they are entitled to.

Working Effectively with Abused Women

How does the professional begin to work effectively with an abused woman?

The best way is to listen to her story and try to imagine what you might feel like in her place. See her alone and ask about the history of her relationship. Be supportive, validating, and active. Ask for specific details about physically, emotionally, and sexually coercive experiences, if she does not offer them. But never push her to disclose information she wishes to keep to herself. She should set the pace and make her own choices. Therapist and lesbian activist Valli Kanuha, who has counseled abused women for many years, offers this advice for the first session: "I always assume that this may be my first and only chance with the woman, given the conditions of her life. I listen, support, and clarify. But I think the risk/safety assessment is the most important first step. A risk assessment and safety plan need not be elaborate, but it's an extremely powerful tool to confirm, affirm, educate, and give something concrete to a woman in crisis."[14]

Your client may be unclear about the next steps she wants to take. Her reluctance, fear, or uncertainty may make you uncomfortable, especially if she is in danger. But if she needs time to think and decide, you must not push her to make decisions. Keep in mind that many abused women feel extremely undermined—"brainwashed," some of them say—by the time they see a professional. Often a woman's partner has played with her perceptions of reality, put her down, and blamed her for every problem imaginable. As a result, she too may blame herself for everything that goes wrong. She may have lost confidence in herself and in her own judgment. You can help her regain it. You might want to point out that she has functioned fairly well in extremely trying circumstances.

A number of abused women seek out therapists to "fix" the controlling partner. It's a logical request, and it speaks well for her own mental health, since she correctly identifies the problem as his. It will help her if the two of you work together by reading Chapter 5 of this book, "Can Your Partner Change?" But whatever may happen to the controlling partner, your main role is to support the woman who is victimized. Safety assessments and planning should become an ongoing, continuous part of your work together. Always let a client know when you think she is in danger. Since many women survive by minimizing danger, they sometimes don't realize how frightened they actually are. Keep in mind that when your client decides to take steps toward becoming more self-sufficient and leaving an abusive partner, she is most vulnerable to serious attack.

If you are uncertain about the best way to help a client plan for her safety, alert the police and seek advice from the local program for abused women. The staff can help you and your client evaluate various alternatives, such as using the court, moving to a shelter or safe home, or fleeing to another community. Never underestimate the danger your client faces.

Your local shelter or battered women's program may provide many other valuable services for your client—including twenty-four-hour emergency service—all of which will make your job easier. They may provide advocates to help your client with social services, legal matters, housing, and dangerous emergencies. More important, they may provide a support group where your client can overcome her sense of being "the only one," make friends, receive consciousness-raising information about family violence, and per-haps take part in empowering social and political action designed to raise public awareness about family violence and persuade pub-lic institutions such as the police and courts to be more responsive. As an adjunct to therapy *every professional should refer battered women to advocacy groups run by a shelter or battered women's program.*[15]

If your client doesn't want to join, however, you must be pre-pared to give her the sort of information she would find there. Helping a woman untangle the confusion engendered by a control-ling partner is one of the most meaningful interventions you can provide. Most women report that they have found information about psychological abuse and other controlling tactics extremely useful in making sense of their own experiences. One way to begin is to read together chapters of this and other books for abused women (see the bibliography for other recommended readings). But in addition to "learning by doing" with your client, you should seek specialized training in these matters on your own.

As you work together, remember that your goal is to help your client end her isolation and restore control over her life in safe and strengthening ways. As long as she remains in the relationship with the controlling partner, your emphasis should be on *what he gains,* not on why she stays. (See Chapter 3.) Believe and support her, and consistently offer these messages:

1. Violence is wrong. Rape and assault are criminal acts. Emotional abuse is wrong. She deserves better treatment.
2. She does not cause emotional or physical abuse. She cannot change the controlling partner, and neither can anybody else. He will change only if he wants to.
3. She can change her life. She can recapture the hopes and dreams she once had for herself, or she can follow new ideals.
4. There are alternatives to living with controlling partners. Thousands of other women have chosen alternatives and have been very happy with their decisions. Getting reestablished is hard work, but it pays off.

How to Handle Official Reports

As a professional dealing with abused women, you must be particularly sensitive in filing reports and making a diagnosis. If you are legally required to report child abuse, you should inform your client of this obligation at the beginning of your conversation. Many women believe that they will lose their children if they disclose any family abuse, so be honest with her from the start. Offer her help to escape her abusive partner, with her children; and if you do have to file a child abuse report, stand by her.

Recording a diagnosis of an abused woman is even more problematic, particularly because so many professionals misunderstand abuse. In workshops we've offered around the country, we hear professionals describe abused women over and over again in the same old ways. The women are depressed, therapists say. They seem flat, passive, affectless. They minimize. They are distrustful. Many drink too much or take too many pills. Their self-esteem is low. Always, baffled clinicians ask the same question: Why don't they assert themselves? Isn't this the reason they are abused?

Symptoms of numbing, depression, paranoia, fear, and alcoholism, we explain, are the *consequences* of living through emotional, physical, and sexual abuse. Precisely how a woman acts often depends on the kind of abuser she is living with. Her behavior is a consequence of her abuse, rather than a cause of it. If you must label the abused woman, it is best to diagnose her as a victim of posttraumatic stress.

Remember that the diagnosis you give her will follow her. Her abusive partner may petition the court for custody of their children, alleging that she is mentally ill and subpoenaing your records as proof. To protect her, you must carefully document the abuse she undergoes and the efforts she makes to find help for herself and her children. Otherwise, your diagnosis may become part of yet another victimization of your client.

TRYING TO HELP: CARE

Bernice was twenty years old when she fled from her controlling partner with her nine-month-old daughter. After tracking her to her sister's house in another town, her partner literally dragged her to the car, took her home, and gave her the worst beating of her life for "leaving him." When the beating was over, Bernice felt blood gushing from her ear. She managed to drive to a hospital, and in the emergency room she met the doctor who, she says, saved her life.

"I felt like a fool," Bernice says, "so when the doctor asked me what happened, I said I fell off the bus." The doctor explained that she'd "fallen" only a hairsbreadth from a fatal injury. He insisted that she see him every day for the next week so that he could monitor her progress. Every day she went to see him, and every day he told her he was very worried about her narrow escape. At the end of the week, when Bernice thanked him for his care, he asked her for a favor in return. "Please stay off the bus," he said. "Then I won't have to worry about you." That night Bernice fled once again from her hometown and went into hiding.

Bernice told us this story ten years after it happened. To this day she remembers the doctor's words and his face. "He gave me the nerve to leave again," she says. "He cared and I knew it."

Notes

Chapter 1

1. See Susan Schechter, *Guidelines for Mental Health Practitioners in Domestic Violence Cases* (Washington, D.C.: The National Coalition Against Domestic Violence, 1987), p. 4.

Chapter 3

1. See Joan Kaufman and Edward Zigler, "The Intergenerational Transmission of Child Abuse," *Child Maltreatment: Theory and Research on the Causes and Consequences of Child Abuse and Neglect,* ed. Dante Cicchetti and Vicki Carlson (Cambridge: Cambridge University Press, 1989), pp. 52–54.
2. See Carol Tavris, *Anger: The Misunderstood Emotion* (New York: Simon & Schuster, 1982), pp. 143–50.
3. Lundy Bancroft and David Douglas, interview, June 1989.
4. Ellen Pence, interview, July 1989.
5. See Ellen Pence, "How Society Gives Men Permission to Batter," audiotape produced by the Domestic Abuse Intervention Project, Duluth, MN, n.d.; Fernando Mederos, interview, July 1989.
6. See R. Emerson Dobash and Russell Dobash, *Violence Against Wives: A Case Against the Patriarchy* (New York: Free Press, 1979), p. 95.

Chapter 5

1. Anne Ganley, personal communication, January 1991.
2. Fernando Mederos, interview, June 1989.
3. See Edward W. Gondolf, *Man Against Woman: What Every Woman Should Know About Violent Men* (Blue Ridge Summit, PA: Tab Books, 1989), p. 75.
4. Don Chapin, interview, November 1989.
5. Charles Niessen-Derry, interview, November 1989.
6. David Adams, "Identifying the Assaultive Husband in Court: You Be the Judge," *Boston Bar Journal* (July/August 1989), p. 25.
7. Edward W. Gondolf with Ellen R. Fisher, *Battered Women as Survivors* (Lexington, MA: Lexington Books, 1988), p. 66.
8. Gondolf, p. 85.
9. Gondolf, p. 95.
10. Jeffrey Edleson, interview, November 1989.
11. Chapin, interview.
12. Fernando Mederos, interview, July 1989.

Chapter 7

1. R. Emerson Dobash and Russell Dobash, *Violence Against Wives: A Case Against the Patriarchy* (New York: Free Press, 1979), pp. 144–45.
2. "Money Income and Poverty Status in the United States, 1989," U.S. Department of Commerce, Bureau of the Census, 1989.
3. "Poverty in the United States: 1988 and 1989," U.S. Department of Commerce, Bureau of the Census, Series P-60, No. 171.
4. Edwin E. Niemi, *A Study of the Effects of Battering on Heterosexual Relationships Over Time,* unpublished dissertation, Union Institute, December 1988, pp. 72, 100.
5. Marie M. Fortune, *Keeping the Faith: Questions and Answers for the Abused Woman* (San Francisco: Harper & Row, 1987), pp. 15–17, 35.
6. See Fortune, p. 26.
7. Marie M. Fortune, personal communication, July 1990.
8. See Diana E. H. Russell, *The Secret Trauma: Incest in the Lives of Girls and Women* (New York: Basic Books, 1986), pp. 103–105.
9. Ginny NiCarthy, *Getting Free: A Handbook for Women in Abusive Relationships* (Seattle: Seal Press, 1986), pp. 25–26.
10. We developed this list through discussions with counselors at EMERGE, a Boston counseling program for abusive men, and with Dr. James Gilligan. Many activists and formerly abused women in the Connecticut Coalition Against Domestic Violence and several survivors of attempted homicide also contributed their ideas. See also Barbara Hart, "Beyond the 'Duty to Warn': A Therapist's 'Duty to Protect' Battered Women and Children,"

in *Feminist Perspectives on Wife Abuse*, ed. Kersti Yllö and Michele Bograd (Newbury Park, CA: Sage, 1988), pp. 241–243; and Jacquelyn C. Campbell, "Nursing Assessment for Risk of Homicide with Battered Women," *Advances in Nursing Science*, Vol. 8, Issue 4 (July 1986), pp. 36–51.

Chapter 8

1. "Recognizing Stages of Breaking Away in Battered Women: What Shelter Staff Can Do to Help," paper developed by Transition House, Cambridge, MA, n.d.

Chapter 9

1. See *Women Need to Know About AIDS*, Gay Men's Health Crisis brochure, 1989; and *10 Minutes That Can Change Your Life*, Gay Men's Health Crisis brochure, 1989.

Chapter 10

1. See Peter Finn, "Statutory Authority in the Use and Enforcement of Civil Protection Orders Against Domestic Abuse," *Family Law Quarterly*, Vol. XXIII, No. 1 (Spring 1989), p. 49. This article includes a state-by-state analysis of the provisions of domestic violence civil statutes.
2. *The Custody Handbook* (Washington, D.C.: The Women's Legal Defense Fund, n.d.), pp. 64–65.
3. See *The Custody Handbook*, p. 65.
4. Laurie Woods, National Center on Women and Family Law, interview, June 1990.
5. See *The Custody Handbook*; Marianne Takas, *Child Custody: A Complete Guide for Concerned Mothers* (New York: Harper & Row, 1987), pp. 31–38; *Fact Sheet: How To Find a Good Lawyer*, Item #17 (New York: National Center on Women and Family Law, November 1990).
6. Woods.
7. *Mediation and You* (New York: National Center on Women and Family Law, 1988), p. 11.
8. See *Mediation and You*, p. 11.
9. Woods.
10. See *The Custody Handbook*, p. 13; and *Mediation and You*, pp. 16–25.
11. *The Custody Handbook*, pp. 62–63.
12. See Marianne Takas, *Child Support: A Complete, Up-To-Date, Authoritative Guide to Collecting Child Support* (New York: Harper & Row, 1985), p. 119.
13. Woods.

14. See *The Custody Handbook*, p. 63.
15. Woods.
16. Joanne Schulman, "Prevention Tips," *Interstate Child Custody Disputes and Parental Kidnapping* (New York: National Center on Women and Family Law, 1983), p. 15-1.
17. See *The Custody Handbook*, p. 57.
18. See Schulman, p. 15-2.
19. See *The Custody Handbook*, p. 58.
20. *Ibid.*
21. Muriel Sugarman, personal communication, December 1990.

Chapter 11

1. Elaine Hilberman, "Overview: The 'Wife-Beater's Wife' Reconsidered," *American Journal of Psychiatry*, 137:11 (November 1980), pp. 1340–1341; see also Peter G. Jaffe, David A. Wolfe, and Susan Kaye Wilson, *Children of Battered Women* (Newbury Park, CA: Sage, 1990), pp. 49–54.
2. Lenore E. Walker, *The Battered Woman Syndrome* (New York: Springer, 1984), p. 59.
3. Muriel Sugarman, personal communication, December 1990.
4. See Anne H. Cohn, *Physical Child Abuse* (Chicago: The National Committee for Prevention of Child Abuse, 1983), p. 1.
5. See Leontine Young, *Physical Child Neglect* (Chicago: National Committee for Prevention of Child Abuse, 1981), pp. 1–4.
6. Cornelia Spelman, *Talking About Child Sexual Abuse* (Chicago: National Committee for Prevention of Child Abuse, 1985), p. 3.
7. See Spelman, p. 9.
8. See Spelman, pp. 5, 9–10.
9. See National Committee for the Prevention of Child Abuse, *Basic Facts About Child Sexual Abuse*, 3rd ed. (Chicago: National Committee for the Prevention of Child Abuse, 1988), p. 11.
10. James Garbarino and Anne C. Garbarino, *Emotional Maltreatment of Children*, rev. ed. (Chicago: National Committee for the Prevention of Child Abuse, 1986), p. 18.
11. Garbarino, pp. 12–13. See also J. Garbarino, E. Guttman, and J. Seeley, *The Psychologically Battered Child: Strategies for Identification, Assessment, and Intervention* (San Francisco: Jossey-Bass, 1986).
12 See Garbarino, pp. 13, 19–20.
13 Jocelyn Tilsen, interview, November 1989.
14. Walker, pp. 59–60.

Chapter 12

1. See Emanuel Peluso and Lucy Silvay Peluso, *Women and Drugs: Getting Hooked, Getting Clean* (Minneapolis: Comp Care, 1988), p. 10.
2. *Ibid.*
3. Vernon Johnson, *Intervention: How to Help Someone Who Doesn't Want Help* (Minneapolis: Johnson Institute, 1986), p. 13.
4. See Peluso, p. 15.
5. See Peluso, p. 16.
6. From Katherine Ketcham and Ginny Lyford Gustafson, *Living on the Edge: A Guide to Intervention for Families with Drug and Alcohol Problems* (New York: Bantam, 1989), pp. 214–215. We have adapted and added to this list.
7. See Peluso, pp. 33–35.
8. *Ibid.*
9. See Peluso, p. 53.
10. Ketcham and Gustafson, p. 240.
11. Ketcham and Gustafson, pp. 240–241.
12. Joel Haber, personal communication, January 1990.
13. Ketcham and Gustafson, pp. 234–237.
14. Ketcham and Gustafson, p. 232.
15. From Ketcham and Gustafson, pp. 233–234. We have paraphrased this list.
16. See Ketcham and Gustafson, pp. 219–220.
17. See *Cocaine/Crack: The Big Lie* (Washington, D.C.: U.S. Department of Health and Human Services, National Institute on Drug Abuse, 1987), p. 3.
18. See *Cocaine/Crack*, pp. 3–4.
19. This test is compiled and adapted from several sources: Claudia Black, *It Will Never Happen to Me* (New York: Ballantine, 1981), pp. 202–203; Johnson, pp. 11–12; "Roots of Addiction," *Newsweek* (Feb. 20, 1989), p. 52, citing a test adapted from the National Council on Alcoholism; Sue Doucette, "Drug/Alcohol Self Assessment for Women in Abusive Relationships," unpublished paper.
20. See L. Ann Mueller and Katherine Ketcham, *Recovering: How to Get and Stay Sober* (Toronto: Bantam, 1987), pp. 114–130.
21. Dan Domench, personal communication, October 1990.

Chapter 13

1. See *Helping the Battered Woman: A Guide for Family and Friends* (Washington, D.C.: National Woman Abuse Prevention Project, n.d.).
2. Joan Duncan, personal communication about her research for the Connecticut Coalition Against Domestic Violence, January 1990.

3. R. Emerson Dobash and Russell Dobash, *Violence Against Wives: A Case Against the Patriarchy* (New York: Free Press, 1979), pp. 144–145.
4. Anne Ganley, personal communication, December 1990.
5. Ganley.
6. See Susan Schechter, *Guidelines for Mental Health Practitioners in Domestic Violence Cases* (Washington, D.C.: The National Coalition Against Domestic Violence, 1987), p. 9.
7. See Teri Randall, "Domestic Violence Intervention Calls for More Than Treating Injuries," *Journal of the American Medical Association,* Vol. 264, No. 8 (Aug 22/29, 1990), p. 939.
8. See Edward W. Gondolf and Robert A. Foster, "Wife Assault Among VA Alcohol Rehabilitation Patients," *Hospital and Community Psychiatry,* Vol. 42, No. 1 (January 1991), p. 74.
9. See Dobash, p. 144.
10. Gerald T. Hotaling and David B. Sugarman, "An Analysis of Risk Markers in Husband to Wife Violence: The Current State of Knowledge," *Violence and Victims,* Vol. 1, No. 2 (1986), pp. 118, 120.
11. Evan Stark, Anne Flitcraft, and William Frazier, "Medicine and Patriarchal Violence: The Social Construction of a 'Private' Event," *International Journal of Health Services,* Vol. 9, No. 3 (1979), p. 474.
12. Jim M. Alsdurf, "Wife Abuse and the Church: The Response of Pastors," *Response* (Winter 1985), p. 10.
13. Angela Browne and Kirk R. Williams, "Trends in Partner Homicide by Relationship Type and Gender: 1976–1987," paper presented at the annual meeting, American Society of Criminology, Baltimore, MD, November 7–11, 1990.
14. Valli Kanuha, personal communication, April 1991.
15. Ganley.

Bibliography

Woman Battering

Browne, Angela. *When Battered Women Kill*. New York: Free Press, 1987.
    —Draws on interviews with 250 abused women, 42 of whom killed their partners, to describe the male need to maintain control and the pattern of escalating violence preceding self-defense.

Dobash, R. Emerson, and Russell Dobash. *Violence Against Wives: A Case Against the Patriarchy*. New York: Free Press, 1979.
    —A ground-breaking book that puts wife abuse in historical context and demonstrates that it is a form of male dominance maintained by social, religious, and judicial institutions.

Dworkin, Andrea. *Woman Hating*. New York: Dutton, 1974.
    —A classic account of the underlying misogyny of our culture.

Gondolf, Edward W., with Ellen Fisher. *Battered Women as Survivors: An Alternative to Treating Learned Helplessness*. Lexington, MA: Lexington Books, 1988.
    —Uses records of 6,000 women in Texas shelters to demonstrate that women are active, courageous, and persistent in the face of abuse and need various kinds of practical help.

Jones, Ann. *Women Who Kill*. New York: Holt, Rinehart & Winston, 1980.
    —A history of American women and homicide. A chapter on battered women who kill argues that they are doubly victimized by individual men who won't let them go and by the male-dominated criminal justice system.

Kelly, Liz. *Surviving Sexual Violence*. Minneapolis: University of Minnesota Press, 1988.

—Draws on interviews with sixty subjects to describe how women experience, resist, and cope with violence over the course of their lives.

Martin, Del. *Battered Wives*. San Francisco: Volcano Press, 1981; first published by Glide Publications, 1976.
—The first, and still first-rate, analysis of wife abuse, its history, and the response of social and legal institutions.

Schechter, Susan. *Women and Male Violence: The Visions and Struggles of the Battered Women's Movement*. Boston: South End Press, 1982.
—The history and politics of the movement to shelter abused women, to make laws, and to change social policy.

Walker, Lenore E. *The Battered Woman*. New York: Harper & Row, 1979.
—An early theory of battering, its psychological effects, and some of the ways women cope.

Yllö, Kersti, and Michele Bograd, eds. *Feminist Perspectives on Wife Abuse*. Newbury Park, CA: Sage Publications, 1988.
—A collection of articles that take gender inequality as the starting point for studying, analyzing, and intervening in battering.

For Advocates and Counselors

NiCarthy, Ginny, Karen Merriam, and Sandra Coffman. *Talking It Out: A Guide to Groups for Abused Women*. Seattle: Seal Press, 1984.
—Helpful information about how to start and sustain a support group for abused women.

Pence, Ellen. *In Our Own Best Interest: A Process for Personal and Social Change,* Facilitator's Manual. Duluth: Minnesota Program Development, 1987.
—An outstanding facilitator's manual, supplemented by videotapes, providing a cogent political analysis of battering, useful in women's support groups for consciousness raising and planning social action.

Schechter, Susan. *Guidelines for Mental Health Practitioners in Domestic Violence Cases*. Washington, D.C.: National Coalition Against Domestic Violence, 1987.
—A 24-page manual filled with suggestions for those counseling abused women.

For Survivors

Fedders, Charlotte, and Laura Elliott. *Shattered Dreams: The Story of Charlotte Fedders*. New York: Harper & Row. 1987.
—A first-person account of abuse written by the wife of a former official of the Securities and Exchange Commission during the Reagan presidency.

Fortune, Marie M. *Keeping The Faith: Questions and Answers for the Abused Woman.* San Francisco: Harper & Row, 1987.
—A guide for Christian women living with abuse and a reminder that many in the Christian community understand and will support an abused woman.

Gondolf, Edward W. *Man Against Woman: What Every Woman Should Know About Violent Men.* Blue Ridge Summit, PA: Tab Books, 1989.
—Straightforward answers from a man to your questions about your violent partner and the likelihood of his changing.

NiCarthy, Ginny. *Getting Free: A Handbook for Women in Abusive Relationships.* Seattle: Seal Press, 1986.
—The first book written for the abused woman, explaining why abuse happens, what she can do about it, and where she can get help.

NiCarthy, Ginny. *The Ones Who Got Away: Women Who Left Abusive Partners.* Seattle: Seal Press, 1987.
—Courageous stories from thirty-five women who left their partners and started over.

NiCarthy, Ginny, and Sue Davidson. *You Can Be Free: An Easy to Read Handbook for Abused Women.* Seattle: Seal Press, 1989.
—A simplified version of *Getting Free.*

Rouse, Linda. *You Are Not Alone: A Guide for Battered Women.* Holmes Beach, FL: Learning Publications, 1984.
—A useful book that provides answers to such basic questions as: "Am I Abused?" and "Why Does It Happen?"

White, Evelyn C. *Chain Chain Change: For Black Women Dealing with Physical and Emotional Abuse.* Seattle: Seal Press, 1985.
—Hope and information for the abused African-American woman who is trying to decide what to do, and very useful to any reader who wants to understand the racial obstacles African-American women face.

Zambrano, Myrna M. *Mejor Sola que Mal Acompanada: Para La Mujer Golpeada/For the Latina in an Abusive Relationship.* Seattle: Seal Press, 1985.
—Very helpful material for the Latina in a physically, emotionally, or sexually abusive relationship. Important information for all women about the problems of undocumented women and of those who speak little or no English.

For Lesbians

Lobel, Kerry, ed. *Naming the Violence: Speaking Out About Lesbian Battering.* Seattle: Seal Press, 1986.
—The first book about abuse in lesbian relationships, including personal stories, discussions of homophobia, and suggestions for starting programs and helping lesbians who are battered.

Rape and Sexual Abuse

Brownmiller, Susan. *Against Our Will: Men, Women, and Rape*. New York: Simon and Schuster, 1975.
— The classic feminist analysis of rape sees rape as an act of power and domination.

Butler, Sandra. *Conspiracy of Silence: The Trauma of Incest*. San Francisco: Volcano Press, 1985.
— An excellent feminist analysis of sexual abuse of children.

Herman, Judith Lewis. *Father-Daughter Incest*. Cambridge, MA: Harvard University Press, 1981.
— A pioneering analysis of incest, challenging the dominant legal and therapeutic practices that have ignored male incest perpetrators and blamed their child victims.

Rush, Florence. *The Best Kept Secret: Sexual Abuse of Children*. New York: McGraw-Hill, 1981.
— A ground-breaking study documenting the historical and cultural roots of child sexual abuse and the silence that surrounds it.

Russell, Diana E. H. *The Politics of Rape: The Victim's Perspective*. New York: Stein and Day, 1974.
— A feminist analysis of rape as domination, based on a study of ninety women.

Russell, Diana E. H. *Rape in Marriage*. New York: Macmillan, 1982.
— The first systematic work to document the high incidence of rape and sexual abuse in marriage, based on a study of 930 women.

Russell, Diana E. H. *The Secret Trauma: Incest in the Lives of Girls and Women*. New York: Basic Books, 1986.
— Valuable evidence, based on a study of 930 women, of the high incidence of incest and sexual abuse and the effects on victims.

Sanday, Peggy Reeves. *Fraternity Gang Rape: Sex, Brotherhood, and Privilege on Campus*. New York: New York University Press, 1990.
— An anthropologist's enlightening account of how young men in one segment of the culture learn to disdain and abuse women.

For Survivors

Bass, Ellen, and Laura Davis. *The Courage to Heal: A Guide for Women Survivors of Child Sexual Abuse*. New York: Harper & Row, 1988.
— A comprehensive classic that details the steps to recovery for women who were sexually abused as children.

Bass, Ellen, and Louise Thornton, eds. *I Never Told Anyone: Writings by Women Survivors of Child Sexual Abuse*. New York: Harper & Row, 1983.
— A reassuring collection of stories of women who survived childhood abuse.

Brady, Katherine. *Father's Days: A True Story of Incest.* New York: Dell, 1979.
——One woman's straightforward story of father-daughter incest.
Gil, Eliana. *Outgrowing the Pain: A Book for and About Adults Abused as Children.* San Francisco: Launch Press, 1983.
——A helpful, easy-to-read guide for adults about the effects of childhood abuse, of any kind, and the process of healing.
McNaron, Toni A. H., and Yarrow Morgan, eds. *Voices in the Night: Women Speaking About Incest.* Minneapolis: Cleis Press, 1982.
——A collection of first-person accounts by both heterosexual women and lesbians, about childhood sexual abuse.

For Abusive Men and Their Counselors

Ganley, Anne L. *Court Mandated Counseling for Men Who Batter.* Washington, D.C.: Center for Women Policy Studies, 1981.
——An incisive analysis and overview for those who work with abusive men, by a pioneer in the field.
Gondolf, Edward W. *Men Who Batter: An Integrated Approach to Stopping Wife Abuse.* Holmes Beach, FL: Learning Publications, 1985.
——A useful explanation of why men batter and a discussion of treatment programs that may help them.
Gondolf, Edward W., and David Russell. *Man to Man: A Guide for Men in Abusive Relationships.* Bradenton, FL: Human Services Institute, 1987.
——A brief analysis that holds men accountable for their abusive behavior, discusses the hard work necessary for change, and offers suggestions and hope.
Pence, Ellen, and Michael Paymar. *Power and Control: Tactics of Men Who Batter.* Duluth: Minnesota Program Development, 1990.
——Widely used educational curriculum, supplemented by videotapes, for working with abusive men, based on the innovative criminal justice model developed in Duluth, Minnesota.
Sonkin, Daniel Jay, ed. *Domestic Violence on Trial: Psychological and Legal Dimensions of Family Violence.* New York: Springer, 1987.
——A useful anthology, including material on the court-mandated treatment of the offender.
Sonkin, Daniel Jay, and Michael Durphy. *Learning to Live Without Violence: A Handbook for Men.* San Francisco: Volcano Press, 1982.
——A workbook for batterers who are in counseling, useful for helping them understand abuse and give up violence.

For Children: About Domestic Violence

The National Coalition Against Domestic Violence, P.O. Box 15127, Washington, D.C. 20003-0127, publishes an annotated bibliography of materials for children and for their counselors and advocates in shelters and social service agencies.

Davis, Diane. *Something Is Wrong at My House: A Book about Parents Fighting,* illustrated by Marina Megale. Seattle: Parenting Press, 1985.
—A very useful book for almost any age group, recommended by the National Coalition Against Domestic Violence.

Paris, Susan. *Mommy and Daddy Are Fighting,* illustrated by Gail Labinski. Seattle: Seal Press, 1986.
—A child's story, designed to help parents, counselors, and teachers talk to children about domestic violence. Discussion guide included. Recommended by the National Coalition Against Domestic Violence.

For Parents: About Child Abuse

Adams, Caren, and Jennifer Fay. *Nobody Told Me It Was Rape: A Parent's Guide to Talking with Teenagers about Acquaintance Rape and Sexual Exploitation.* Santa Cruz: Network Publications, 1984.
—A short, straightforward, and helpful guide.

Adams, Caren, and Jennifer Fay. *No More Secrets: Protecting Your Child from Sexual Assault.* San Luis Obispo: Impact, 1981.
—A practical guide for concerned parents.

Byerly, C. M. *The Mother's Book: How to Survive the Incest of Your Child.* Dubuque: Kendall/Hunt, 1985.
—A brief, practical guide, with a helpful section on resources, to handling your own recovery and your child's as well.

Colao, Flora, and Tamar Hosansky. *Your Children Should Know: Personal-Safety Strategies for Parents to Teach Their Children.* New York: Harper & Row, 1987.
—An excellent guide for parents on teaching children to deal with potential and actual assault.

Fortune, Marie. *Sexual Abuse Prevention: A Study for Teenagers.* New York: United Church Press, 1984.
—Helpful materials for use in a Christian educational setting.

Parenting

Boston Women's Health Book Collective. *Ourselves and Our Children: A Book by and for Parents.* New York: Random House, 1978.
—A book about being a parent, written by parents with a feminist perspective.

Brusko, Marlene. *Living with Your Teenager.* New York: McGraw-Hill, 1986.
—A helpful guide, offering practical information and useful suggestions.

Faber, Adele, and Elaine Mazlish. *How to Talk So Kids Will Listen and Listen So Kids Will Talk.* New York: Avon, 1980.
—A fund of advice and good examples about how to communicate effectively with your children.

Fraiberg, Selma H. *The Magic Years: Understanding and Handling the Problems of Early Childhood.* New York: Scribner, 1959.
—An outstanding book for any parent who is trying to enter and share the world of the young child.

Gordon, Thomas. *P.E.T. Parent Effectiveness Training: The No-Lose Program for Raising Responsible Children.* New York: Peter Wyden Inc., 1975.
—A time-tested, useful guide to effective parenting.

Porterfield, Kay Marie. *Keeping Promises: The Challenge of a Sober Parent.* San Francisco: Harper & Row, 1984.
—A helpful guide for parents in recovery from chemical dependency, useful for anyone who wants to understand what children go through when parents abuse alcohol or drugs, and how to help them.

Divorce

Arendell, Terry. *Mothers and Divorce: Legal, Economic and Social Dilemmas.* Berkeley: University of California Press, 1986.
—An important study of the consequences of divorce for women and their children, documenting the difficulties women experience after they divorce.

Triere, Lynette, with Richard Peacock. *Learning to Leave: A Woman's Guide.* New York: Warner Books, 1982.
—Helpful ideas about how to leave, overcome depression and guilt, help your children, and meet your own emotional and physical needs.

For Children: About Divorce

Gardner, Richard A. *The Boys and Girls Book About Divorce.* New York: Bantam, 1970.
—A helpful, reassuring book.

Krementz, Jill. *How It Feels When Parents Divorce.* New York: Alfred A. Knopf, 1988.
—Nineteen girls and boys, aged seven to sixteen, talk about their parents' divorces.

Child Custody and Support

Armstrong, Louise. *Solomon Says: A Speakout on Foster Care.* New York: Pocket Books, 1989.
—An informative exposé of the foster care system, revealing how social workers and courts regard mothers.
Chesler, Phyllis. *Mothers on Trial: The Battle for Children and Custody.* New York: McGraw-Hill, 1986.
—Wide-ranging discussion of custody issues, including the politics of maternal custody in the "Male State" and the particular problems facing women married to abusive men.
Takas, Marianne. *Child Custody: A Complete Guide for Concerned Mothers.* New York: Harper & Row, 1987.
—A very helpful source of answers to custody questions with a chapter on protecting yourself from a dangerous, intimidating partner.
Takas, Marianne. *Child Support: A Complete, Up-To-Date, Authoritative Guide to Collecting Child Support.* New York: Harper & Row, 1985.
—A guide to winning and enforcing child support awards, with information on child custody, finding your partner's hidden assets, and keeping your family safe.

Alcoholism and Drug Abuse

Black, Claudia. *It Will Never Happen to Me: Children of Alcoholics.* Denver: Medical Administration Company, 1981.
—One of the first and best books for adult children of alcoholics.
Johnson, Vernon. *Intervention: How to Help Someone Who Doesn't Want Help. A Step by Step Guide for Families and Friends of Chemically Dependent Persons.* Minneapolis: Johnson Institute Books, 1987.
—Practical information about how to help a loved one choose to enter substance-abuse treatment.
Ketcham, Katherine, and Ginny L. Gustafson. *Living on the Edge.* New York: Bantam, 1989.
—A very useful source of information on substance abuse.
McDaniel, Judith. *Metamorphosis.* Ithaca: Firebrand Books, 1989.
—Poems and prose by a lesbian recovering alcoholic, offering a recovery story and a helpful discussion on using twelve-step programs to strengthen yourself.
Peluso, Emanuel, and Lucy Silvay Peluso. *Women and Drugs: Getting Hooked, Getting Clean.* Minneapolis: CompCare, 1988.
—Stories of diverse women who became chemically dependent on alcohol or drugs.
Sandmaier, Marian. *The Invisible Alcoholics: Women and Alcohol Abuse in America.* New York: McGraw-Hill, 1980.

—An explanation of why women's alcoholism has been hidden, what's wrong with traditional (male-oriented) treatment, and how to get help.

Swallow, Jean, ed. *Out from Under: Sober Dykes and Our Friends*. San Francisco: Spinsters Ink, 1983.

—An anthology of articles, stories, and interviews by and for lesbian recovering alcoholics, drug addicts, adult children of alcoholics, and their counselors. Includes an important analysis of the politics of addiction.

V., Rachel, ed. *A Woman Like You: Life Stories of Women Recovering from Alcoholism and Addiction*. San Francisco: Harper & Row, 1985.

—Nineteen women from various backgrounds tell their stories of addiction and recovery.

Your Body

Barbach, Lonnie, and Linda Levine. *Shared Intimacies: Women's Sexual Experiences*. New York: Bantam Books, 1980.

—A wide-ranging, informative discussion of women's sexual experiences.

The Boston Women's Health Book Collective. *The New Our Bodies, Ourselves: A Book by and for Women*. New York: Simon and Schuster, 1984.

—The indispensable reference book and guide to your body and women's health care issues. Spanish language edition available by writing to: Nuestros Cuerpos, Nuestras Vidas, Boston Women's Health Collective, 465 Mt. Auburn St., Watertown, MA, 02172.

Kitzinger, Sheila. *Women's Experience of Sex: The Facts and Feelings of Female Sexuality at Every Stage of Life*. New York: Penguin Books, 1985.

—A resource book exploring women's feelings about sex, relationships, sexual life-styles, and life transitions such as menopause.

Resources

Abortion Referral

National Abortion Federation
1-800-772-9100
Hours: 9:30–5:30 EST
> Provides referrals to local organizations and answers questions about legal, financial, and procedural matters.

Abuse and Violence

The National Domestic Violence Toll-Free Hotline
c/o Michigan Coalition Against Domestic Violence
P.O. Box 7032
Huntington Woods, MI 48070
1-800-333-7233
1-800-873-6363 TDD Number for the hearing impaired
> Call toll-free, twenty-four hours a day for information or referral to a support group or battered women's shelter anywhere in the United States.

The National Coalition Against Domestic Violence
P.O. Box 15127
Washington, D.C. 20003-0127
202-638-6388
> A coalition, made up of individuals and organizations, that works for battered women and provides information about domestic violence.

National Gay and Lesbian Task Force
202-332-6483
Hours: 9:00–5:00 EST
> The antiviolence project provides information, referral, and support to lesbians and gay men.

National Clearinghouse for the Defense of Battered Women
125 South 9th St., Suite 302
Philadelphia, PA 19107
215-351-0010
> Provides legal information to women charged with crimes for defending themselves from abuse and to their attorneys.

Center for the Prevention of Sexual and Domestic Violence
1914 North 39th St., Suite 205
Seattle, WA 98103
206-634-1903
> Provides resources addressing religious issues that arise for victims of sexual and domestic violence and for abusers.

STATE TOLL-FREE DOMESTIC VIOLENCE HOTLINES

(You can call these numbers toll-free if you live in one of these states.)

Arkansas	1-800-332-4443
Indiana	1-800-334-7233
Nevada	1-800-992-5757
New Hampshire	1-800-852-3311
New Jersey	1-800-572-7233
New York	1-800-942-6906 (English)
	1-800-942-6908 (Spanish)
North Dakota	1-800-472-2911
Oklahoma	1-800-522-7233
Washington	1-800-562-6025
Wisconsin	1-800-333-7233

Abusive Men, Counseling

Ending Men's Violence Task Group
c/o RAVEN
P.O. Box 24159
St. Louis, MO 63130
314-725-6137
> Publishes and distributes *Ending Men's Violence National Referral Directory* listing programs for men nationwide.

AIDS

AIDS Hotline
1-800-342-2437
> Provides information about HIV and AIDS and referrals to local advocacy groups, physicians, treatment facilities, and test sites.

AIDS Project Inform
347 Dolores St., Suite 301
San Francisco, CA 94110
1-800-822-7422   In San Francisco: 415-558-9051
Hours: 10:00–2:00 PST
> Provides information about drug treatments for those who are HIV positive or who have AIDS.

National Sexually Transmitted Diseases Hotline
1-800-227-8922
Hours: 8:00–11:00 EST
> Offers referrals to local groups and information about sexually transmitted diseases, testing sites, and treatment facilities.

Alcohol and Drug Abuse

Alcoholics Anonymous World Services
P.O. Box 459
Grand Central Station
New York, NY 10163
212-686-1100
Hours: 9:00–5:00 EST
> Provides the numbers of state groups that can refer you to a local program.

Al-Anon Family Group World Services
P.O. Box 862
Midtown Station
New York, NY 10018-0862
212-302-7240
Hours: 9:00–4:00 EST, Monday through Friday
> Provides information for family and friends of alcoholics and referrals to state and local programs.

Alateen
Same address and phone as Al-Anon
> Provides information and referrals to local groups for teenagers.

Alcohol and Drug Counseling
1-800-ALCOHOL
> Makes referrals to local alcohol or drug counselors and recovery groups.

National Council on Alcoholism
12 West 21st St.
New York, NY 10010
212-206-6770
> Write or phone for comprehensive list of publications and resources (including publications on women and alcoholism and fetal alcohol syndrome). Provides referral to nearest local council that offers treatment and support programs or information on local resources.

National Institute on Drug Abuse Information and Treatment Referral Hotline
1-800-662-HELP
Hours: 9:00–3:00 EST, Monday–Friday
> 12:00 NOON–3:00 A.M. EST, Saturday and Sunday
> Provides referrals to local alcohol and drug counselors, support groups, and treatment facilities.

National Cocaine Hotline
1-800-COCAINE
> Provides information about cocaine and makes referrals to local treatment programs.

Cocaine Anonymous
1-800-347-8998
> Offers referrals to local groups or treatment facilities.

Career Education

Displaced Homemakers Network
1411 K St., N.W., Suite 930
Washington, D.C. 20005
202-628-6767
> Makes referrals to local groups that help women with career education and job training.

Child Abuse and Neglect

Child Help National Child Abuse Hotline
1-800-422-4453

Provides information about child abuse and neglect and reporting laws. Offers referrals to treatment facilities for children, parents, and adult survivors of abuse.

National Committee for Prevention of Child Abuse
P.O. Box 94283
Chicago, IL 60690
312-663-3520
Offers free catalog of about sixty publications on topics including parenting, child abuse, and child abuse prevention. Provides referrals to chapters in every state.

Parents Anonymous
6733 South Sepulveda Blvd., Suite 270
Los Angeles, CA 90045
1-800-421-0353
Provides information about child abuse and referrals to local support groups for parents who abuse or fear they may abuse their children.

Child Support

Handbook for Child Support Enforcement
Dept. 628M
Consumer Information Center
Pueblo, CO 81009
Write for a copy of the handbook.

The Child Support Enforcement Network
301-833-0054
Hours: 9:00–5:00 EST
Provides information about state and federal laws.

Child Support
119 Nicodemus Rd.
Reistertown, MD 21136
Provides information by mail about state and federal laws and referral to local agencies for help with enforcement.

National Child Support Advocacy Coalition
P.O. Box 4629
Alexandria, VA 22303
703-799-5659

Provides information about your legal rights and how to get help to enforce a support agreement. Send $3.00 and a self-addressed stamped envelope for reading and referral lists.

Custody and Legal Resources

National Center on Women and Family Law
799 Broadway, Room 402
New York, NY 10003
212-674-8200
Hours: 9:00–5:00 EST, Monday through Friday
    Provides information to clients and attorneys.

NOW Legal Defense and Education Fund
99 Hudson St., Suite 1201
New York, NY 10013
    Write for Violence Against Women Legal Resource Kit and referrals to local legal services and support groups.

Center on Children and the Law
American Bar Association
1800 M St., N.W.
Washington, D.C. 20036
202-331-2200: ask for "child support" or "child custody"
Hours: 9:00–5:00 EST
    Provides information and referrals, primarily to attorneys.

Lesbian Rights Project
1663 Mission St., 5th floor
San Francisco, CA 94103
415-621-0674
Hours: 9:00–5:00 PST
    Offers legal advice, counseling about custody, and referrals to local help.

Custody Action for Lesbian Mothers
P.O. Box 281
Narberth, PA 19072
215-667-7508
    Provides consultation and referral to legal services and lesbian support groups, and, for those who live in the Delaware Valley Region, legal representation.

Lesbian Mothers Resource Network
206-325-2643
    Offers referrals for legal help and counseling and support services.

Divorce

Parents Without Partners
8807 Colesville Rd.
Silver Spring, MD 20910
1-800-637-7974
> Provides information and referral to local groups that are open to anyone who has been separated thirty days or more.

Parental Kidnapping

National Center for Missing and Exploited Children
2101 Wilson Blvd., Suite 550
Arlington, VA 22201
1-800-843-5678
> Hotline provides information, including publications and resources, and technical assistance to parents who are searching for missing children or trying to prevent a parental abduction.

Child Find, Inc.
P.O. Box 277
New Paltz, NY 12561
1-800-I AM LOST
> Provides referrals to help locate lost children or find support and legal advice.

Sexual Assault

Incest Survivors Anonymous
P.O. Box 5613
Long Beach, CA 90805-0613
213-428-5599
Hours: Wednesday and Friday afternoons PST
> Makes referrals to local groups and offers information and support.

VOICES (Victims of Incest Can Emerge As Survivors)
Box 148309
Chicago, IL 60614
312-327-1500
> Provides information about VOICES chapters around the country. For information, write or leave a message with your address.

Index